THE REMAINS OF REASON

THE REMAINS
OF REASON

On Meaning after Lacan

Dominik Finkelde

Northwestern University Press
Evanston, Illinois

Northwestern University Press
www.nupress.northwestern.edu

Printed in the United States of America

10 9 8 7 6 5 4 3 2 1

Library of Congress Cataloging-in-Publication Data

Names: Finkelde, Dominik, author.
Title: The remains of reason : on meaning after Lacan / Dominik Finkelde.
Description: Evanston, Illinois : Northwestern University Press, 2025. | Includes
    bibliographical references.
Identifiers: LCCN 2024041445 | ISBN 9780810148093 (paperback) | ISBN
    9780810148109 (cloth) | ISBN 9780810148116 (ebook)
Subjects: LCSH: Psychoanalysis and philosophy—21st century. | Philosophy—
    21st century.
Classification: LCC BF175.4.P45 F56 2025 | DDC 150.19/5—dc23/eng/20241121
LC record available at https://lccn.loc.gov/2024041445

Contents

Foreword by Eric Santner   vii

Prologue: Epistemology and Psychotheology   3

Part 1. Introduction   **9**

Part 2. In Conflict with the Negative   **23**

1   Trauma, Interpellation, and Enigmatic Signifiers   25

2   Freud and Kant: Illusions of the Mind and Illusions of Reason   38

3   Madness and the Loss of Language: Daniel P. Schreber
and the Failure of Symbolic Investiture   49

4   Hegel: Negativity as a Structural Moment of the Concept   63

5   The Metaphysics of Contingency   83

Part 3. The Human Being and the Symbolic Order   **95**

6   In the Mirror, the Image of My Enemy   97

7   Lacan's Graph of Interpellation   107

8   Infinite Desire   130

Part 4. Ideology as Ontology   **139**

9   Sublime Objects   141

10   Fantasy Maintenance and Transgression   154

11   Longing for Leadership: The Time of Haste   158

12   Betrayal in Times of Overdetermination   167

Part 5. Enjoyment as an Ontological Factor 173

13 Jouissance 175

14 In Violation of the Pleasure Principle 183

15 The Thing 187

Works Cited 199

Image Credits 209

Index 213

Foreword

Eric Santner

Dominik Finkelde's new book is among the clearest and most compelling works I have encountered among the many recent attempts to elucidate the zones of intersection and interference between philosophical thinking and psychoanalytic theory and practice. It is important to underline that Finkelde includes under "philosophical thinking" its own set of fissures, antagonisms, and seeming incompatibilities. He speaks with equal clarity and authority about the so-called Continental tradition—above all the work of Kant, Hegel, and those who take up the challenges of German idealism—and a variety of representatives of the analytic tradition, among them Quine, Davidson, Dennett, Putnam, McDowell, and Brandom. His main points of reference on the psychoanalytic side of things are Freud, Lacan, and Laplanche. The quite rich set of examples that Finkelde deploys to concretize concepts and moves in his argument are taken from literature, film, politics, public life, and what Freud characterized as the psychopathologies of everyday life. The ways in which Finkelde occupies and stakes his claim in the complex network of theories, discourse, and practices with which he engages place him in close intellectual proximity to Slavoj Žižek, with whom he furthermore shares a profound appreciation for the place of religion in human life. Finkelde's writing thankfully manifests a profound pedagogical commitment that is lacking in most philosophical work: he has something to teach us, and he is a very skilled, patient, and generous teacher. No child is left behind in this carefully, beautifully paced set of lectures. The pedagogical dimension is, of course, already signaled in the generic specification that the chapters are conceived as lectures.

The red thread running through this set of sixteen lectures concerns what might be called the *remains of reason*, the bits that, so to speak, remain on the cutting-room floor of our unceremonious initiation ceremonies into the space of reasons, the space of normativity in which we are answerable to others for what we claim and do and where we reasonably expect the same level of answerability on the part of others. This space of normativity, which Hegel called "spirit" or *Geist*, is, as Finkelde underlines from a variety of different perspectives, one that endows each human subject with a fundamental kind of recognition: that of being a legitimate player in the game of giving and asking for reasons. Finkelde's psychoanalytic point is that our legitimation or authorization as properly spiritual beings—we know that throughout human history, many human beings never got to enjoy such legitimacy—involves the dimension of what Freud called transference, an erotically charged and largely unconscious "relation" to an ultimate source of legitimacy, an ultimate source of recognition, the virtually real "big Other." The drama of this ultimately impossible relation is what gets played out below the level of our intentionality and becomes manifest in unconscious mental activity familiar to us in the form of dreams, symptoms, parapraxes, repetition compulsions, fantasies, and obsessions; its materials are, as it were, those bits of film that didn't make it into the final cut—Freud would have called it the Oedipal cut—of our socially recognizable, socially legitimate, authorized selves, and that remain "obscene" to them. For Finkelde, the dimension of transference is what philosophy is unable to think, unable to account for. Put somewhat differently—and "psychotheologically"—human beings don't just naturally become reasonable; becoming a rational animal is always an answer to a call, one to which we can, at our psychic and existential peril, fail to respond, fail to muster the courage of the "Here I am" that allows us to establish our place in the human world. One might say that "providence" involves the provision that we have been provided with a call.

As Finkelde emphasizes, this call is profoundly *exciting* (*ex-citare*, to summon, call out); it is an occasion of those persistent psychosexual excitations that Lacan subsumed under the heading of *jouissance*. As Finkelde furthermore argues, this is precisely the dimension that is forgotten in the major philosophical movements of the last years that have, in various ways, tried to conceptualize the mind-world relation. Here he includes not just neo-pragmatists like Brandom and McDowell but also figures like Markus Gabriel, who has developed a "field theory" of meaning in which human beings always occupy multiple, semi-autonomous *Sinnfelder*; and Graham Harman, whose "object-oriented ontology" promised to offer a new theory of everything on the basis of a radical concept of objecthood in which objects themselves are seen as providing the excess that can never be fully brought into the space of reasons.

This book provides a much-needed guide not just to those already interested in this contested zone at the border of philosophy and psychoanalysis, but also to newcomers who will continue to seek a lucid, well-written introduction to the most advanced thinking at this borderland. I can also say that as someone who has, as he graciously mentions in his book, had some influence on Finkelde's thinking, I have learned enormously from this book and would use it myself in classes. Even where he claims to be following my lead, I inevitably find myself in the place of the student very gratefully learning from the master.

THE REMAINS OF REASON

At the end of Fellini's *La Dolce Vita,* a tired party crowd meets fishermen who, at dawn, pull a large ray out of the sea caught in a net. Everyone looks with amusement at the dying animal, which returns their gaze. Lacan describes the eyes of the ray in *Seminar VII* as the site of a fissure. The character of Marcello comments on them by saying: "E questo insiste a guardare"—"It keeps on looking."

Prologue

Epistemology and Psychotheology

This book is based on a lecture series given in the autumn semester of 2018–19 at the Munich School of Philosophy as an introduction to philosophy. It is centered on Jacques Lacan and the intertwinement of his thought with classical questions concerning truth and falsehood, knowledge, and the relation of mind and world. The topics presented were expanded in the process of reviewing the manuscript. Questions concerning the relation of psychoanalysis and epistemology were developed in more detail and shaped several theses in the book. One thesis stands out: the relationship between mind and world as it is influenced by psychotheological demands emitted from social institutions. Human beings equipped with reason and an unconscious in the very midst of this reason are not only invited to understand states of affairs and define facts in a "world" that is "all that is the case" (Wittgenstein). The human mind is also called upon through these demands to be an existential "answer," a "living response" to reality, even if what reality is about never receives a final answer. As a result, all kinds of interpellations emerging from spaces of reasons lure the individual into clusters of facts, norms, fantasies, and desires to find its proper place *as a place-out-of-place*. Specifically, the philosophy of psychoanalysis in the tradition of Freud, Lacan, Laplanche, and Santner—but also its entwinement with the philosophy of German idealism as presented in recent years by Žižek, Dolar, and Zupančič—is devoted to this topic. This book follows their lead with the goal to show how epistemological questions are intertwined with psychotheological and psychopathological motives which have, through interpellation, an impact on how a sapient being may be driven and unconsciously animated to be an answer to questions that are not well-posed. As such, this investigation is not primarily interested in the presentation of multiple debates in which, for example, a priori (Kant, Strawson), process-teleological (Hegel, Brandom), semantic (Quine, Davidson), or holistic-pragmatic (Rorty, Putnam) conditions of knowledge are thematized. Rather, it is concerned with the impact of patterns of interpellation that carry metaphysical weight and affect the human mind precisely in the presence of a failed clarification of that mind's relation to its surrounding reality. These patterns, as enigmatic demands and exhortations, are involved in what one might call an epistemic entanglement—even smearing—of the demarcation line between *Mind and World*, to mention John McDowell's famous 1994 monograph. Therefore, in acts of cognition, a solipsistically distorted treatment of that which is *not* absorbed in the relation between mind and world plays a central role. This refers us to the unconscious as analyzed by Sigmund Freud at the fin de siècle. The unconscious is that part that has no part. It *in-exists* and affects the mind-world relation epistemologically and ontologically at the same time. At least, this is what the following sixteen lectures want to unveil: paths into a Lacan-inspired psychotheological theory of knowledge.

The investigations of Eric Santner (1996, 2001, 2011), presented in numerous publications at the intersection of cultural theory, comparative literature, and psychoanalysis in particular, must be mentioned here. The term "psychotheology" is borrowed from his (2001) study on Franz Rosenzweig and Sigmund Freud, and his research on the "Schreber case" is also repeatedly referred to in connection with the efficacy of symbolic investiture in processes of subjectification (Santner 2010, 2018).

But what exactly does a "Lacanian psychotheology of knowledge" refer to, and what role does it play in introducing basic questions of philosophy? The following lectures try to give multiple answers to this question. As already hinted at, the unconscious will play a central role. It turns out to be not only a psychoanalytic category, but—despite Freud's critique of religion—both a theological and, going beyond Freud and toward the research of the Ljubljana school of psychoanalysis, an epistemological one as well. Since every process of subjectification, in the course of which a human organism locates itself in a world of facts and states of affairs, is never capable of subjectifying everything in the organism of each individual on its way into an intersubjective space of experience, a remainder necessarily "flocculates" out of the processes, as in a reaction in colloid chemistry. This remainder resists any equivalence of a universal (i.e., of an entity with clearly defined elements establishing, like a set, coherence and identity) and thus defies the coextension of mind and world, as it is searched for again and again in philosophical debates from antiquity to the present, from Plato to McDowell. Precisely for this reason, however, the unconscious infuses "noise" into mind and world behind the control center of our cognitive and social-pragmatic abilities. It calls us humans into our own niche of the reality surrounding us and gives us not only a place in reality, but also a place-out-of-place as well. Our social-pragmatic and cognitive abilities, then, guarantee in large part the coherence of our experience; but they have no direct influence on the vocational patterns we live by; that is, the singular and individual mode of ourselves being reality's response, the answer to certain facts in question. This kind of calling and being interpellated affects, and even grants, the unconscious, as can only be hinted at here for now. The latter must not be interpreted as a more substantial self at the bottom of our individuality. As I mentioned, it is that part which has no part, since it does not operate under the rule of the law of identity as the fundamental principle of knowledge, reason, and justification. As such, it cannot join the sum total of, for example, parts within the space of giving and asking for reasons (regarding facts, beliefs, deeds, desires, etc.). This is also why the unconscious is always a source of indeterminacy, of experiences running counter to the rule of the law of identity as the basic rule of "all that is the case." It can protrude the mind-world relation and provoke unanticipated events of strangeness with regard to ourselves, as well as with regard to the reality principle guiding our experience. For this reason, we may then wake up one night in our marriage bed at three o'clock in the morning and experience a disturbing irritation with regard to our place within a certain genealogy of our being. Or we may suddenly find ourselves, like Daniel Paul Schreber after the symbolic act of his appointment as president of the Third Circuit of the Appeals Court in Dresden, in a world of Zoroastrian gods. In the first case, it may cause us to step out of bed into a world that, from now on, leans toward us differently. In the second case, we may be doomed to remain prisoners of alien powers that incarcerate us in *their* minds and in *their* worlds.

The fact that, until today, a large part of the philosophical literature beyond the narrow limits of the philosophy of psychoanalysis does not thematize this indeterminate entity that Freud calls the unconscious, Franz Rosenzweig the "self" (Rosenzweig 1985, 69), and Žižek, following Lacan, the subject, which "is in the subject more than itself" (Žižek 1999, 30), for epistemological purposes is incomprehensible. After all, the first traces of philosophical interest in the unconscious were already laid in the nineteenth century in the works of Friedrich W. J. Schelling, Eduard von Hartmann, and Arthur Schopenhauer (Nicholis and Liebscher 2010); that is, long before Freud achieved his theoretical breakthrough. Sadly, they were neglected soon thereafter, with the effect that questions of cognition in contemporary debates are almost exclusively concerned with conceptual and judgmental determinations of facts analyzed, for example with regard to a Sellarsian "space of reasons" (Brandom 2000; McDowell 1994), theoretical frameworks of supernumerary fields of sense (Gabriel 2016), object-oriented ontologies (Harman 2018; De Landa 2017), and hermeneutic interpretations of realism (Benoist 2021; Koch 2016), to name just a few current debates. None of these takes into account the unconscious as the hidden third, and always epistemically smeared, element in the dichotomy of mind and world. As such, the aforementioned debates neglect what is most crucial for Lacan's epistemology: the

Other in the ego as the zero point of its predicative content, protracting into the mind-world relation as that which belongs to the subject and nevertheless remains external to it. In certain situations, this Other is capable of inverting the mind-world relation from the inside out. Experiences like these can be detected in religion, politics, art, and science (Finkelde 2017, 2019).

To investigate subject matters of this kind is only possible if the mind-world relation is not being exhausted by conceptual definitions that repeat the rule of the law of identity (be they holistic, semantic, hermeneutic, sense-field-theoretical, etc.). The anti-metabolic surplus of the subject of the unconscious (subverting the rule of the law of identity both in the individual and in societies) has to be taken into account. This surplus could be eliminatively explained away as a widespread "indeterminacy of translation" or as an overdetermination of conflicting reasons with reference to states of affairs, in terms of the American philosopher Willard V. O. Quine (2013, 202). But this is not what Freud and Lacan are concerned with. They are not concerned with the indeterminacies of incommensurable "manuals of translation" (ibid., 25) or acts of "radical interpretation" (Davidson 2001a, 148) among people of different cultures talking within different conceptual schemes. Rather, they are concerned with an indeterminacy of reason (and meaning) within reason's own unreason, an unreason caused by the unconscious that—because of its lack of participation in the rule of the law of identity—has no other way than to overtax the individual with regard to the latter's place in the world. Or, to put it differently: no reality concerning us humans can be constituted without the indeterminacy of patterns of interpellation in the very midst of overdetermined facts and their phantasmatic binding into "all that is the case," because subjects, equipped with an unconscious, define what is the case. The advantage of philosophy's extension through questions regarding a psychotheological theory of knowledge helps us see why individuals may subvert—out of nothing—old states of affairs and enter new ones emerging against the hitherto valid structures of universal causes. This topic is not reflected in contemporary debates examined under titles such as "new realism" (Gabriel, Ferraris), "speculative realism" (Harman, Meillassoux), "new materialism" (Barad, Bennett), and "hermeneutic realism" (Benoist, Koch). The following lectures, in contrast, will try to lay the ground for this field of investigation. They are structured as follows.

Some remarks on the symbolic status of subjectivity are presented in this book's introduction, in which the talk of a "first" and biological nature of humankind becomes retrospectively comprehensible from the genesis of a socially mediated "second," or symbolic, "nature." The second set of lectures, "In Conflict with the Negative," is devoted to the influence of negativity as a category that decisively shapes the relation of mind and matter, or word and object. Three analyses reveal subjectivity's dependence on normative orders and the patterns of interpellation radiating from them, underlining Graham Greene's word that we should be thankful not to be able to "see the horrors and degradations lying around our childhood, in cupboards and bookshelves, everywhere" (Greene 2015, 14). In this, subjectivity proves to be shaped by minimal traumas in its onto-genetic development as well as by enigmatic signifiers. Emerging from the forces of political institutions, enigmatic signifiers penetrate the human organism from birth on. They put it on the trajectory of a vocation which is always marked by excessive fantasies as well. This vocation shapes the bond between mind and world long before an individual with conceptual capabilities locates him- or herself in a social space administered with norms, values, and fantasies by rational animals. Theories on the epistemic status of enigmatic signifiers are addressed, as are Immanuel Kant's and Sigmund Freud's analyses of the mind as a source of illusion and imagination shaping multiple objects of experience, be they abstract or empirical. Subsequently, and in line with investigations of the Ljubljana school of psychoanalysis, reference will be made to Hegel's understanding of negativity. I will try to show to what extent the relation of subjects to facts is to be understood as a correlation between knowledge and truth characterized by a missed encounter. The world of facts proves to be at odds with itself, not only because it is smaller than the quantity of its parts, but also because of subjects that revolve—as epistemic sources of facts—around deficient formations of their reflexivity with regard to the parts. Because of this, subjects are able to performatively establish new worlds in sometimes psychotic flights of fantasy.

The third set of lectures, entitled "The Human Being and the Symbolic Order," follows this path with an interpretation of Lacan's "graph of desire." It serves to answer the question of why subjectivity cannot enter into self-relation without the restlessness of invocations that remain overdetermined. The fourth set of lectures, "Ideology as Ontology," adds insights from Žižek's comments on "sublime objects of ideology" to the theses so far presented. What distinguishes sublime objects from the "middle-sized objects" of (roughly speaking) everyday life is a paradoxical combination of meaning and the lack thereof, without which the space of reasons evoked by philosophy in various contexts, from Habermas to Brandom, could not exist at all. Word leaders, masters, and prophets play crucial roles in the grounding of these spaces with sublime authority. As centers of processes of transference, they are able to evoke existential love in their followers within clusters of ratiocinations. But equally, they can suddenly become objects of hatred by the same followers due to an unforgivable deceit for which they bear responsibility.

The last set of these lectures, "Enjoyment as an Ontological Factor," finally places Lacan's notion of a pathological enjoyment, called jouissance, at the center of analysis. Without this kind of enjoyment, symbolic forms could not come into being, since enjoyment proves to be an essential political and ontological factor of utmost importance. Only within a world that can be enjoyed excessively can human beings feel at home, even if such excess puts this world on the brink of destruction time and again.

Part 1

Introduction

(Lecture 1)

1

In everyday life, we meet all kinds of people in an almost disconcerting variety. One way to explain this diversity is the extent of different cultural interpellations that shape human beings. There is, for example, the priest who sees himself as a disciple of Christ (embodied here by Don Camillo, *below, left*). But there is also the Bororo man (*below, center*), who finds himself in fraternity with a parrot. And there are quantum physicists (here Albert Einstein and Niels Bohr, *below, right*) who look at their environment from the framework of their science and neither understand what a parrot nor what a man from Galilee, who lived roughly 2,000 years ago, may have to do with reality. These three types of subjects, mentioned here only in passing, are grounded in a diverse range of consciousness which is, for its part, oriented toward diverse forms of pleasure. For all three subjects literally swim in libidinous structures, that is, erotic-psychic patterns of motivation, which run like a sticky mass through all symbolic orders in which these subjects live. The Catholic

priest, for example, will think of himself as a "faith and reason"-uniting clergyman who rejects the animism of a Bororo as an outdated form of esotericism. A Protestant pastor, in turn, may condemn the Catholic clergyman as a pre-Enlightenment Christian because he still clings to the concept of transubstantiation,.that is, the "real presence of Christ" in the eucharist. And a physicist may regard the Protestant as an impostor, who actually should know better than the Catholic what kind of fairy tale Christianity is.

These three types of people are all subjects of ideological interpellation, since they experience themselves as autonomous beings in their everyday life. For this reason, these types of people (or better: these individual tokens of people-types) are also, metaphorically speaking, *answers* to the most diverse demands, which, coming from social institutions, act on the human mind, but also on the unconscious in the very midst of this mind. The priest and the pastor mentioned are answers to the calling of Christ. The Bororo man is an answer to the interpellation of his tribal culture, whatever that may be. And the physicists see themselves called out to by the truth of science, which they must obey—for, today, which kind of truth could be more convincing than scientific truth, especially under the banner of naturalism? But Hilary Putnam has already indicated the ideological character of naturalism itself. The enthusiasm to label oneself with this tag reminded him of the allegiance with which scientists in the former Soviet Union put themselves at the service of "Comrade Stalin" (Putnam 2012, 109–10).

All the individuals mentioned (priest, pastor, Bororo, physicist) will consequently see their relation to the world as a more or less legitimate access to the reality surrounding them, without thereby necessarily seeing recognized standards of scientific knowledge called into question. The French psychoanalyst Jacques Lacan, who combined insights of Freud with the structuralism of his time, was interested in these processes of subject-formation through interpellations of all kinds. As a medical doctor with a specialization in psychiatry, he recognized, through his work at the Centre Hospitalier Sainte-Anne in Paris, what happens when complications in processes of interpellation occur. Such processes begin from earliest childhood on and continue even into old age, since the "calls," or appeals that emanate from symbolic institutions never cease to send messages that are both normative and enigmatic. These appeals can emanate from the family, the sports club, or the university, but also from the judge before whom we are brought one day in the course of a divorce. Even the psychoanalyst who we meet after a psychic breakdown triggered by a completely arbitrary event belongs to this world of institutions. The reference to the Freudian concept of the unconscious, to which we will repeatedly return, proves to be central in these processes, since ideological invocations concern the subject's relation to itself—but specifically also to its unconscious. The interpellations are interwoven with our most intimate longings, fantasies, and idealized self-images. For example, as we've surely all experienced, an advertising billboard in a subway station can have an effect on us and make an impression. We need not consciously notice how we have just been called by a message. By means of such a trivial example, our inner experience proves to be always already invaded by an other, a stranger to us, which originates from a semantic field (of overdetermined messages) that surrounds us from birth and has an incessant effect on us—at once overtaxing and calming. The reasons for this kind of impact can be an inherent lack of self, much commented on in the history of philosophy, and/or a fundamental eccentricity of the human mind. In this context, the concept of "overdetermination" means that the reception of reality is always a selection process for which we often cannot sufficiently determine the criteria applied. So, consciousness is always confronted with an extract of reality that is, by definition, smaller than the set of its parts. Between the act of cognition and the object cognized lurks a difference. Consciousness cannot subsume this difference under the rule of the law of identity. This may explain the multiplicity of subjects presented at the beginning of this lecture; it goes back to the abundance of differences that open up between objects and the places in which they become components of clusters of experience. There simply is no homologous existential quantifier $\forall(x)$ of reality that establishes a purely logical subject-formation formula for all people. If there were such an existential quantifier, we humans would all take on a homologous form, just like Agent Smith from the *Matrix* films with his innumerable duplicates. We would resemble each other like copies, not in outward appearance but in acts of cognition, desires, hopes, and fantasies.

The ego's inherent strangeness, for which Freud's concept of the unconscious stands, accompanies man over the span of his life. And this is good news. It affects not only ourselves as subjects, but also the diverse cultural spheres surrounding us. For just as in subjects, there is in cultures always more as well: untamed signifiers that can sometimes be activated, sometimes silenced, but never managed and administered simultaneously.

Slavoj Žižek's philosophical explorations, which he has presented in over fifty books, are particularly illuminating in the context of these issues. He shows that our understanding of ourselves and the reality surrounding us is shaped by collective virtualities, idealizations, and repressed antinomies. These concern our social environment, in which we both passively live and actively participate. We are thereby both the beneficiaries of these virtualities and the providers of their energy. Living amidst these virtualities produces a discomfort that in turn forms the condition of existence for linguistically and symbolically gifted beings such as we humans are. And, not infrequently, this discomfort can overcome us in such a way that we—like Neo in his incubator in a famous scene of the first *Matrix* film—want to break out of this reality.

According to the film's storyline, Neo experiences a computer simulation of reality fed into his nervous system in order to drain the energy of his body for alien purposes. In this way, the Wachowski siblings presented an updated version of Marx's theory of alienation. Proletarians suffered the same fate as Neo: to be robbed of their life's energy like a Duracell battery by alien powers (capitalists) and to be unable to see this circumstance of their exploitation.

2

Every banknote, no matter what the currency, illustrates this virtuality that, like a second nature, surrounds the first nature of our biological bodies. Its symbolic value is imprinted on both sides and its value is guaranteed by the stability of a social contract. This value cannot be compared to, for example, the hundred buns of bread that I can buy with it. The buns have use value in an empirical form—I can eat them. The banknote has no similar empirical form, because empirically it is nothing but paper. The virtuality of its content, however, does not prevent the bill causing empirical effects: namely, to enable the purchase of buns of bread.

However, when doubts arise in the collective consensus about a belief in the incarnation of value in this piece of paper, the social contract of shared imagination becomes irritated. This can happen abruptly. Suddenly, the baker at the corner begins to devalue the banknote, because the flour supplier may do so as well. In everyday dealings, however, this kind of imbalance is kept to a minimum. Normally, when the social contract works, we treat the value, in the substantial form of the bill, with absolute self-evidence. I don't have to promise the saleswoman in a department store that the bill embodies substantial value, independent of its being paper. It's no wonder that I am not relieved when the exchange succeeds—that is what money was invented for. It subtracts the use value of a commodity and makes it formally equivalent to all other commodities in the world. As long as this kind of social contract runs unconsciously and keeps all irritating influences from the circulation of commodities, the banknotes are tokens of substance-types.

These mechanisms of collective virtualities, which shape beliefs and justifications, are the subject matter of the following lectures. Virtualities impact individuals with regard to sets of facts and states of affairs. Instead of a banknote, one could also speak of the virtual authority of a justice department, or of faith in a constitutional state, or of faith even in physics or in contemporary naturalism. We humans in particular, as symbolic beings, can do what no other creature in the animal kingdom can do. We can stick to the most absurd belief systems, even if all empirical facts disprove what we take to be true. The so-called "ideologies of the twentieth century" (fascism and Stalinism) have especially demonstrated this.

But it would be a misunderstanding to think that this dealing in symbols, or social life in this unconscious virtuality of practices and beliefs, is "merely virtual" compared to what is real. So, we are not talking about an ideological failure of human cognition, which could be either corrected by the natural sciences or overcome with their understanding of objectivity and truth. (Strangely enough, this conviction is still very common.) Modally robust sciences, like the natural sciences, are part of the virtual worlds as modally vague forms, because their genesis is shaped by worldviews—the term "naturalism" embodies this. "Naturalism" as concept is *by definition* a worldview. Our everyday interaction with virtual worlds in the form of symbols, memes, internalized concepts, and collective traumas and aspirations is simultaneously virtual and empirical. Worlds, co-created by virtual forces, create empirical reality from banknotes to atomic cloud chambers, worlds that we never find in the animal kingdom.

A dog can very well give me a sign that he is hungry. He runs to his food bowl and waits for me to fill it. What he cannot do, however, is reveal to me that his hunger is symbolically *as great as* the food bowl is wide. He would have to use the food bowl as a symbol or—better—as a *signifier* for the concept "hunger." This turns out to be impossible for the animal. The dog cannot—metaphysically speaking—execute a transubstantial property exchange, at the end of which the following equation would stand: big empty bowl = big hunger, similar to the banknote mentioned: 100 dollars = 100 buns of bread = 50 baguettes, and so on. Were the dog to act like this, the world of symbolic forms would open up immediately. All kinds of things would be, from then on, potential media of communication. The feeding bowl itself would, as signifier, as symbolic entity, incorporate infinite amounts of meaning, which the dog could adopt in multiple contexts. But as I said, the dog is excluded from the world of the signifier because of his epistemic poverty as a sentient being. He can understand signs and give signs, but signifiers, as carriers of abstract concepts, are inaccessible to his mind.

The judge who may one day preside over the proceedings of my divorce may be the worst judge ever. But as soon as the judge puts on her robe as a symbol of her authority and pronounces the verdict in the name of the people, it does not matter at all whether she is bad or good. She represents, even as the worst of all possible judges in this world, a universality: the universality of the law that is embodied spatiotemporally in her particular person. If we humans would rebel against these symbolic dimensions of states of affairs and, for example, subtract the virtuality of the symbolic from facts that empirically shape our everyday life, our world would collapse like a puffed-up dough. The world would no longer exist, at least not as a stable framework of one's ego function. Hierarchies of clusters of meaning would break down together with the structures of desire that produced and maintained them. Conditions of enjoyment, so important for the social contract, would dry up immediately.

I imagine that most of us have experienced these forms of phantasmatic loss of reality in times of lovesickness and romantic grief, for example. There are trees, streets, houses, and cars; everything still exists. But what exists has the appearance of being emptied out, deflated, lacking sense and meaning as if, speaking with Kant, the transcendental "I" of pure apperception could no longer carry out its task undisturbed: to synthesize sensory impressions, with the help of concepts, into experiences worth living in. The coordinates that make everyday life ordinary are displaced in cases like these, so that getting out of bed can be a difficult task.

Consequently, we are psychologically healthy when we are part of unconscious symbolic processes of thought and practice that enable us to deal with priests, judges, norms, and so on as the condition "of what [robustly] is the case." Therefore, it is more than naive to claim that today, in our age of neoliberal democracy (or at least in "Western democracies"), we live in a non-ideological epoch. The belief in the end of ideologies spread after 1989, when hammer-and-sickle emblems were cut out of national flags in eastern Europe. Not only was the Marxist-Leninist unity of the working class (hammer) and of the peasant class (sickle) considered to be finished, but the last true ideological worldview on earth seemed to have been overcome (Fukuyama 1992).

But this is obviously false, and the opposite belief is today a commonplace. At all levels of our everyday lives, we swim as subjects of ideological interpellation in a matrix of administered fantasies, norms, and values. This matrix of unconscious symbolic processes manifests our second nature, without our being able to fundamentally rationalize or cognitively encompass it in its multiple networks of justification. The networks that give both us as rational agents and our unconscious justification and prescribe "what is the case" are simply too complex and eccentrically interwoven, with other clusters of justification nested in further clusters, and so on. Our second nature, which defines us as symbolic beings, cannot be imagined intimately enough in a symbiosis with our bodies (i.e., our first nature). The aforementioned scene from the first *Matrix* movie sums up this condition fittingly. The slime-like fluid that envelops Neo in his incubator surrounds his biological body as a divided unity. Neo is himself within an Other. This is a further reason why it is impossible for us humans to strip off our second nature like a mask. Were we to stand in front of a mirror and remove the mask, we would not recognize ourselves. We would face an animal that does not know who and what it is.

The philosophy of psychoanalysis deals with this deficient union of the two natures (first and second) of the subject, which is experienced as a painful contradiction between the biological (material) and the symbolic (abstract). It reveals why the two bodies cannot unite without glitches. This insight set the philosophy of psychoanalysis at the end of the nineteenth century on the path of its scientific inquiry. When our biological body can no longer subjectivize and perform various symbolic roles (the mother role, for example, or the role of a master chef or pop star), a discomfort arises in our subjectivity. A painful difference between body and symbolic investiture opens up. In such situations of mental discomfort, people try, like Neo, to break out of a structure of interpellation that conditions their body like an unpleasant, oppressive, and suffocating slime.

3

From the perspective of the philosophy of psychoanalysis, ideology is not a false worldview. It is the condition to access the realm of experience shared with other symbolic beings. It is a place maintained with justifications, commitments, entitlements, and fantasies that are not bound like fixed taxonomies to the basic structures of reality (whatever these may be). We constantly invest our energy into this realm of shared experiences in the form of taxes, work, desires, and so on, to receive in return the right to know and to enjoy. Ideology is consequently a condition of our existence, without being generally allowed to be recognized as such. It is the unconscious structure of facts that, as such, minimizes epistemic stress and allows us to experience ourselves as autonomous among states of affairs. Ideology is the way we become subjects in a medium that generally relieves us of asking how things or facts (as they are in themselves) actually are.

According to a famous saying of Lacan, everything depends on how the subject "positions" itself to the symbolic (Lacan 1988a, 80). The former, the subject, is defined by the latter, the symbolic, without being entirely absorbed by it (Lacan 1990, 106). This place is what determines whether someone "has the right to, or is prohibited from, calling himself *Pedro*" (ibid., 80). To simplify greatly, the symbolic stands for prevailing norms that are linguistically mediated amidst established practices and historically developed concepts and values. These norms form a cultural space and administer, among other things, diverse fantasies as a community's way of imaging and enjoying itself. Like water in a sponge, ideology permeates experience, incarnating properties of the Lacanian "big Other."

The subject decides, both consciously and unconsciously, what can bring it to the brink of insanity or what it wants to perform in relation to the big Other, the simultaneously personal and anonymous metastructure of its (the subject's) being. It is we who decide what we recognize with respect to our own self-image. But unfortunately, this is not us at all. A stranger in us has already made presuppositions about our desires and fantasies before we have the capacity to be autonomous and rational agents of our deeds.

In this context, the experience of German fascism in the twentieth century was an outstanding event in the history of ideological fantasies that constitute the symbolic as the realm of objects of experience. It shows that a symbolic order can radically descend into collective psychosis. And even if the majority within this body politic suspects that this symbolic order, this big Other (and the people at the top of it), is misguided, that it is corrupt and hollow, there may nevertheless be such immense collective insecurity in judgment to confront this fact that an actual change of the political psychosis is impeded.

The big Other as a condition of the possibility of established norms and values is obviously virtual, but this does not mean that the big Other is an illusion. The piece of paper printed with "One Hundred Dollars" is likewise virtual, but nevertheless enables me to buy 100 rolls of bread. We humans always move on the level of an unconscious reality-formation that has been declared coherent long before we appear within its rules as participants with our doubts and suggestions for change. The big Other can even be absent without any problems and still keep a collective and headless body politic alive, because everybody is afraid that—were the big Other to abdicate completely—everything would become worse. Adolf

Hitler in the Berlin *Führerbunker* shortly before his and his wife's suicide exemplifies such an absent big Other. The 2004 film *Downfall*, directed by Oliver Hirschbiegel, stages this scenario in a striking way. It is April 1945. The war is hopelessly lost and yet orders are passed back and forth, documents are stamped, death sentences pronounced and carried out. The Führer, as a paragon of the big Other, has been cut off from the outside world for days in his compound of interconnected bunkers, but his orders still buzz through the ether of the German administration.

Here we encounter, in exemplary fashion, the symbolic body of a state, which trembles at its extremities as if in its death throes. Yet the same body politic cannot see that, by clinical standards, it has already died. The state resembles the "walking dead." It represses the reality of its current demise to the very end. All kinds of political revolutions, including that of 1989 in East Germany, illustrate the collapse of virtual worlds that have carried empirical facts in multiple networks of justification for decades. The government of the German Democratic Republic still believed in the corridors of its administration, which good reasons guaranteed the right to exist. But its citizens protested on the streets, knowing very well that this right had expired. The desire to continue building a collective project or maintaining the social contract was gone.

In situations like these, revolutions become a conflict of interpretation over reality and its virtual supplement, since the question arises as to who can defend his or her fantasy against the political enemy. Which party can prove the symbolic death of the political rival, especially if various political body parts of this same enemy still exist and function smoothly (administration, jurisdiction, chains of command)? The power of the virtual must never be underestimated here, since, as I have said, there would be no empirical reality for us human beings if the virtual did not maintain it. Against this background, the democracies that surround us in central Europe today represent virtual narratives, as do totalitarian regimes. They must take care through the media, trade unions, churches, civil societies, and so on that the dissonances in webs of opinions and fantasies do not diverge too far from a collectively shared sense of "reality," as we are currently experiencing in the United States in 2022. When such divergence occurs, a polity can, in the worst-case scenario, no longer agree on facts. This is not because we live in an age of "post-truth politics," but because judgmental premises are no longer shared as conditions of a universal space of giving and asking for reasons. So, democracies are no less sheltered from the delusion of the symbolic than totalitarian regimes are, because delusion is part of the symbolic itself.

Delusions inform the authority of speech and reason. They drive us and torment us. This is another reason why human beings are the only creatures on earth that can fall for even the hollowest authority. This tendency to surrender to an authority of the Other feeds on a "lack of being [*le manque de l'être*]" inscribed in the subject (Lacan 2006a, 428). This lack permanently pushes the individual to compensation, to the search for a fullness of identity. The eradication of an existential deficit can then be found, for example, in a charismatic leader or in a cultural space with excessive fantasies and promises. The social lifeworld is interpreted in this context as a semantic field of justifications and meanings. It seeks to cure the lack of its subjects in order to be able to form stability with regard to the rule of the law of identity. As such, the social lifeworld exemplifies a famous drawing of a paradoxical staircase drawn by the Dutch artist M. C. Escher.

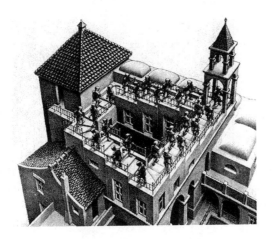

The never-ending loop of stairs exemplifies allegorically the loop of communal desire that cannot come to a standstill because of an inner antagonism that the drawing obscures through mixed perspectives. The loop embodies a search for inner coherence and stability that is never met, and yet must be phantasmatically defended as an attainable goal. If the antagonism would surface, the phantasmatic application of the law of identity of meaning would be endangered. And this concerns democracies as well as totalitarian polities. Every state must therefore take itself—in spite of inner antagonisms—absolutely seriously at all levels of its tasks. As soon as it fails to do so (because of the insight into its virtual theater), it runs the risk of ceding its monopoly of power through a collective loss of imagination.

Myths and narratives, but also political rituals such as Bach concerts in parliament on Holocaust Memorial Day, establish a seemingly stable network of authority around these traumatic nuclei at the center of political life. In this network of rituals, fantasies, and desires, we subjects are supposed to recognize ourselves. The authority in action, though, is based on a lack of legitimacy; that is, it is always based on an infection or illness of one's own culture and tradition, since tradition has never been, by definition, wholesome, sane, and sound. Culture as a space of political reality is consequently the constantly failing process of reconciling immanence with transcendence. Being a subject across the range of experience, in a community, however politically and socially shaped, is hence described by Žižek as a process of constant struggle to come to terms with identifications and interpellations that are socially thrust upon us from birth on. The society that surrounds us in the sovereignty of a particular culture and its tradition is then in fact a "matrix" in its purest form that feeds our identity for the purpose of its own preservation. At the same time, we are always already more a part of this matrix than we can recognize with regard to ourselves. In its eccentricity it determines our intrinsic properties of identity and our cognitive abilities. But it also determines our evolution to what we have not even dreamt of becoming. We do not simply face facts, but are epistemically inscribed into them as their subsets against the background of an unconscious structure of reality mentioned above. Facts have called upon us and continue to do so—from the crucifix in the Munich Immigration Office to the iPhone in the New York Apple Store. As such, we embody in the logics of worlds surrounding us a paradoxical self-inclusion and self-exclusion, a syllogism that produces its own refutation and is known as "Russell's Paradox."

When we go to bed at night, we not only enter a virtual space of dreams, but also free ourselves from the virtualities that have governed and defined our everyday life. We litigate our self-awareness with an imag-

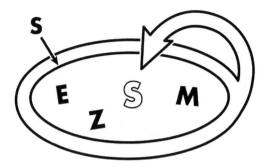

ination running riot. It is no longer subject to what Freud calls "secondary processes"—that is, formal conditions of logic, argumentative coherence, and rationality. Instead, "primary processes" govern our mental states. The results are all kinds of fantasy scenarios, which we are all too familiar with. The ego slowly decomposes and processes the virtual worlds it has had to submit itself to. In these processes, our mind not infrequently spins a riddle of images (a rebus) around the day's fragmented memory remnants, at the origin of which, according to Lacan, an indeterminate desire lurks, as in a seedless shell. Freud speaks of the "dream's navel" (Freud 1981, vol. 5, 525). By this he means an unfathomable condensation at the center of our dream that cannot be deciphered. But—and this is the guiding thesis of this book—these virtual dream-worlds correlate with the realities that we, as anti-individualistic subjects, subjectify anew every day. Or, to put it differently: our dreams form a complementary structure to the virtual worlds that our second, or symbolic, natures experience anew in waking life (see Finkelde 2021a).

After all, the symbolic roles we play are worth living only because we spend a third of the day processing their influence on our bodies and minds according to laws that are not yet scientifically transparent. The symbolic roles of our everyday lives turn out to be holograms of an Other in us for our mind in the state of dreaming, just as our dreams in return are holograms for our ego-function in everyday life. Analyzing this complementary structure of our dreams and the virtual worlds of everyday life helps us to understand the extent to which a clear frontier between dreaming and being awake cannot be drawn. Rather, we humans live in mental states of "non-wakefulness" (Finkelde 2020a) through the unconscious structure of the facts and practices that surround and define us. Philosophers of German idealism, to whom we will repeatedly refer in the following lectures, already addressed the virtuality of reality in yet undeveloped ways. They knew about the fragility of facts due to their intrinsic form as appearances and not as things-in-themselves. After all, the concept "appearance," as coined by Kant, expresses one of the most important insights of German idealism: that appearance and truth do not cancel one other out, but mutually depend on each other. In Adorno's words: "The appearance of identity is inherent in thought itself, in its pure form. To think is to identify. Conceptual order is content to screen what thinking seeks to comprehend. The appearance and the truth of thought entwine" (Adorno 2004, 5, trans. changed).

Part 2

In Conflict with the Negative

1

Trauma, Interpellation, and Enigmatic Signifiers

(Lecture 2)

Freud's theory of psychoanalysis is associated with the concept of the unconscious. And although Freud was not the first one to discover unconscious mental activity, *The Interpretation of Dreams* was nevertheless the first publication to confront it with scientific precision. In doing so, Freud took into account the psychophysical debates of his time and developed his own insights into semiotics as the science of signs and symbols. The decisive breakthrough, however, resided in what at first sight seemed counterintuitive. It rested in the discovery that unconscious mental activity is in part mechanical and even machine-like in nature. Talking of machine-like activity can best be illustrated by strange patterns of behaviors, like an uncontrollable impulse or tic. It can affect us without being explained by a mental chain of rational causation directing our acts of will under normal conditions. This can be the innocent tic of a certain way of moving one's body through the streets or that of a trembling eyelid while speaking in front of an audience. But it can also be the extreme obsessive-compulsive disorder that forces a person to think about painful issues he or she wants to forget, or to rub disinfectant gel on one's hands far too many times a day. The persons affected know very well that their actions and thoughts are absurd and irrational, and yet a physio-psychic energy forces them to do it again and again. In Nietzsche's words, in situations like these the subject experiences his ego precisely not as "the condition of the predicate 'think.'" A "thought [or a symptom as a placeholder of thought] comes when 'it' wants, and not when 'I' want." "It [the thought or the symptom] thinks" and to suppose "that the 'it' is just that old famous 'I' . . . is just an assumption or opinion, to put it mildly and by no means an 'immediate certainty'" (Nietzsche 2002, 17). Self-reflection and self-observation cannot keep the unconscious repetition under control.

We all recognize such tics both in ourselves and in others. Often they are normal, sometimes funny, rarely distressing, and very rarely extreme and life-threatening. Tics of this kind have even become part of our entertainment culture. Heroes of popular culture embody them with exemplary traits. We only have to think of TV series like *Dexter, Monk, Psycho* (the series), or movies like *Halloween I–V*. They place, at the center of their stories, mechanisms of inner psychic forces that cannot be brought under control by the rational agency of the protagonists. The plot of the stories is then often based on an attempt to find "a signifier" as the compulsive disorder's cause, since the symptom is a symptom of a missing link in the order of meaning within the mind. In almost all cases, though, the obsessive-compulsives portrayed enjoy their symptoms. Dexter, who works as a forensic scientist for the Miami Police Department and practices vigilante justice in his spare time, is unable to let go of repetitive loops in his mind and thus cannot let go of his compulsions to kill. There is something more in himself: another agency that places him time and again "*an einen anderen Schauplatz*—at another scene" (Freud citing Fechner, Freud 1981, vol. 4, 48). In this he resembles some of the patients analyzed by Freud, who suffered from traumatic front-line experiences in World War I. They couldn't let go of their traumatic experiences in the trenches during sleep and found themselves time and again at the same point of their distress (Freud 1981a).

Dexter is a compulsive assassin because of a childhood trauma, with something alien in him enjoying the sawing and cutting of his victims in the psychotic acts of his justice. It is as if he could find in the entrails of his victims the aforementioned signifier that was lost.

One of Freud's most important discoveries was therefore a negative one: the insight that in attempting to analyze the persistence of unconscious symptoms, one cannot simply approach them with an interpretation that remains strictly within the register of meaning and a pragmatic space of reasons. After all, the very persistence of a symptom is immune to the question, "Why are you doing this?" If someone like Dexter wakes up at night covered in sweat from recurring nightmares, one cannot say to him, "Have a glass of milk and calm down." Equally unsuccessful is pointing out the absurdity of compulsive neurotic hand-washing. The person in question knows the absurdity of her/his deeds. And yet he/she cannot transform this knowledge into a mental causation in such a way that the compulsive course of action dissolves with what Jürgen Habermas calls "the better argument." Propositional knowledge does not lead to the translation of a tic into an act of free will. For this reason, it can be argued that the birth of psychoanalysis is tied to the recognition of gaps in consciousness that are caused "by repression" (Freud 1981, vol. 16, 298).

The early Freud analyzed mental illnesses with a theory of latency put forth in his *Studies on Hysteria* (1895, with Josef Breuer). He discovered in what way the "construction of a symptom is a substitute for something else," something that has been omitted or that has not happened. "Some particular mental processes should normally have developed to a point at which consciousness received information of them. This, however, did not take place, and instead—out of the interrupted processes . . .—the symptom emerged" (Freud 1981, vol. 16, 280). Since 1895, that is, since his *Project for a Scientific Psychology*, written in exchange with Wilhelm Fliess, Freud had searched for the "sense of symptoms" (ibid., 258–72). Symptoms are bearers of what at first sight appears to be a "senseless idea" (ibid., 270). But the sense must be found in a "past situation," Freud says. For in this, the sense, which provided consciousness with a gap, was justified as a certain "idea and the action [of displacement] served [a] purpose" (ibid., 270).

As in dreams, the lack of translating an experience in the order of meaning shows up in the symptom, hence Freud's interest in the homology between symptoms and dreams. If symptoms are defined by that which "has not forced their way into consciousness" (ibid., 278), then, with regard to dreams, Freud underscores that not only can there be no such thing as a symptom-free consciousness, but also that symptoms cannot simply be overcome at the level of epistemic acts of cognition and semantic acts of reasoning. In the examples mentioned above (from *Dexter* to war-neurotics), the body overwrites acts of consciousness from psychophysical sources that are difficult to access. In individual cases this can even put the individual's life in danger. In such cases, a non-semantic residue escapes the sovereign authority of our intellect and, according to Freud, can only be bound by means of a discourse that attempts to approach the psychophysical "dimension of symbolization 'below' the level of intentionality" (Santner 2001, 28). That is, this non-semantic core of our symptoms (and our dreams) can only be approached indirectly and asymptotically. This happens in an analysis, for example, by talking about dreams and fantasies, or about what the patient literally "babbles away" when he or she starts talking freely in the presence of the analyst. In Nietzsche's words: the "it" in "it thinks" is called upon to emerge, not the "I" as "the condition of the predicate 'think'" (Nietzsche 2002, 17). What is repressed and unbound in the mind cannot be compared to an act of self-deception that, in principle, remains responsive to the question "Why don't you know what is wrong with you?" Our dreams are always wrong, so to speak, they can never be right. But the way dreams or symptoms are wrong expresses how they are right.

Freud himself suggested that the human mind is determined by motivations of which the individual subject is supposed to have no clue. A defense mechanism protects the psyche from too much insight into its motivations. So, it is not just that we can never be masters in our house of consciousness. Psychoanalysis says more: we are not allowed to be at home in this house. A form of non-being, the absence of the landlord is necessarily inscribed into consciousness. A certain form of non-being is the condition of being.

2

Lacan deepens Freud's insights with the tools of phenomenology and the linguistic and anthropological structuralism of his time. He thus arrives at the thesis that unconscious mental activity is organized around and with the help of signifiers. As stacks of data, signifiers are elements of inferential meaning networks and at the same time are the building blocks of our second nature—and, thus, of our consciousness and our unconscious.

Signifiers are both embedded in our biological bodies (transforming them into biopolitical ones) and omnipresent in the world structured by us and our fellow beings. They are the building blocks that split us apart into the ego as a particular social entity within the universal frame of society and that which is more than this particularity: a remainder crisscrossing any law of identity and any order of being. Signifiers are present, for example, in newspapers, traffic lights, legal practices, laws, and monuments; conversely, they also show up in our dreams, hallucinations, desires, and fantasies. As instances of symbolic force, signifiers are omnipresent. They establish beliefs, values, and norms between objects within collective networks of meaning. Precisely because of this, our mental states are symptom carriers of chains of signifiers; that is, of an Other we are part of, and who, in reverse, is part of us. This persistence of an Other in oneself, the symbolic order with its coherence-theoretical structured laws of identity, can be stressful, but involves libidinous dimensions as well. We, or something in us (the Other, the stranger, that which is more in us), experiences a paradoxical pleasure of displeasure through the non-integration of that which is mindless within the mind. And this experience continues even if it stands in contradiction to our pragmatic interests, where pleasure is sought and displeasure is supposed to be discarded. This paradoxical enjoyment that Freud detected in war-neurotics, among others, and that Lacan calls jouissance (more on this later), is diametrically opposed to the classical conception of humanity shaped by the various humanist traditions of antiquity, the Renaissance, and the Enlightenment. In these traditions, the rational animal often features a soul in which the rational part dominates spirit and appetite.

So, the rational part of the mind is by no means associated with a hidden, sadomasochistic enjoyment of its mindless tics and mental aberrations—anything but.

Freud detects this enjoyment of agony in "patients suffering from traumatic neuroses" (Freud 1981, vol. 18, 32). He exposed it in the behavior of patients tormented with traumas from World War I (Freud 1981a), in defensive reactions to the positive tendencies of therapy, and in various forms of masochism (Freud 1981b). But this causes theoretical problems, since this strange form of enjoyment contradicts Freud's pleasure principle, which as a principle of homeostasis is directed to find an equilibrium between pleasure and displeasure. The psyche can fall out of its mind-world relation through distressing glitches in experience, with these same glitches—as self-contradictory as this may sound—being the universal conditions of what subjectivity may essentially be about.

3

Under the influence of Wilhelm Fliess and the psychophysics of his time (especially as represented by H. v. Helmholtz, T. Fechner, and W. Wundt), Freud interpreted the brain as a relay station of libidinal and energy-laden data-stacks in his draft paper of 1895, *Project for a Scientific Psychology* (Freud 1981c).

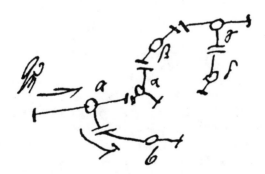

In doing so, he came to the conclusion that the internal structure of the brain has to be interpreted as an interface between internal and external bodily stimuli, constituting an unconscious as a background structure of an emerging ego. For just as every organism needs a boundary that enables it to individuate, the ego, as a mental entity with its experience of selfhood, also needs such a boundary: in relation to the flux of diverse stimuli, impressions, thoughts, associations, and fantasies from without and within. Five years later, this thesis is specified in the famous seventh chapter of the *Interpretation of Dreams*. Freud describes the mind as a succession of memory-layers enshrined between perceptions on the one hand and acts of motor agency on the other. Between the layers, successive transcriptions take place. Through processes of mutual overwriting, these open up a realm of personal experience with present and past in a constant exchange of meaning-formation (Freud 1981, vol. 5, 533–49).

In contrast to modern neuroscience, Freud's primary interest in the human mind was not so much focused on the psyche's ability to shift energy-quanta concerning memories, libido, desires, and so on, but on the question of how the streams of energy-quanta affect processes of transference between an individual and the symbolic world it is part of. Psychoanalysis thus focuses on symbolic relations in which the ego-function is located in its communal and corporeal-biological genesis. It is interested in how the ego responds to the virtual and empirical worlds that open up spaces of experience for the self, for others, and the relation of meaning and truth among them. And since the mind must locate itself with regard to a world of shared experiences, these communal structures of inference do not so much raise questions of the localization of neural regions of the brain responsible for semantic, emotional, or sensorimotor capacities, but questions of authority and authorization. Psychoanalysis is thus precisely not interested in questions of modern psychology (and debated, among many others, by Dennett 1991; Churchland 1995; Deacon 1997; Metzinger 2009; Millikan 2019). Rather, the psychoanalytic way to understand subjectivity is concerned with the role of symbolic interpellation and its impact on the mind-world relationship. Factors such as family and childhood become crucial, while disorders at the level of neurotransmitters (like serotonin or dopamine), despite their undoubted influence on the mind, fade into the background. In the words of Eric Santner: psychoanalysis deals not with biological but with "biopolitical life" (Santner 2001, 30). If we look closely at this biopolitical (rather than biological) life that interests psychoanalysis, we see that it is strongly affected by the riddle of authority and authorization within the framework of a meaningful order. And this is what the following sections of this lecture will be about.

According to Freud's "pleasure principle," displeasure arises from a stressful gridlock of energy quanta wanting to be discharged. Pleasure, by contrast, arises in the moment of release. Take the example of a person sitting at a desk all day. He or she may experience discomfort at the lack of movement. The desire to get up will increase with regard to the mounting frustration of not having moved at all. The pleasure principle motivates us to cancel this distress. The "reality principle," however, will hold us back when we are sitting in an opera. We will not get up in the tenth row of the concert hall to stretch our legs. Consequently, the pleasure principle strives to avoid displeasure (i.e., excessive stimuli from within), while the reality principle subjects this urge to an act of cognitive assessment. The so-called "primary processes" are subject to the pleasure principle, the "secondary processes" to the reality principle. Freud now asserts that the human mind loses its integrity and innocence beginning in early childhood by being repeatedly exposed to all kinds of arousing streams of energy-quanta. How to deal with these must be learned. Sources of excitement can have their origin externally (for example in the parents), but also internally in the body (hunger, thirst, sexual drives). Often, they produce displeasure because in infancy the child cannot know why an empty stomach causes pain. We have all experienced situations where parents stand around their screaming toddler trying to calm it down. Does it want the balloon? No. The pacifier? Does it want to get out of the stroller? No, again. The child continues to cry.

This is mentioned to underline the multitude of situations that can have traumatic qualities from a toddler's perspective. A dinner plate falls down and the child, shocked by the accident, starts crying. A fissure in the matrix of everyday life opens up. But moments later, all is well again—for example, due to a lollipop held out to the child. Or think of the situation when a balloon pops. The toddler appears to be as upset and devastated as an adult who has suffered a terrible loss. But unlike the adult, two minutes later the toddler is no longer distraught at all. It laughs as if nothing had happened. The World War I soldier lying on Freud's couch fails to spontaneously forget. He repeatedly wakes up from his dreams soaked in sweat. One cannot simply disconnect him from the repetitive loop of hallucinations in the same way as one can soothe the child with a pacifier. The impact of excitation has fundamentally damaged the mind, bringing it into conflict with itself. But, according to the pleasure principle as a principle of homeostasis, the mind has no interest in the return of a stressful situation—quite the opposite. Therefore, as Freud discovered, the repetition of a nightmare makes no sense at all. Why should the mind be interested in repeating a terrible event?

Freud, considering this paradox, formulates the thesis that the traumatic experience has not been internally symbolized by the patient's mind. "An 'anticathexis' on the grand scale is set up, for whose benefit all the other psychical systems are impoverished, so that the remaining psychical functions are extensively paralyzed or reduced" (Freud 1981, vol. 18, 30). In this case, we have an experience that, strictly speaking, was no experience at all. Something which is too much to bear overwhelms the mental states of consciousness and fissures them. The mind collapses. It may eventually regain its balance, but the cause of the mental breakdown resists conversion into a meaningful experience. Freud now claims that every trauma arises from "an excess in demand [*Zuviel von Anspruch*]" (Freud 1981, vol. 23, 73). Santner, following Freud, speaks fittingly of "too muchness" (Santner 2001, 8). "Too muchness" illustrates the fact that a trauma leaves a particularly lasting mark on the mind precisely when the disturbing impact was not processed and continues to be resistant to future processing.

Freud had already stumbled upon this fact in his and Breuer's *Studies on Hysteria*. Focusing on sexual assaults experienced by pre-adolescent patients, among other matters, the authors dwell on the intrusion of an Other in the mind due to an unsymbolized excess of sexual excitement. The mind of "Katharina" (Freud 1981, vol. 2, 125–34), for example, is unable to process the sexual transgression experienced in an earlier phase of her life. Freud and Breuer show how this surplus or "excess in demand" lingers in latency and is experienced as traumatic in a phase of life that—at first sight—has nothing to do with the original situation of transgression mentioned. Consciousness proves to be caught within a time loop reversing past and future. It is unable to understand how an event in the past, which at first sight has no direct causal relationship with the original traumatic experience, can suddenly be activated from the future. In such aberrations of excessive streams of energy-quanta, Freud believed to have found an explanation for the formation of neurotic symptoms and for meaningful content within the absurd hallucinations of dreams.

4

A demand, as well as the act of being addressed by a demand, requests responsiveness in return. It is directed at our mental state of attention: to be aware of something. Traumas burst through this attention. The lack of experience is the result of it. What remains in the individual's mind is not an oblivious disappointment as in the toddler's experience of a popped balloon, but a "non-place," a gap in the fabric of the mind's inner reflexivity. The very lack of an experience allows the mind to "boot up" anew, like a computer program, but the catastrophe may return again.

In the state of sleep, so-called secondary processes wane along with the power of repression, and the primary processes mentioned by Freud come to the fore. This is when the mind, like in the film *Groundhog Day*

(1993), seeks to return to the primal scene of injury. While asleep, various instances of censorship loosen and the unsymbolized and meaning-lacking past can emerge as something that continues to exist in its paradoxical state of in-existence. As Freud says, traumas enact "an excess in demand." They embody a surplus of meaning barred from translation into inferential and cognitive truth values. Traumas have obstructed the translation of horrific events into meaningful experiences.

No later than the 1920s, Freud became convinced that no interpretation of a dream can completely illuminate or clarify it. The human mind is simply confronted with too many demands from birth on. And this is obvious: we have demands toward ourselves, demands emanating from our parents and various institutions, and so on, and we often cannot live up to them as we would like. This can lead to nightmares, symptom formation, and slips; and in rare cases, to severe psychological disorders. Most of these demands, however, are not eruptively traumatic. No one is going to claim that her or his childhood was a succession of traumas. In this respect, many of the demands made on us are not overwhelming, but are rather part of the training program that Freud calls the Oedipus complex: the subjugation of the individual to norms and values of which the child is never the source. And yet, to a certain extent, interpellations within these training programs leave behind enigmatic traces.

An important scholar in the philosophy of psychoanalysis who has examined these traces of transference against the background of their enigmatic properties is Jean Laplanche (2002, 2005). His work is centered on the concept of "enigmatic messages" and enigmatic signifiers (Laplanche 2005, 166–96). Laplanche explores the mystery that unfolds within the child's inner-psychic experience in confrontation with this Other as the source of touch, food, sexuality, and speech-acts. He recognizes that the subject's inner alienation, which is sometimes identified with the unconscious, is essentially the result of a traumatic encounter with the enigmatic presence of the desire of the Other. This Other is first and foremost embodied in the parents. For when parents care for their child, a desire intrinsically accompanies their acts. But the child does not yet comprehend what is going on. It does not understand why eating is necessary or why sleep is indispensable. It is not much more than a vegetative organism lacking self-consciousness. It satisfies many of its needs on the mechanical level of biological functions. As such, the child is nevertheless called upon in the numerous tactile ways of dealing with its body. This kind of tactility is expressed in caressing and feeding the child. Acts like these convey norms and values, but enigmatic demands as well. They have meaning without being meaningful for the child. Laplanche uses Saussure's vocabulary of "signifiers"; he speaks of "enigmatic signifiers" as essential building blocks in processes of transference. Signifiers transmit meanings and concepts of all kinds in their physical form of sound, image, or grapheme. A stop sign is a signifier. It embodies the command: "Stop, or be punished!" For a toddler, signifiers emanate from parents, even if the child is not able to decipher them. The work of education starts here with token-training of type-words and type-norms. It consists of teaching what signifiers stand for. For example, the concept "lunch" signifies something which has to be put into the mouth and not on the head. Beyond that, however, a surplus of meaning in terms of content is always transferred as well (since the signifier, in its contextual deployment in signification, always signifies more than the signified). The surplus is a by-product of intersubjective relations. This explains for Žižek why a child may follow the demands of the mother and "demonstrate how well-behaved he is, ready to fulfill his mother's demand to finish the plate and to do it properly, without dirtying his hands and the table." Desire and pleasure are channeled. "Pleasure is 'barred,' prohibited, in its immediacy, i.e., insofar as it involves taking a direct satisfaction in the object; pleasure is permitted only in the function of complying with the Other's demand" (Žižek 1993, 72).

A few years ago, I witnessed in a family of close friends a situation of transference with similar demands, interpellations, and even angst going back and forth between toddler and parents. This time the context was marked by the signifier "deficiency of motor skills." Doctors suspected this kind of deficiency in the behavior of the child. This caused the parents to look at him with great concern for several weeks, not knowing if the deficiency had neurological reasons or was just an arbitrary delay in development. And even if the child in question did not yet know what it means to lack motor skills, one can assume that he received messages from the parents' distress in subtle processes of day-to-day contact. "What do my parents want from me?" "Why do they look at me in fear?" The mind of the child encounters expressions of authority in combination with care and concern in the form of riddles and enigmas. "What is it that makes me different, a source of fear?"

I do not claim that toddlers are capable of posing these kind of questions in the first three years of their life. Nevertheless, memory fragments may contribute to intrapsychic interpretations of this kind at later stages of development and change the past through the future via retrospective acts of interpretation. The individual may one day learn to retrospectively understand something about the gazes of his parents, who were too anxious for many months and therefore too puzzling in the eyes of the child.

Laplanche paradigmatically mentions the mother's breast as an enigmatic signifier with sexual properties located between mother and child. As one of the most important organs of care, it can be the medium of a particular form of interpellation. "For the breast is not only an organ for feeding children but a sexual organ . . . in the woman's sexual life" (Laplanche 2005, 78). Enigmatic messages impose themselves through the breast, which is charged with a desire unknown to "the mother herself" (ibid., 97). Laplanche, recalling Freud, speaks of a "primal scene" of the birth of sexuality. "There is . . . the other who addresses me, the other who 'wants' something of me" (ibid., 78) out of the disturbed spirit of fundamental dependence, which at the same time invests early childhood sexuality with an "interrogative core" (Santner 2007, 34). What does the Other, as a source of food and sexuality, want from me? What is his or her desire? Why am I called to be desired? Enigmatic messages go back and forth without a clearly detectable message.

Laplanche speaks in this context of a precognitive drama of legitimation and underlines the correlation between sexuality and the confrontation with the question of where the individual is located in the desire of the Other. One source of his line of argument goes back to Freud, especially to Freud's notion of so-called *Wahrnehmungszeichen* ("perception signs," trans. changed). Freud mentions this term in a letter to Wilhelm Fliess of December 6, 1896. It marks proto-subjective acts of perception. *Wahrnehmungszeichen* stand for the "first registration of . . . perceptions . . . incapable of consciousness" (Freud 1981, vol. 1, 234). Freud could have made more of this concept, Laplanche argues, as he, Freud, interprets the signs of perception primarily in their indexical function to determine states of affairs. However, for Laplanche, it is precisely the sign-like nature of *Wahrnehmungszeichen* (perceptual signs) with regard to both the parents and to the lack of a clear meaning that is of importance. *Wahrnehmungszeichen* "make *a sign* in a double, linked sense—they acquire the force of signs and this is because, isolated by the sender, they are addressed to the subject" (Laplanche 2005, 75). *Wahrnehmungszeichen* are more than mere instruments of reference a toddler learns. Inscribed in them is a message that even the caregivers or parents themselves, as senders, may have no clue about what the message's content actually is. Questions regarding the impact of interpellation and the dependence on the desire of the Other become meaningful for us not only when we go to kindergarten, school, or work. They affect us as subjects even before our birth, and continuously thereafter. Perceptual signs cannot be remembered as primordial tokens at the origin of the genesis of our consciousness. Consciousness needs unconscious inscriptions as a condition of conscious ones. At the origin of consciousness, "consciousness and memory are mutually exclusive" (Freud 1981, vol. 1, 234). In these inscriptions the Other is always present. So, as toddlers we are involved in the formations of desire that help shape our own desires. The "primordial scene" is then, according to Laplanche, an individual's confrontation "with signifiers emanating from an adult" that are related to the satisfaction of existential needs. But beyond that, these signifiers "convey the purely interrogative potential of other messages— and those other messages are sexual. These enigmatic messages set the child a difficult, or even impossible, task of mastery and symbolization, and the attempt to perform it inevitably leaves behind unconscious residues. These are what Freud . . . terms *fueros*" (Laplanche 1989, 130).

In its existential dependence on its caretakers, the infant is involved in a stream of transference. It is confronted or fed with an abundance of signifiers even if these are initially accessible only as demands (*Geltungen*) lacking meaning (*Bedeutung*). Laplanche's talk of "source objects of the drives" (Laplanche 1989, 130) denotes the constant effort of translation due to the parent's desire projected into the child. At this level, the infant resembles the famous ethnologist that Willard V. O. Quine speaks of in *Word and Object* (Quine 2013, §§7–8). He attempts to translate the word "Gavagai" as pronounced by a native of an indigenous tribe when a rabbit passes the scene. As Quine reveals, however, a correct translation between languages is never possible. Quine uses this example to illustrate the "indeterminacy of translation," but also to underline the always overde-termined relationship between mind and world that can never be cogni-tively ordered into clear hierarchies of clusters of semantic meaning. And just as Quine's anthropologist can never be certain he has dissolved all epistemic remainders between himself and the representative of the for-eign culture in his translation manual, so too is Freud's and Laplanche's infant unable to know what is ontologically meaningful or fatefully hidden in the "enigmatic messages" that are simultaneously tactile and linguistic.

Classical philosophies of subjectivity, from Kant to Charles Taylor, for example, approach the subject differently. For them, our entry into the social structure of Being is tied to our cognitive formation by con-cepts and their semantic roles in thoughts and actions. In contrast to these, a psychoanalytic perspective understands the entry into the shared realm of experiences as being primarily characterized by the indetermi-nacy of translation, due to the intrusive strangeness of the Other and the reception of enigmatic signs/signifiers emanating from this Other. Psychoanalysis thus suggests that the entry into the socio-symbolic order depends on the encounter with an enigmatic Other. This encounter, in turn, triggers excitations as patterns of transference via "source objects of the drives" (Laplanche 1989, 130).

The subject's intrinsic patterns of desire are fatefully shaped by the aforementioned processes of transference, patterns that are never fully transparent to reason. Subjectivity is indeterminate to itself. Unconscious transmissions of alien desires lie at the bottom of our individual idiosyncratic forms of consciousness. In this context, Santner speaks of "the undead" (Santner 2001, 25) as something that in-exists in the mental life beyond life and death. He infers this expression from Freud's concept of the "death drive" as presented in *Beyond the Pleasure Principle*. According to Žižek, the death drive characterizes the "vanishing mediator between nature and culture" (Žižek 2002, 207). He refers to the "subject prior to subjectivization" in the form of "pure negativity . . . prior to its reversal into the identification with some new master-signifier" (Žižek 2000a, 160). Santner follows this interpretation. His talk of what is "undead" in the human mind refers to alien animations of our desires "prior to subjectivization." They can lead us into aberrations and force us to miss the fullness of life for incomprehensible reasons. This interpretation of the concept of the "death drive" is diametrically opposed to the common understanding of sinking back into inanimate matter. The death drive proves to be a force of life, not of death, though it has destructive properties.

To summarize: from the child's encounter with the desire of the Other, a drama of legitimation unfolds. Freud is the first to point out the uncanny vitality of our psychic life as an effect of this process. He describes it as the perseverance or persistence of something that inhabits our ego function through infiltrations of the desire of the other. And even if we suffer from the drama mentioned, experiences of pleasure in displeasure may have their impact as well. The discontents of civilization are thus also discontents in and of ourselves. Laplanche, in his further development of Freud's investigations, points out that our cognitive integration into social relations is also bound up with an existential integration revolving around enigmatic signifiers. The unconscious, as a hoard of signifiers, enigmatic signifiers, and repressions, does not resemble an archive. It does not stand for something formerly conscious that we can no longer remember. Rather, the unconscious is a "memory cut off from its origins and from its access routes, isolated and fixed, reduced to a trace" (Laplanche 2005, 152) and, as such, functions as a condition of the possibility of experience. It stands for that which has escaped the realm of well-ordered memories. The unconscious is not a memory but a "reminiscence" (ibid., 65, 152).

2

Freud and Kant

Illusions of the Mind and Illusions of Reason

(Lecture 3)

1

Freud develops his psychoanalytic concepts in an effort to give rational justification for mental illnesses as the precondition of treating them. With reference to neurotic disorders whose sources lie, for example, in the experience of trauma, psychoanalysis asks why traumatic experiences can repeatedly return and resist being forgotten. After all, the repetition of a stressful situation—having, for example, the same nightmare again and again—contradicts Freud's pleasure principle. Freud's own explanation for the mind's dilemma starts with postulating psychic "quantities of energy [*Energiequantitäten*]" (Freud 1981, vol. 1, 304). In such a case, the quantity of energy overtaxes and overburdens the psyche in the traumatic moment and so cannot be processed adequately into an experience of everyday life. A split in the psyche is the result. It leads to a confusion in the mind's internal organization of energy-quanta, with their psychic and libidinous properties. Hence, the trauma marks a failure of the psyche's evaluation of experience. As such a lack of experience, as a rupture in the fabric and pattern of everyday mental life, the unprocessed event returns because of its presence as a missing link. Or, in Lacan's words: the trauma resists translation into the order of the so-called "signifying chain" (Lacan 2006a, 418).

However, excessive quantities of psychic energy are not only significant for trauma patients. Every human mind has to react to energy-charged impressions (sense data) from outside and inside that produce pleasure and displeasure. They accompany the production of stratified memory layers through rejection, cathexis, and absorption. The mind's procedural task is therefore to shift energy quantities without producing too many stressful perturbations. In these shifts, experiences of pleasure and displeasure motivate, for example, the establishment of experience one can live by. These processes ultimately lead to the establishment of the reality principle as the antipode to the pleasure principle's dominance. The mind needs to find an equilibrium between stimuli from within (drives, instincts, and feelings such as hunger and pain) and those from without (in the form of spoken words and commands from parents, for example). This prevents both the complete sacrifice of the inner realm of psychic desires to the outer world of social interaction and its converse: the corruption of the intersubjective world of normative demands by an idiosyncratic mind and its impulses. External impressions may be the words of the parents, which the infant does not yet understand, while inner impressions may be feelings of hunger or sexual desires that create physical stress by preventing the discharge of quantities of energy. The multiplicity of energetic sensations that require psychic processing can never be completely metabolized by the mind. This has been indicated by Laplanche. There are necessarily enigmatic signifiers which resist comprehension and, as a result, leave inner-psychic traces behind.

Traces of this kind characterize a layer of consciousness which, as an other in the ego, forms the basis of unconscious mental activity. However, as I indicated in the prologue, the unconscious is not the true self behind our ego function. It is the part which has no part in the realm of universal rules and relations; that is, in the realm in which every entity is and must be submitted to the rule of the law of identity. The unconscious is not the hoard of a supplementary content that remains stored away like in an archive, or a cellar. It is not something from which, by inner psychological scrutiny from the ego's rational perspective, repressions can be recovered like corpses in a grave. "Because if something thinks in the floor below or underground, things are simple, thought is always there and all one needs is a little consciousness on the thought that the living being is naturally thinking and all is well. If such were the case, thought would be prepared by life, naturally, such as instinct for instance. . . . But the unconscious has nothing to do with instinct and primitive knowledge or preparation of thought in some underground" (Lacan 1970, 189). The unconscious generates supernumeraries and surpluses that cannot be negotiated like an exchange value. The unconscious is proverbially marked with a missing cause, a missing legitimacy, which existentially ties the human to distress and awe, to the weird and the eerie. But it also ties the human being to the possibility to incorporate judgmental properties as part of its second nature. This process retrospectively causes the first nature—the biological body—to become an entity in its own right. The aforementioned remainders, which might be caused by the enigmatic words and actions of parents and caretakers, can appear repeatedly as unprocessed residues in our mind-world relations and trigger unexpected experiences of strangeness. In these cases, they may thwart our relation to facts and states of affairs or our understanding what "the good life" is commonly about.

As mentioned, Jean Laplanche is interested in enigmatic processes of transference in the early stages of child development. Here, the human organism is involved in an ongoing process of managing internal and external stimuli due to its long-lasting dependence on parents and caretakers. Patterns of visual recognition have to be trained, as must the communication of personal needs and the response to the desires of others. In places where energy quanta, with their epistemic remainders, leave deep traces in an individual mind, they can, among other things, produce neurotic symptoms—anxiety attacks, phobias, psychosomatic reactions, and so on—without the person in question knowing exactly what is going on.

Such symptoms indicate the insistence of something non-mental, which at one time overtaxed the mind and has continued to act on it latently ever since. Such disorders can have purely biological causes. They can be disturbances on the level of neuronal messenger substances such as serotonin or dopamine, which are investigated by psychology and psychiatry. Psychoanalysis, however, is not interested in biological causes. It sees its task as the investigation of symbolic processes in the genesis of subjectivity, rather than in the neuropsychological analysis of messenger substances in the brain. This does not mean that mental disorders cannot have biological causes. On the contrary, neurotic tics cannot be explained without their biological causes. But for psychoanalysis, the biological factors can in turn be the outcome of mental factors—that is, those arising in processes of symbolic mediation.

In *Beyond the Pleasure Principle*, Freud thematizes one such stressful experience in which a mind is struck by a parent's enigmatic behavior, by referring to his grandson, an eighteen-month-old child who was living under Freud's roof at the time (Freud 1981, vol. 18, 14–15). In contrast to his and Breuer's *Studies on Hysteria*, Freud's attention here is not focused on how the mind suffers a symptom-like "dent" due to a traumatic injury, which then erupts after a period of latency. Instead, he analyzes an opposite experience: how the mind of a toddler can overcome an experience of negativity by inventing a symbolic space through the help of a signifier used to calm itself. Freud's observation has been interpreted as the origin of human culture via the sublimation of experiences of negativity.

Freud is specifically interested in the child's ability to console himself over his mother's absence by playing with a spool of string. The handling of the spool is, according to Freud, a playful repetition of the unpleasant experience of the mother's departure insofar as the child reenacts the experience repeatedly. He repeatedly throws the spool away, saying "fort" (away), and pulls it back to himself, saying "da" (here). The absence of the parent is dealt with via a simple practice of cultural compensation. The child was "passively" affected (overtaxed) by negativity and actively liberates himself through a signifier. Freud writes: "It was related to the child's great cultural achievement—the instinctual renunciation (that is, the renunciation of instinctual satisfaction) which he had made in allowing his mother to go away without protesting. He compensated himself for this, as it were, by himself staging the disappearance and return of the object within his reach" (Freud 1981, vol. 18, 15).

The American philosopher Jonathan Lear comments on Freud's interpretation of this "fort-da" game. He argues that the toddler overcomes an abyss of negativity through a state of play on a symbolic, or sign-mediated, level. In the face of the enigmatic absence of the mother, a symbolic structure of appeasement and reassurance emerges. "If we are trying to respect the child's point of view, we cannot even say that the game is prompted by loss. For it is only after the game is installed that the child will begin to have the concept of loss or absence. Only when the game is established will the loss be a loss for him. The outcome of the game is to convert what would otherwise be a nameless trauma into a loss. The child had been inhabiting a less differentiated field of 'mother-and-child': it is this field that is disturbed by the mother's absence" (Lear 2000, 92).

According to Lear, the original experience of negativity was not an *experience* in the true sense of the word. It had no symbolic expression. It is only with the play's initiation, the spool as signifier, as proxy for the absent mother, that negativity acquires symbolic meaning through the play of presence and absence. This meaning, though, is not the experience of negativity prior to the play. It arises retrospectively *through* the play.

Freud's interest in the child's fort-da game reflects his concern with the origin of cultures and the use of symbolic archetypes to sublimate a stressful past and the traumatic loss of an allegedly paradisical beginning in time. Cultures, as collective structures of the unconscious, assemble patterns of imagination and options for social action. Freud sees in them an analogous way of handling pre-symbolic stress. This stress can only be cognitively recovered through symbolization. This does not only concern ancient cultures and the "horde of brothers" that Freud discusses in his theory of an original patricide at humanity's beginning in *Totem and Taboo*. In reference to our time, one can claim that numerous sociopolitical rites achieve just what Freud's grandson accomplishes. These rites control contingency through repetition by bringing a negative experience into a game of symbolic ceremony. This is done at the expense of the original stress in its traumatic, ineffable dimension, which is now inaccessible. Holocaust commemoration, with its widespread predilection for sentimentalism in, for example, film, television, and literature, is exemplary of this. Ritualization makes the supposedly incomprehensible trauma emotionally tangible, and yet it does not do justice to the original atrocity as an empirical fact. The ritual formally transforms all participants involved into better people.

This mechanism is reflected in the difficulty of the human sciences to adequately determine the epistemic moment of transition from a "state of nature" to a "state of culture." For as soon as culture has emerged, the chaotic state of nature is only accessible from the former. This may explain why, from the lack of a transparent transition from the state of nature to the state of culture, the imaginary idea of a romantic paradise arises in many cultures as well. What has been lost, the state of nature as paradise, emerges as a fantasy to compensate for a lack of meaning in the state of culture. The loss of origin is not an event that can be dated with exactitude. It ascends as an effect of a symbolic order, which, due to its impossibility to close itself off, repeatedly experiences itself as threatened by crises of all kinds.

Freud's reference to the game with the wooden spool is an allegory for how human beings deal with prehistoric stress such that negativity is dealt with in a playful and compensatory way. The child whom Freud discusses finds a way to transfer the excess of negative excitement to a signifier. One could therefore say that he discovers the power of a fiction under the influence of a small catastrophe. The toddler enters a widening horizon of meaning in which, from now on, the difference between mother's presence and mother's absence no longer exclusively governs the child's emotional household. From now on, the mother's presence and absence can be re-celebrated. The newly mediated form of life, though, continues to be marked from now on by a trace of absence (the spool as signifier).

2

Playing with the spool reenacts the loss of the mother as a ritualized compensation. What is not represented, however, is, as I mentioned, the original distress. It prompted the child to create the symbol as a pattern of sublimation. To put it pointedly: the symbolic order itself is based on the lack of what cannot be recovered. It is grounded on an inherent crisis. Eric Santner, referring to the fort-da game and Lear's interpretation thereof, describes this circumstance as follows: "The form of life the child now inhabits is haunted by *the trace of a missing link*, the lack of a signifier for the initial trauma, the namelessness of the rip in the fabric of life that called forth—ex-cited—the child's creative capacities in the first place" (Santner 2011, 71). This fits Lear's diagnosis: "The name of loss requires the game of loss: it requires inventing ways of living with the loss that one has just named. Once the game is established, once the child can face his loss courageously, once the mind can function according to the pleasure principle, the question of what lies beyond (or before) gets covered over. What gets hidden is the nonteleological occasion for courage: the disruption of the fabric of life to which courage can only be a retrospective response" (Lear 2000, 95).

In other words, the fort-da game demonstrates the performance of the human mind at a rudimentary level in an interplay of cognition, symbolic representation, language, and contingency management. The child masters the unexpected by opening up the symbolic order. An ideal way of dealing with absence and presence emerges, which rests on an experience of negativity that is from now on repressed. This idea is important for my further course of argument, since the human psyche's mode of functioning, indicated by Freud in the child, can also be found on a higher level of abstraction in Immanuel Kant's work. According to Kant, a world of phenomena can only be built up by human understanding (*Verstand*) if it is supported by fantasies internal to reason (*Vernunft*). Kant calls the postulated fantasies "ideas" (freedom, soul, the world, God). They cannot be recognized in space and time like objects of experience, since every attempt to do so entangles reason in paralogisms (fallacies) or antinomies. And yet they prove to be phantasmagorical, formal conditions of our fact-perceiving consciousness. Ideas give the realm of mere understanding systematicity that cannot be justified by this realm (*Verstand*) alone. Without reason's fantasies, the abundance of scientific experience would be a singular chaos. No hope would drive us to transform multiplicities of multiplicities into order and systematic harmony.

But Kant also unfolds another reality-constituting fiction besides the ideas of reason (as postulates) with his concept of a "*focus imaginarius.*" Kant introduces this term in his *Critique of Pure Reason* in accordance with his conviction that the phenomena surrounding us in daily life can only be confronted with regard to the fantasy of a world (as totality) that they are part of. The term "world," though, has no referent. There is no world we can contemplate like the coffee mug next to me on the table. Yet, the term "world" gives phenomena, like the mug, the property of being in the world next to abstract entities like numbers, moral maxims, all kinds of social institutions (from money to insurance), and so on.

One can also think of the *focus imaginarius* as the vanishing point in an architectonic drawing. This point lies either inside or outside the drawing as the guiding focus of all horizontal and vertical lines. It helps the architect to bring the objects drawn into harmony according to their proportions. Kant now claims that our mind adopts this fictive point automatically as a target inscribed a priori into the form of the understanding. The *focus* helps us encounter a world as an entity constituted of sub-elements to be potentially ordered in the present as well as in the future. Thus, the idea of *focus* gives our mind "a certain goal" in acts of understanding. It centers "the lines of direction of all its rules" into "one point, which, although it is only an idea (*focus imaginarius*)—i.e., a point from which the concepts of the understanding do not really proceed, since it lies entirely outside the bounds of possible experience—nonetheless still serves to obtain for these concepts the greatest unity alongside the greatest extension" (Kant 1998, 591 [A644/B672]).

As Petra Bahr has pointed out, Kant borrows the term *focus imaginarius* from eighteenth-century art theory, and more precisely from the technique of drawing objects with the help of auxiliary lines forming a perspective grid. Bahr writes: "The *focus imaginarius* is that invisible vanishing point at which all objects can be placed in the correct proportion to one another. It is added artificially to an image in iconographic analyses in order to make its unseen ordering structure manifest" (Bahr 2004, 249, my trans.).

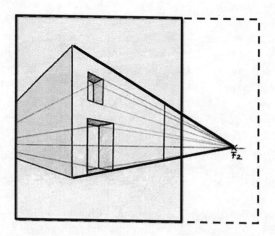

Kant thus uses the term to underline that our mind is oriented toward a vanishing point of cognition—even when the point in question is only a fiction and lies outside the limits of experience. "The illusion . . . awakens the pretense that the goal of total knowledge is 'objectively' conceivable"

(ibid., my trans.). It creates a point of transition in which reason sees itself as its own medium of totality. This necessary illusion is the result of reflection, and the "idea of totality is [. . . reason's] self-portrait" (Kaulbach 1990, 74, my trans.). The *focus imaginarius* is not part of the drawing but evokes a totality of the world depicted, coherent in proportions, rendered visible. It is, as a fiction, indispensable for the experience of facts and states of affairs.

I mention Kant's concept in order to illustrate the meaning of a "transcendental illusion" in this system. Kant refutes the skeptics' conviction that the concept "world" is meaningless. He encourages us, instead, to think that the "world" may very well be a great delusion; that is, a chaos of multiplicities that can never be ordered and brought into a coherent world picture. But the illusion of a world as the totality of what is and will be the case is "nevertheless indispensably necessary" (Kant 1998, 591 [A 645/B673]). Or, expressed in a more complex way: the illusion of a world as the totality of facts and states of affairs assumes, as a noumenon, a purpose within the manifold of phenomena. Multiplicities of contradicting facts can come into focus for us because the illusion of an intelligible world (without contradictions) holds them together. The focus is a transcendental illusion, which, as a condition, enables understanding's synthesizing power to perceive what is the case. And yet the illusion has to be repressed (see also Allison 2004, 426).

If we relate this insight back to Freud, the following is striking. Just as the child of the fort-da game symbolically captures the mother's absence and controls her contingent, arbitrary departure in the form of a signifier (the spool), Kant argues that understanding (*Verstand*) relies, for its cognitive performance, on reason's signifiers, since reason (*Vernunft*) imposes fictions on understanding for the formation of a potentially coherent world of experience.

In addition to the *focus imaginarius*, Kant names at least four such fictions constitutive of human cognition and action: freedom of will, the immortality of the soul, God, and the world as the totality of what is or will be the case. But his conception of humanity's teleological progression toward a moral future and his belief in the purposiveness of nature, discussed in several anthropological essays in the *Groundwork of the Metaphysics of Morals* and in *Critique of the Power of Judgment*, can also be counted among them. In this context, the *Groundwork* develops the following idea, which is close to the concept of the *focus imaginarius*: "Teleology considers nature as a kingdom of ends, morals considers a possible kingdom of ends as a kingdom of nature. In the former [where nature is interpreted teleologically as being equipped with an intrinsic purpose], the kingdom of ends is a theoretical idea for explaining what exists. In the latter [where the realm of moral determination is analyzed], it [the talk of a 'kingdom of ends'] is a practical idea for the sake of bringing about, in conformity with this very idea, that which does not exist," since morality cannot be found in the world like an object in space and time, "but which can become real by means of our conduct" (Kant 2006, 44).

So, according to Kant, at least two ideas accompany our theoretical cognition and our practical action. The first concerns nature as an ordered and fine-tuned realm of purposes. We adapt this idea automatically to understand, for example, natural processes as meaningful and nature as a holistic organism. The second idea, that of our moral genius, serves to reinforce our self-understanding as autonomous agents, even if we know full well that under purely empirical conditions of observation, the true motivation of our moral deeds may be shockingly egoistic. This subject matter remains relevant and complex in contemporary debates on free will (see Dennett and Caruso 2021).

Without the idea of nature's inner purpose and inner harmony, rational agents could not only not discover meaning and morality in the world, they could not even locate the trees in the park and the cars on the streets in a space of experience. We would perceive no facts and states of affairs accessible to reason at all—or, at best, we would do so in a frame of widespread cynicism: "It's all an illusion" (the motto of the Club Silencio in David Lynch's *Mulholland Drive*). The world would likely present itself to us as a misanthropic place and any form of social policy, intended to make the world a better place, would be misinterpreted as a conspiracy to maintain the power of the political class. In other words, we would suffer from mental illness and be alienated both from ourselves and from our fellow human beings. But we must be careful. Kant's teleology is not a relapse into classical metaphysics, but is conceived as a transcendental philosophy. It is assigned to the hermeneutic circle in which human beings receive their reality according to the conditions of their experience. Whether the reality of a river surrounding the nest of a beaver is indeed intrinsically meaningful and perfectly "designed" (by an intelligent designer), so that the animal's ability to build a dam as shelter points to a metaphysical principle of order designed for perfection, does not follow. The only conclusion we can draw from the dam as shelter is that it makes sense to project some kind of order in the harmony of an ecological niche. Our mental health as well as our cognitive capacities depend on postulates like these. In other words: the world, literally, calls upon us, as reasonable agents, to be perceived as a potential "kingdom of ends," a place of order striving for perfection with our minds being inclined, via reason's ideas, to give its approval.

3

The operation of the faculty of reason in Kant's philosophy is analogous to the modes of reaction of the infant's psyche in the case of Freud's grandson and his fort-da game. Just as the infant symbolically compensates for the contingency of the mother's absence and presence, so the faculty of reason triggers the necessary vision of a world, the teleologically shaped meaningfulness of phenomena, and the idea of a morally redeemable humanity in the "kingdom of ends."

The infant surrenders himself to the spool as a symbol (or signifier) after being passively frightened by the absence of his mother, just as the virtual worlds of reason (*Vernunft*) come to the aid of understanding (*Verstand*) in its confrontation with contingencies of all kinds. The *focus imaginarius*, as signifier, gives the mind a mirror image of its own totality. The illusion of "a world" sustains our grip on facts and states of affairs, norms and values. In doing so, the individual assumes, literally, the status of being a response to Being. He or she is urged to conform with reason to states of affairs as if reality asks to be ordered and understood via the human mind. (I will discuss this more later.) In a nutshell: Kant's postulates of reason (God, freedom, immortality of the soul, world, teleology in nature, kingdom of moral ends, etc.) inject phantasmagorical signifiers of an ideal harmony into human understanding through the higher faculty of reason. This unites our world with what is beyond (transcendent) and gives us rational beings the possibility to live toward a horizon of what is objective, good, beautiful, and eternal. According to Kant, human consciousness is bound to such self-imposed fictions, since metaphysical desires are, literally, inscribed into the human DNA. These are transcendental in character, that is, they are conditions of the possibility of knowledge and practical reason. One can therefore say that Kant identifies with his so-called "postulates" (God, soul, world, freedom, etc.), in the Freudian sense spools in our mind without which, according to Kant, we could neither explain nor enact cognition nor morality. The postulates constitute the objectivity of phenomena as virtual ideas, fantasy objects, the fictional building blocks of our mind. But they are, as Kant explicitly states, merely subjective functions of representations (Kant 1998, 248–49 [B136–38]). Constitutive determinations are by definition subject-"*immanent*" (Kant 1999, 249). They condition the horizon of objective knowledge as a goal to be achieved. This even has the paradoxical effect that God's reality is literally nothing, or rather, *a nothing* in which we nevertheless must believe and to which we must relate as embodied answers to a call.

Let me summarize once again the central line of argument that has been given so far. Freud's interpretation of the fort-da game shows the human mind characterized by an idiosyncratic interplay of cognition, symbolic representation, language, and contingency management. Freud sees basic cultural achievements at work in his grandson's actions. They tell us phylogenetically something about the contingency management of human cultures in general. The child masters contingency by opening up a minimal symbolic order. Analogously, Kant asserts that the faculty of understanding needs the higher faculty of reason, reason's figments, so to speak, for its cognitive performance and its moral freedom. Kant's postulates are a priori "spools" for the understanding to cope with all kinds of antinomies. In dealing with experiences of negativity, reason works with the same means as the mind of the infant. It works with abstract spool-like signifiers, a symbolic meta-world, which opens the first-order world, that is, the world of immediate experience, toward another, second-order world, a world of a metaphysical order.

3

Madness and the Loss of Language

Daniel P. Schreber and the Failure of Symbolic Investiture

(Lecture 4)

1

I pointed out in the previous lectures that the entry of human beings into the social world of symbolic forms only partly concerns the correct acquisition of stimulus patterns, the training of semantic processes in holistic systems of meaning, and the familiarization with customs and traditions. Jean Laplanche drew our attention to the insight that the impact of enigmatic signifiers on the mind must also be accounted for, under both epistemic and ontological perspectives. His recourse to Freud and Lacan shows to what extent the psyche is confronted with the desire of an Other (or others) in early childhood development. Humans are situated in a relational space not primarily of reasons but of desires and unconscious transference patterns. Actions are only partly based on reasons and concepts. They are also rooted in unconscious processes of transference of beliefs, desires, fantasies, and expectations.

These circumstances give rise to the small drama of our existence through the uncanny liveliness of our inner mental life. We cannot eliminate this vitality of an Other in us through the assignment of a psychophysical inventory of memories, traumas, repressions, and so on. The most radical reductive materialist among the naturalists of our era, among whom I would place Alex Rosenberg first and foremost, cannot illuminate this fact. The enigma of existence cannot be eliminated with the help of purely scientific criteria. The output would be similar to Rosenberg's *Atheist's Guide to Reality*, with reality being exactly that entity that, in the course of this insightful book, is lost (Rosenberg 2011).

The aforementioned drama is inscribed in the inner strangeness that characterizes every rational being as a condition of the very possibility of responding to and asking for reasons. Often this internal strangeness is accessible to us only indirectly: in dreams, hallucinations, psychic crises in which we have exhausted ourselves, slips, or psychophysical symptoms. In the following, I will once again refer to Laplanche's work and focus on the origin of this inner strangeness with reference to the structures of interpellation as emanating from enigmatic signifiers (gestures, words, expressions).

As already discussed, Laplanche is interested in signifiers that appeal to us without the need of a rational understanding of what the signifiers denote or stand for. A signifier's force of interpellation may even have more impact the more its meaning is undermined through the lack of understanding. But why should a message lacking comprehensibility interpellate (and captivate) us more successfully than a clear, comprehensible message? Is it not the meaningful content of a message, rather than the enigmatic form in which it is conveyed, that determines how we receive it? The answer to this question lies in the fact that, similar to traumatic experiences mentioned in the second lecture, the signifiers in question receive importance in their very failure to be translatable and, as a result, they captivate the mind. Laplanche writes: the "productive side to Lacan's use of the notion of the signifier is, in my view, to be found in the episodic but vital distinction he makes between its two aspects: it is both a signifier *of*. . . , and a signifier *to*. What comes to the fore at certain moments is that aspect of the signifier which signifies to someone, which interpellates someone, in the sense that we can speak of an official signifying a court decision, or issuing a distraint order or prefectoral decree. This foregrounding of 'signifying to' is extremely important, as a signifier can signify *to* without its addressee necessarily knowing *what* it signifies. We know *that* it signifies, but not *what* it signifies. . . . We know that *there is* '*a signifying*' somewhere, but there is not necessarily any explicit signified" (Laplanche 1989, 44–45).

Laplanche describes in this quotation an interpellation without identification, which is devoid of any meaningful content. It nevertheless gets "under our skin"—so says Eric Santner, whose interpretation I follow (Santner 2001, 27). We make this impact of distressing irritation permanent in the psychopathologies of everyday life. For example, a colleague at the office gives me a strange look. "Why did he do that? What is wrong?" I may ask. I don't know what the look means, whether it was directed at me, and if so, with what intention. But perhaps the colleague had noticed my outrage about his promotion at the staff council two weeks ago. Is his look the exposure of my disapproval? Did someone tell on me? Precisely *not* knowing what a look means can push the mind into a chain of fantasies to fill the gap of the enigmatic interpellation.

This trivial example of an irritation in everyday life and an unconscious urge to produce fantasies as a reflex-like response, touches indirectly upon a famous dispute between Walter Benjamin and the Kabbalah expert Gershom Scholem in the first half of the twentieth century. The dispute concerned whether a call can have "validity" without "meaning"; that is, whether a calling can exist without being already deciphered, since the calling's source, for example, is lost in oblivion. The cause of conflict was the Jewish theological legacy that Franz Kafka's prose is allegedly endowed with. Is Kafka's oeuvre, with its enigmatic novel-fragments and surreal stories, necessarily to be interpreted against the background of certain traditions of Jewish theologoumena? Characters like Gregor Samsa and Josef K. seem to struggle with metaphysical problems, and the answers they want to give to their families, superiors, themselves, and so on is not practical and pragmatic but metaphysical. The first wakes up without explanation as a beetle. The second is repeatedly confronted with the question of his symbolic mission as a law-abiding citizen vis-à-vis an anonymous apparatus of administration that puts him on trial without explanation. Or is this play with enigmatic interpellation just another chimera that doesn't shy away from ironizing the tradition of Jewish theologoumena itself? One can interpret certain films by the Coen brothers in this fashion, among which the movie *A Serious Man* from 2009 stands out.

Scholem argues that Kafka's work is an expression of Jewish metaphysics insofar as it paradoxically expresses the "nothingness of revelation." He writes to Benjamin: "You ask what I understand by the 'nothingness of revelation'? I understand by it a state in which revelation appears to be without meaning, in which it still asserts itself, in which it has validity without meaning. A state in which the wealth of the meaning is lost and the appearing, as if reduced to a zero point of its own content, nevertheless does not disappear (and the revelation is something appearing), there its nothingness emerges [*da tritt sein Nichts hervor*]. This is obviously a borderline case in the religious sense" (Benjamin and Scholem 1989, 142, trans. changed).

Scholem mentions the expression that is of interest to us: "validity without meaning." With this expression, he emphasizes that Kafka certainly alludes to the Jewish heritage, insofar as it still has validity, but its metaphysical meaning is lost. In other words, Kafka's texts have a religious-metaphysical dimension of revelation, but what revelation stands for is only marked by its absence (see Mosès 2006, 70). Paradoxically formulated, one can say that Kafka's work is non-religious and non-non-religious at the same time. It addresses Jewish eschatological motifs, but only vis-a-vis the absence of their meaning. Scholem writes that revelation's "nothingness emerges." Or, to put it another way: Kafka describes a world at the beginning of the twentieth century in which norms of traditional, metaphysical truth still have the force of interpellation, but their meaningful reception is lost.

Consider, for example, the fate of the aforementioned Josef K. in the unfinished novel *The Trial*, written in 1914/1915. In it, the protagonist is confronted with an indictment that, in the course of the novel, neither has a justification, nor needs one. Josef K. experiences the validity of the law—after all, he is supposed to appear in court. However, what exactly the court demands of him never takes the form of a comprehensible accusation within multiple series of reasons and justifications (see Žižek 1989, 44). Is his traumatic arrest by two policemen, depicted in the opening scene of the novel, a misunderstanding? Is the administrative apparatus of bureaucratic life simply reluctant to admit an error? Is there, within the administrative apparatus, "a subject supposed to know" (Lacan, n.d.), an instance of competence and oversight? In Lacan's words: a big Other? The thrill of Kafka's novel is built on these questions. In their shadow, the drama unfolds with the lack of legitimacy in the calling of a mystic entity (the Law) having a direct influence on K's mental well-being. Kafka obviously does not describe this condition of "interpellation without meaning" as a harmonious one. The mental state it incites does not grant the subject in question freedom from institutions lacking sense. On the contrary, Kafka describes it as a state in which human beings become increasingly neurotic.

The particularization of modern society into ever larger conglomerates of "singularities" (as analyzed in contemporary sociology; see Reckwitz 2020) may be a modern version of this kind of neurosis. Due to the decrease of traditional agents of symbolic authority and force (king, aristocracy, military, clergy, etc.) and their hegemonically embodied way to represent validity *with meaning*, so-called Western nations demand that the symbolic authority be supposedly open to its other, constantly. Advocates of radical democracy theory see the ideal of an open society precisely in this expansion of the combat zone through new singularities in the emphasis on the constitutive absence of the big Other. This has a variety of effects. One is that singular social groups face each other with increasing distrust in the struggle for their hegemonic appeal to be heard, taken into account, and taken care of. Here lies, to some degree, a collateral damage of democratic processes as presented by such diverse authors as Ernesto Laclau, Claude Lefort, Jacques Rancière, and so on. Instead of the big Other, the "empty place of power" (Lefort 1988, 17) of the body politic is acclaimed. It produces victim groups, but these exist not in demarcation from the state apparatus (as in Kafka), but among themselves. Since democracy has to resist the desire to fill in the empty center with fixed identities, it sees itself as a zone of constant struggle and conflict, with the state of political fulfillment to be eternally postponed (see Finkelde 2024). There is always something in the body of the people which, as excluded, has a right to its irreducible selfhood in the void of its representation, be these right-wing nationalists or left-wing cosmopolitans. But are all citizens not then always potential perpetrators if they are not victims? If so, then perhaps Kafka announces not only the state of decay of modern bureaucracies, but also that of modern democracies as well.

What Kafka interprets as an inscrutable state apparatus of blind authority concerns, in today's Western societies, the normative status of singularities and their individual norms. A contemporary Josef K. is therefore likely to be neuroticized not only by the enigmatic messages of a political superstructure that has validity but no meaning, but by interpellations toward an increasingly open society. As Matthew Flisfeder shows, the role of the now decentered big Other provokes new forms of compensation. The big Other's social role is taken back, according to Flisfeder, by modern internet platforms such as Instagram, X (formerly Twitter), and Facebook (Flisfeder 2021). In them, subjectivity unfolds in structures of market-oriented subordination more unconsciously than consciously.

The experience of "validity without meaning" that Kafka describes is not foreign to us. One only has to think of people who go to church only on Christmas, that is, exactly once a year. Many of them do not believe in the specific metaphysical concepts on which Christianity as a monotheistic religion is built. It is not a resource for them of transcendence in regulating the metaphysical dimension of their lives. But they may still be absorbed in devotion when, on Christmas Eve, the organ plays or the priest holds up the chalice. Churchgoers may know that the ceremony is nothing but a ritual and that Christianity has long since ceased to dominate the lives of citizens as it once did. Nevertheless, there will be remnants of interpellations in gestures and words. In this situation, the concept of Christianity has validity, but no longer metaphysical meaning. This form of validity without meaning should not be underestimated. It may be that, precisely because of this validity without meaning, individuals are much more under the spell of faith even if they do not consciously subscribe to this faith.

Scholem articulates a similar line of thought with regard to Kafka's work. Texts such as "Before the Law" or "In the Penal Colony" seem to be infused with Jewish metaphysics. They revolve around riddles of interpellation, desires, and demands. What is Josef K. accused of, and by whom? Why was he ordered to *The Castle*? With what purpose are verdicts tattooed into the skin of convicts "In the Penal Colony"? Kafka's texts do not provide an answer, and it is precisely this avoidance of answers that Scholem, if I (following Eric Santner's and Stéphan Mosé's interpretations) understand him correctly, calls the "nothingness of revelation." In the context of ideology and symbolic order, it is precisely the "nothingness of revelation," that is, the validity that seems to have no meaning, that has a very particular grip on us. In Freud's words, a fixation is established. "Every neurosis includes a fixation . . . , but not every fixation leads to a neurosis" (Freud 1981, vol. 16, 276).

It is the "nothingness of revelation," this surplus of validity over meaning, that occupies the imagination of the protagonists in Kafka to such an extent that they cannot, after all, disassociate themselves from this thing from which they endlessly seek to distance themselves. Žižek aptly sums up this idea as follows: "The starting point in Kafka's novels is that of an interpellation. . . . But this interpellation . . . is an *interpellation without identification/subjectivation*." The subject "does not understand the meaning of the call of the Other" (Žižek 1989, 44).

Kafka's novels expose, in an outstanding way, the power of ideological interpellation. The affected protagonists do not succeed in disengaging their subjectivity from the gap that is hidden at the center of the demands directed at them. On the contrary. As the symptom is formed through what "did not take place" in experience (Freud 1981, vol. 16, 280), the lack of meaning has an effect. Therefore, rational explanation cannot necessarily bring relief. In Freud's words, "The patient knows after this [after his treatment] what he did not know before—the sense of his symptom; yet he knows it just as little as he did. Thus we learn that there is more than one kind of ignorance" (Freud 1981, vol. 1, 281). And the ignorance to know one's symptom, even if one knows it just a little, is one that shapes psychophysical dynamics.

The subsequent attempt to transfer this gap, via imagination, into meaning drives the individual all the more in submission. Therefore, the interpellation does not allow for subjectification, in the sense of: "Yes, I am guilty, I have committed X. You have proven my guilt." Rather, Kafka unfolds a poetics of neurosis through "interpellation without identification" (Žižek 1989, 44), which, in Santner's words, is devoid "of any propositional content" but "nonetheless gets under the skin and has some sort of (hindered) revelatory force, . . . as Scholem puts it, validity without meaning" (Santner 2001, 39).

2

Let us again recall in this context Freud's statements about traumatic experiences. They stand for the insistence of an "anti-cathexis [*Gegenbesetzung*]" in the energy circuit of the mind, "for whose benefit all the other psychical systems are impoverished" (Freud 1981, vol. 18, 30). The persistence of "validity without meaning" does something analogous. As a trauma-like irritation, it leaves a mark. "What is happening? Why am I on trial?" The mind lapses into hysterical dynamics similar to hallucination, bypassing the cognitive faculties of consciousness. In Santner's words, it may even be the specific form of disorientation, the idiomatic way in which "one's approach to and movement through the world is 'distorted'" that most concerns our lives and our mind-world relation (Santner 2010, 39).

Kafka seems to suggest something similar in his references to institutions of symbolic force. They have become unstable in the early twentieth century through economization, massification, bureaucratization. But instead of our gaining more freedom through their loss of meaning, the opposite seems to be the case—an increase of neurotic symptoms like insecurity in one's own identity. The translation of (enigmatic) signifiers into reasons fails due to the surplus of validity over meaning. This surplus can call upon the human imagination as an organ of fantasy production to literally transform the missing meaning into a "bound variable" (Quine), an entity within the law of the order of identity. And Kafka's protagonists try to do this. They try to find explanations for their predicament. They imagine answers to the question of why they are at the center of anonymous forces of interpellation that have validity but no meaning. This matches the involuntary fantasy production of some of Freud's patients. Freud comments on their resistance to the psychoanalytic treatment, especially when they enter dangerous territory. The patients camouflage their real motivation of resistance and repression with self-produced fantasies. Freud gives apt examples of these mechanisms of fantasy formation. For whenever patients in psychoanalytic sessions find themselves in need of putting the unspeakable into words, they give reasons, more unconsciously than consciously, for not having to enter the terrain of what cannot yet be confronted (Freud 1981, vol. 16, 289–302). They arrive late, miss an appointment, or express their dissatisfaction with the psychoanalytic process as a whole. In these cases, the mind, in its intrinsic state of irritation and confusion, is autopoietically misled by itself and its fanciful excuses.

However, fantasies do not only emerge as barriers against negative feelings. More importantly, they shape the coherence of our everyday lives. For this reason, too, one's lifeworld can turn out very differently compared to the lifeworld of someone else, even if that person appears to be "one of us," of the same age, social class, and so on. After all, the lifeworld is shaped according to the way our imagination as an epistemic faculty, supporting understanding and reason, reacts to interpellations, to inferential webs of reasons, antinomies therein, and enigmatic remainders permeating the act of cognition and the perceived object of it. Every individual's existence thus consists in a solipsistic distortion, via the power of imagination, of certain states of affairs prejudiced by desires, repressions, ideals, and libidinous transmissions of the desires of others as representative of the big Other. This guarantees the preservation of an equilibrium of facts to be constantly renegotiated. This is also why the individual cannot simply liberate her- or himself from the big Other. According to Žižek, "the Kafkaesque illusion of an all-powerful Thing paying no attention to us [Kafka's heroes in The Trial and in The Castle are ignored even though they feel permanently threatened and watched] is the inverse-symmetrical counterpoint to the illusion that defines ideological interpellation—namely, the illusion that the Other always-already looks at us, addresses us" (Žižek 2000a, 108).

The experience that the big Other is always already looking at us is familiar to anyone who has ever stepped out of a porn store. He or she probably felt afraid of being recognized. We are necessarily under the illusion that the Other recognizes us because our anxiety places this Other as a judging counterpart into the street to expose us. It is as if, within a few meters, the gaze of the Other becomes omnipresent and the symbolic texture around us precariously fragile. We feel rightly accused and indicted, but without a true rational foundation. Again Žižek: "Far from simply deranging/distorting the 'proper balance of things,' fantasy at the same time *grounds* every notion of the balanced Universe: fantasy is not an idiosyncratic excess that deranges the cosmic order, but the violent idiosyncratic excess that *sustains* every notion of such an order" (Žižek 2000b, 86).

As I already mentioned, these remarks come very close to the arguments presented by Kant. Freud understands psychoanalysis, among other things, as an attempt to intervene in this dimension of fantasy production, especially when the latter provokes life-impeding burdens for the individual. Such a burden can be the illusory hope of becoming the most important pop singer in the world, the best father for his children, a successful entrepreneur, and so on. In cases like these, therapy may help the analysand to liberate him- or herself from life-consuming interpellations and interchange them with life-affirming ones. A quasi-idiosyncratic reinscription of subjectivity into new symbolic coordinates is necessary. Here, the act of setting the coordinates anew is analogous to Kant's concept of a "revolution in the disposition" (Kant 1996, 92). Freud wrote the *Interpretation of Dreams* for people like those we find in Kafka's novels; that is, people who are haunted by experiences they cannot understand and which they try to make sense of with ever new fantasies. What is at stake in Freud's work in this regard is the question of whether there is a possibility of healing, of unbinding our fantasies in such a way that the subject no longer remains driven by her or his symptoms.

In the Schreber case, as commented on by Freud and Lacan, the motif of interpellation once again becomes significant on a social level. For this reason, Schreber's fate is discussed in the following and final section of this lecture.

3

Freud became aware of Daniel Paul Schreber, the son of the founder of the so-called "Schrebergarten" movement, through his *Memoirs of My Nervous Illness*, published in 1903. Exactly ten years earlier, in 1893, the Austrian advocate had been appointed president of the Third Circuit of the Appeals Court in Dresden. Due to mental distress, he subsequently fell ill and resigned from office in October of the same year. In the report published by Freud in 1911 under the title *Psychoanalytic Notes on an Autobiographical Account of a Case of Paranoia (Dementia Paranoides)*, the founding father of psychoanalysis interprets Schreber's delusions as a phantasmatic manifestation of a homosexual panic. I am only indirectly following Freud's rather unconvincing interpretation. If I mention this case file, it is in order to analyze (once again) how subjectivation is inter-related with processes of interpellation, causing legitimation (of fantasies, desires, antinomies, and ideals) and all kinds of psychic events. My reflections are guided by the studies of Thomas Dalzell (2011), Wilfried Ver Eecke (2019), and Eric Santner (1996). Admittedly, these reflections remain highly speculative in nature. In fact, no scientifically validated diagnosis of Schreber's mental illness can be derived from the empirical material on the case. The following remarks, therefore, do not claim to do final justice to the Schreber case as such.

What makes Schreber's memoirs interesting for philosophical purposes is the fact that the author makes fruitful connections between psychoanalysis, epistemology, and theology simultaneously. This becomes apparent especially when the text is read as a phenomenological description of the inner events of a schizophrenic mind trying to get a grip on all kinds of glitches and slips (*Fehlleistungen*) in the relation of mind and world. Schreber's memoirs repeatedly deal with questions of revelation (similar to Kafka's). For example: Schreber considered his mental distress to be of theological and metaphysical provenance. He suffered a psychological breakdown and presents his partial recovery in theological and not in medical terms. The addressees of his memoirs were not the psychiatrists educated in neurology and forensics, but theologians and philosophers. The latter may draw, like Schreber, useful insights from his experiences. Schreber was, in other words, convinced that his psycho-physical distress had to do with a disorder of his soul. His mental states had nothing to do with the malfunction of his brain as a biological organ on a neurological level. His accounts touch exclusively on the impact of symbolic investiture, that is, of the insertion of an individual mind into collective forms of virtuality.

Given that Schreber fell ill shortly after his appointment as president of the Third Circuit of the Appeals Court in Dresden, it is plausible to see a source of his suffering in the act of his symbolic investiture (see Santner 1996, 14). But what exactly do we mean by someone's symbolic investiture? In highly simplified terms, the concept denotes a social act by which a certain title or mandate is conferred on an individual. The assigned mandate is associated with a novel social status and a new role within a social world. In this way, one becomes a husband, a professor, a judge, a psychoanalyst, and so on, and comes to enjoy various predicates and powers as integral parts of one's new social form.

The talk of "enjoyment" and of "enjoying" one's social mandate is meant literally, since libidinous aspects come along intrinsically with the new status of authority. We are familiar with them when, for example, the U.S. president is sworn in, when a judge puts on her robe, or when soldiers take an oath to the flag. No matter what status is conferred by these rites, the personalities experience enjoyment in the transubstantiation, because they incorporate an extension of their biopolitical body through symbolic authority. They are now part of a semantic structure that transcends the individual understood as a biological machine with its drives and needs.

The minister of justice, who granted Schreber the legal title "president of the Third Circuit of the Appeals Court in Dresden," on the one hand simply makes Schreber's credential for the job official. His statement publicly establishes that, from now on, Schreber is the presiding judge. But on the other hand, he does more than that. The conferred title changes Schreber's ontological status as a subject among subjects. The eccentric incorporation of a particular subject into hyper-individual structures of authority has an impact on this individual's mental states, especially from the perspective of his first, or biological, nature. "Commitments" and "entitlements" (Brandom 1998, xi–xxv) of a higher social status—concepts of much importance in Robert Brandom's philosophy of inferentialism—from now on play an important role. In short, it makes a real or an ontological difference whether or not a biological body receives a symbolic mandate imposed on it—regardless of whether we are talking about the ordination of a priest or the appointment of a judge. Symbolic inaugurations are performative acts. They do not depict facts, they create them. A power of being "judge-in-itself" is transformed into a power "for me" who, from now on, is the judge-in-itself-as-myself. An abstract attribute is transferred to an individual who incorporates a judge's universal status on the level of his or her particularity. The attributes of a judge's office pass performatively into the attribution of a human mind. The proximity to J. L. Austin's speech act theory is not accidental. What is crucial is not the symbolically appointed individual, but the social structure without which the appointment and accreditation cannot take place.

It would be a misunderstanding, however, to interpret this ontological change of status of subjects in writs of symbolic investiture (their very personal transubstantiation in a truly metaphysical sense) as only an irrational act that concerns primarily religious communities. The most secularized society cannot function without the magical powers of this kind of transference. When, for example, a woman in the German Democratic Republic (East Germany) of the mid-1980s became a representative of the "Party of the People," she became part of a body politic which, according to the Marxist-Leninist conception of history, incorporates both

metaphysically and materialistically the very victory of the proletariat in
the history of mankind. A tremendous social status had to be accepted
as the incarnation of mankind's path to freedom through the morass
of history. As a result of transferring attributes and not attributions, the
new politically invested woman is more than herself. That which appears
to be only an external property, such as a title, a task, or an extension of
political competence, changes the individual intrinsically as well. It affects
a mind's reflexivity without the subject having to explicitly consent to
the change of status or to apprehend the intervention psychologically or
philosophically. The individual does not have to perceive this intervention like an operation in a hospital. But in fact, it is very close to being
just that: an invasion of the biological body, which in Schreber's case had
disastrous consequences.

What the examples mentioned above (priest, politician, judge) underscore is the dominance of symbolic worlds that can be as secular as
possible, and yet must retain a metaphysical residue of the meaning of
what it means to be called, appointed, interpellated. The symbolic (as
one of Lacan's three registers) cannot be hierarchized unambiguously or
reduced to matter (*Materie*) in justifications of the hard sciences. Every
subject is a subjectum "of the word" as part of an abstract realm of entities emerging within processes of transference through language. "The
word" splits matter (*Materie*) into appearance and its noumenal residue/
remainder/remnant (the thing-in-itself), and splits individuals into their
sociocultural identity (see Bourdieu 2005, 103ff.) and that which the splitting leaves unaccounted for: the unconscious as consciousness's backside,
among other things. Symbolic institutions cite this "word" in its metaphysical sense of the Gospel of John. As soon as a judge puts on her
robe, she automatically speaks on behalf of this word and its metaphysical
force of transubstantiation—now in the name of the people. She does not
merely pass judgments on states of affairs in the world that are either true
or false. The judge's verdict brands facts; it imposes on empirical reality
the status of identity within the normative substance of being.

Now, one thesis put forward by Santner regarding Schreber's fate
is that Schreber's psyche was apparently unable to endure this personal
union with his symbolic role after he was installed as president of the
court (Santner 1996; see also Ver Eecke 2019). His mind was unable to
process the subjectification of an attribution; that is, to incorporate the
magical effect of his investiture according to which he would have been
able to proclaim his verdict *im Namen des Volkes*, "in the name of the
people." The insertion of an authority mediated with signifiers into his
psychophysical self-image failed. Likewise, a priest with neurotic tics can
struggle at the altar. The investiture of his metaphysical mission, to bring

the body of Christ down to earth, overwhelms his mind. Pierre Bourdieu speaks in this context of a "performative magic" (Bourdieu 1991, 106). He calls every transformation that adds no attribute other than the decisive attribution via title or name the formula underlying the performative magic of all acts of investiture. "An *investiture* (of a knight, Deputy, President of the Republic, etc.) consists of sanctioning and sanctifying a difference . . . by making it *known* and *recognized*" (Bourdieu 1991, 119). "The process of investiture . . . exercises a symbolic efficacy that is quite real in that it really transforms the person" (ibid.). This illustrates what this lecture tries to pin down: that the world of symbolic orders is per se a miraculous, metaphysical, ambiguous world, one that cannot be entirely secularized or eliminatively reduced to so-called empirical facts, be they physical, mathematical, or Darwinian. Schreber drops out of this world when the entitlement is imposed on him. The diagnosis he gives to himself is "soul murder" (Schreber 2000, 33). His soul was murdered through the infiltration of symbolic too muchness.

Let me conclude this lecture by summarizing what has been said so far. When a mandate is handed down, the attributes of an office are transformed into attributions. A judge does not play being a judge-in-itself. She *is* judge and this is what she is for-herself, for others and the office. She is existentially the performative expression of an intersubjective, and therefore overdetermined, mandate. In this sense, one can say that Schreber was confronted with an ideological interpellation of normativity in such a traumatic way that his only escape was to psychologically "duck away." This is not surprising: every office as office forces the biological body into a necessary split between "being-for-itself" and "being-for-others-in-itself." Robert Brandom acknowledges this force of entitlements. He recognizes the symbolic power of attribution in normative webs of belief, according to which rational beings mutually ascribe commitments, entitlements, and trust to one another. His inferentialist semantics of conceptual roles rests on these insights. Curiously, however, he addresses the subject matter in his pragmatic inferentialism exclusively from the point of view of the positive-normative power of attributions (Brandom 2000). Hence, Brandom's unbroken and even positivistic faith in "trust," as presented in his latest book on Hegel (Brandom 2019), makes him a Right Hegelian and distinguishes him radically from Left Hegelians such as Žižek and Badiou. The extent to which entitlements and commitments may also be inherently dangerous for individuals and necessarily burden the mind through the overdetermination of symbolic forms is, as far as I can see, not touched upon in his work. But it is crucial to not only acknowledge the limits of "trust"—so dear to Brandom's interpretation of Hegel's *Phenomenology*—but to also acknowledge questions of ideology that should play an important role in inferentialism if this theory is to have a true explanatory function (Finkelde, forthcoming).

Schreber fled from the aforementioned interpellation and thus, at the same time, from the world of objective experience. The mandate crushed his imaginary self and subsequently founded his delusion as a psychophysical compromise. It gave his biological body the opportunity to continue living under the condition that his experience of being free was lost. From now on, his mind phantasmatically explains the loss of experience through divine powers (taken from Indian mythology). These powers make him, Schreber, a victim of submission and sexual harassment. The external control takes on explicitly lascivious connotations when he describes himself as a "slut" in the hands, and at the voluptuous disposal, of foreign gods. Schreber is unable to enjoy being a president and judge. The enjoyment of symbolic investiture is psychologically reversed into its opposite. He experiences himself within a world of harassing signifiers that his mind cannot cope with, and he becomes a victim of sexual violence, as if he were permanently raped in accordance with his new ontological status of being, in his own word, a *Luder*, a "slut." This is what Schreber's term "soul murder" denotes: the collapse of the symbolic dimension through speech acts in their psychophysical function of inscription. Schreber's universe is not only delusional in the sense that he can no longer bring his self-image into the structure of established norms, but his imagination invents a cosmos in which rays of libidinous pleasure constantly traverse his body. It is as if the libidinous dimensions, which in the infant can convey confidence, stability, security, and acceptance through skin contact with the parents (the sources of signifiers), suddenly express exactly the opposite: permanent rape, constant transgression, and harassment. Consequently, what Schreber discovers is that the process of symbolic investiture conveys an invasive core (that which escapes understanding) and, in doing so, introduces too much reality into the subject, at least under certain circumstances. The psychotic suffers, in Freud's words, "an excess in demand [*Zuviel von Anspruch*]" (Freud 1981, vol. 23, 73). The symbolic order has first subjectified Schreber, only to de-subjectify him later on.

4

Hegel

Negativity as a Structural Moment of the Concept

(Lecture 5)

1

The previous lectures have dealt with different issues of negativity. They concern the noncoincidence of the sociopolitical space of a body politic, which never forms a harmonious whole. But they also concern the noncoincidence of human identity. This identity is invested with enigmatic signifiers, equipped with patterns of latency, infiltrated by the unconscious, and retroactively redefines itself constantly through time. Both modes of noncoincidence are metaphorically depicted in the first two illustrations below, by the Dutch graphic artist M. C. Escher (1898–1972). They illustrate what we have revealed so far through recourse to Freud, Lacan, and

Laplanche; that is, to what extent reflexivity is composed across a lack and various distortions of perspective that have to do with the enigmatic confrontation of an Other in the ego-function of our selves. The ego emerges in the midst of processes of transference that originate in interpellations and, producing epistemic remainders, extend into the relation of mind and world. Interpellations emanate from parents and from all kinds of institutions of symbolic agency (state-apparatuses, universities, etc.).

It is important to remember, however, that educators and social agencies are codependent results of unconscious processes of transference. They are part of the cultural space in which they operate. Every culture neurotically circles around the deficient legitimacy of its origin in time, just as every father and mother struggle with their symbolic roles lacking perfection. Although one cannot claim that a culture is endowed with an unconscious just like a human being, it is affected nevertheless through the unconscious of every member of the body politic.

But let us return to the concept of negativity in more detail. Freud looked at it in relation to a child's playful use of a wooden spool as a way of overcoming an experience of agony (the absence of the mother) through the invention of a symbolic game (the fort-da game). The reference to Kant's notion of the *focus imaginarius* was then presented as a transcendental account to compensate for negativity in a different way. Kant unfolds the concept in accordance with regulative ideas of reason vis-à-vis the limits of understanding. Reason produces ideal imaginations to desire what can only be thought, while understanding determines what it means to exist. The example of Daniel Paul Schreber was then presented as a diametrical counter-example to the child's play with his woolen spool as proto-signifier. Schreber drops out of everyday life due to the impact of the "too-muchness" of symbolic force that his mind cannot withstand. Schizophrenia is the compromise his psyche comes up with, but it imposes on him the belief that he is tormented and controlled by alien gods. Schreber is now a victim of constant abuse and uses the word "slut" (*Luder*) as the proper term of his destiny. This is another reason why, from now on in Schreber's world, the unconscious primarily regulates his mind-world relation. It openly dominates the ego-function. The oppressive gods are hyperreal and omnipresent to him. They rob Schreber of the possibility to ironically distance himself from the injunctions surrounding him. Schreber is incapable of opening up any kind of distance between himself and the facts. The gods in his world are too real to be criticized or ironically subverted. As foreign powers, they have stripped him of his freedom and keep him unambiguously under control.

The third illustration shows the Hungarian flag in 1989 with the hammer and sickle cut out. Only a hole in the place of meaning is left. The Soviet empire is no more. As such, the flag illustrates the aforementioned lack in political structures. Even if every society is concerned with camouflaging such an inner lack, political crises prove the often unexpected return of this lack. It is the return of a truth that was cut out from the beginning. Cutting out the insignia of symbolic force proves that politics is unable to reconcile transcendence with immanence. Its very foundation has only an illegitimate claim to "what is (politically) the case."

In this lecture, the topic of negativity outlined so far will be discussed with reference to the philosophy of Georg W. F. Hegel. The research of the Ljubljana school of psychoanalysis in the last three decades has shown that negativity concerns psychoanalysis and German idealism in a similar way. For both disciplines, the mind, or mind in general, is affected by negativity in its ontogenetic development up to the establishment of a coherent self-image and worldview. The mind is also affected by negativity in its phylogenetic development of mental or cognitive processes in the evolution of "spirit" (Hegel) as the meta-medium which keeps mind and world related, but not in a unity. "Spirit" is a metaphysical category to denote the basic structures of reality as being in a constant disharmony of clusters of meaning, belief, and justification, which cannot be harmoniously ordered according to one homological existential quantifier. In order to explain this in more detail, we will take a detour via some central insights of Kant's epistemology. It offers access to an array of philosophical problems associated with the second half of the eighteenth century, upon which Hegel presents his understanding of negativity as encompassing mind and matter simultaneously. From here on, the relation to the philosophy of psychoanalysis will become apparent.

2

In the "Transcendental Dialectic" of the *Critique of Pure Reason*, Kant famously opposes three disciplines that are endowed with false claims to truth. They shaped the metaphysics of his time: first, rational psychology based on the insights of Descartes, Leibniz, and Malebranche regarding the subject matter of the "soul" defended by Christian Wolff and his school (Kant 1998, 413 [B403]); second, rational cosmology, which postulates the "world" as totality (ibid., 470 [B455]); and third, rational or natural theology, with its subject matter "God" and the proof of his existence (ibid., 569 [B631]). These philosophical fields of research are problematic for Kant because of their epistemological ambition to derive "from the possibility of the concept (logical possibility) . . . the possibility of the thing (real possibility)" (ibid., 566 [B 624]). They uncritically presuppose an isomorphism between thinking and being. The various ontological proofs of God can be mentioned here as a much-cited example. Such a proof claims to deduce the real existence of God from the features of the concept of God. Were the concept of God not to include real existence as one of its predicates, it would not be the concept of such a supreme being. Such a lack of real existence would undermine the truth of this concept, hence this being must exist in reality.

Kant recognizes in this the erroneous conclusion of deriving "synthetic a priori cognitions from things in general" (ibid., 358 [B303]). This is wrong, since any talk of things-in-themselves (referring to God, soul, world, freedom) no longer commits us to our five epistemic senses of registration: smell, touch, sound, vision, and taste. God verified by pure thinking alone would be such a thing-in-itself. To ascribe the predicate "to exist" to God does not hold to the premise of empirical knowledge, since the existence of objects of experience presupposes sensible intuitions (*Anschauungen*). It was precisely from the senses that the first generation of empiricists in the British Enlightenment established the cornerstones of modern epistemology. And according to Kant, one cannot step back from this insight. The five senses have to be integrated into the equation of perception, knowledge, meaning, and truth. With this insight, Kant arrives at the thesis that the knowledge of objective facts is possible. The condition for this, however, is the rejection of an ultimate metaphysical certainty of what it means to exist. In contrast to deductive forms of truth in logic and mathematics, empirical facts can only have the ontological status of appearances (*Erscheinungen*) due to reason's limits. So, when Kant argues in the first *Critique* that "being is obviously not a real predicate, i.e., a concept of something that could add to the concept of a thing" (ibid., 567 [B626]), he expresses his conviction that being cannot be a meaningful concept in the metaphysical sense of the word. The term "being" has no spatiotemporal referent in the way that a car or a bike can be counted in the set of "vehicles." There is no referent falling under the concept "being." "Being" has exclusively the logical function of the copula in a proposition, that is, the role of "is" in, for example, the proposition "The car *is* blue." Kant's Copernican revolution is to be located here. From now on, the copula does not express a real property of the subject of a proposition, but only states of affairs within the conceptual limits of human experience. This implies that pure reason as the medium of our epistemic(-metaphysical) capacities is not able to think the unity of the world with the proof of God's real existence, as proposed by Descartes in his *Meditations on First Philosophy*. Nor does it grant the foundation of knowledge a final truth value in all possible worlds with regard to a *res cogitans*. Knowledge can only be the result of temporal experiences.

As such, experiences resemble, allegorically speaking, the self-portrait of subjectivity's own becoming. According to Claus Artur Scheier, this explains why Montesquieu, Voltaire, and Hume emerged primarily as historians (Scheier 2008, 244). But the contemplation of this self-portrait within historical experience may be as shocking as the one described by Oscar Wilde. In his novel *The Picture of Dorian Gray*, the protagonist is confronted with a magical painting that shows the traces of his corrupted soul. The portrait is not sublime or lovely, but rather littered with deformations and mutilations. But this is very similar to the sum total of humanity's experiences with regard to Kantian metaphysics. From now on, "custom" and "habit" become the new foundations of subjectivity as it unfolds in contingent, historical chains of events, with reason being a helpful capacity of the mind to fantasize a deeper truth of meaning. Or, to put it another way, a first ground of experience can only be provided by experience itself, not by reason, as Hume famously pronounces (Hume 2007, 76–78), thus losing faith in an asymptotic approach to divine perfection culturally attainable by man. To express the argument of Scheier: "S c P" is replaced by "S + P" (Scheier 2008, 244). A logic of cultural addition (+) is left where, in former times, the copula (c) still was able to *metaphysically* connect the subject (S) in a judgment with the predicate (P). Friedrich Hölderlin's talk of an *Ur-Teilung*, a primordial or primary division, as expressed in his 1795 text *Judgment and Being*, has become void and meaningless. A judgment does not separate and unite what the basic structure of reality grants as an essential unity of a proposition's meaning. A judgment rather unites what can only be related under contingent, that is, historical conditions. Thinking and being are forever disconnected, and what is lost can no longer even be comprehended as loss.

Freud and Lacan extend Kant's Copernican turn. They deepen the realm of experience with further categories (death drive, the unconscious, *Vorstellungsrepräsentanz*, etc.) and so present more dimensions of the human mind that are salient to the establishment of a shared space of experience. Roughly speaking, the focus of attention here is not so much the classical dichotomy between subject and object, or mind and matter, but the relation of singularity and objectivity as that which precedes every domain of facts and states of affairs. More on this later.

Kant follows Hume's critique of human imagination, in which the mind unreflectively equates its experiences of states of affairs with states of Being—for example, the fact of causality as an intrinsic property of chains of events in the world (Hume 2007, 70–83). This leads to the idea of a self-sufficient world of objects where apparently things-in-themselves stand to each other in relations—for example, causal relations—as these relations are in themselves. This is wrong. Facts as experienced by human beings with the help of their five senses cannot be equated, according to Hume, with facts of reality as it is in itself. Kant confronts this problem with an epistemology that heads off such a naive ontology of things-in-themselves. Appearances are accessible through sensibility in intuition (*Anschauung*) and through concepts of understanding (*Verstandesbegriffe*), but things-in-themselves are not. They drop out of understanding's sovereignty, but attain a special status as "things-in-themselves" necessary for reason (not for understanding). For even if we have access only to appearances, these must affect us from somewhere, that is, from things-in-themselves, and this means that appearances are more than mere appearances. There is something more to them than they can warrant. Kant's Copernican revolution consists precisely in this insight. It rejects both a reality as it is in itself and the idea of a thinking substance as the foundational principle of cognition. Beside an apparently "absolute conception of reality" (called "transcendental realism" by Kant; Kant 1998, 426 [A369]) on the one hand and the human mind on the other, a third realm arises. It is a hybrid connection mediating between mind and world. It neither coincides with a reality that can claim an ontological and epistemological independence from us, nor does it coincide with the individual brain as the source of patterns for the psychological (or better: neurological) construction of reality. The content of our beliefs is instead dependent on their integration into supra-individual networks of signifiers as our capacity to judge, similar to the condition of the Borg in *Star Trek*. These are cybernetic organisms linked to each other in a swarm mind called "the collective." Since, as Wittgenstein showed, the idea of a private language is self-refuting, there can be no private truth claims, except for a paranoiac like Schreber. Thus, too, for Kant as for Lacan, the sapient, rational subject is necessarily split in theoretical philosophy, just as the moral subject is in practical philosophy.

"What is the case" can only be determined by animals capable of thinking. However, this does not mean that what is the case depends solely on the thinking subject. Categories do not produce sense data. They process sense data with the help of the faculty of imagination. As the example of "dark matter," much discussed in contemporary physics, shows, this can go so far that an entity is denoted without knowing what it actually is. It is presented as an "ideational representative [*Vorstellungs-repräsentanz*]" (Freud 1981d, 177), the representation of what is unknown, and, as such, denotes a gap in our holistic explanatory networks. (For

Freud *Vorstellungsrepräsentanz* is an unconscious representation, in the form of an idea or thought, of an instinctual impulse.) "Dark matter" is literally a "nonsensible-sensible intuition" about which it is simultaneously meaningful and senseless to make judgments. The term acts as a proxy for a fissure. It has something positive in its negativity, because with its help, non-knowledge is marked.

The world surrounding us becomes accessible to us via our five senses. It is bundled by processes of categorial filtering and is transubstantiated into a judgmental structure open to revision through communication between rational animals. This judgmental structure of facts has a retroactive influence on sensibility and intuition. This is why a toddler, similarly to an animal, sensibly intuits very differently compared to an adult. His or her rational capacities have not yet affected the senses, so to speak, but do so retrospectively in the genesis of a process of rational formation. What is intuited by the adult, however, is categorically structured. John McDowell has defended this thesis in many places, in order to close off the gap left open by Kant in his distinction between the content-conditions and form-conditions of perception (McDowell 1994, 2013).

Beings endowed with language can exchange information about facts. But the nexus of states of affairs is shaped according to the limits of reason, not vice versa. It is not the sum-total of what is true in, or of, reality that conditions our perception; rather, our perception conditions what is the sum-total of truth. An insect that sits next to me on the garden table has no mental state of perception of the table *as a table*. It perceives inhumanly, so to speak, by which I mean that the insect has, according to its evolution, its own filters to suck a world of experience out of the slice of space-time where I perceive a table. Many decades before Kant, John Locke called attention to the multiplicities of potential realities surrounding us, depending on the organism of perception. "Had we senses acute enough to discern the minute particles of bodies, and the real constitution on which their sensible qualities depend, I doubt not but they would produce quite different ideas in us; and that which is now the yellow colour of gold, would then disappear, and instead of it, we should see an admirable texture of parts of a certain size and figure" (Locke 1997, 273).

The world of experience is necessarily smaller than the sum total of its parts, since it is only given by virtue of parts that have no part in what is known. Different organisms (like cats, bats, microbes, etc.) with different forms or modes of sense-registration, and other categorial filters (of aliens, angels, gods, etc.) distill multiple objects from a realm of "multiple multiplicities," a term used by Alain Badiou. Or, to mention a famous expression of the former U.S. secretary of defense Donald

Rumsfeld, "There are things that we know we don't know. But there are also unknown unknowns—the ones we don't know we don't know" (Rumsfeld 2002).

The American author of fantasy and horror fiction stories H. P. Lovecraft (1890–1937) builds the universe of his texts from this blissful ignorance of "unknown unknowns." The texts portray fragile worlds of appearances, concealing multiple untamed multiplicities as places of abysmal horror. This explains why he writes that "the most merciful thing in the world, I think, is the inability of the human mind to correlate all its contents. We live on a placid island of ignorance in the midst of black seas of infinity, and it was not meant that we should voyage far" (Lovecraft 2020, 9).

Kant must introduce the "thing-in-itself" into his metaphysics because stimulus receptors and categories have to receive their material from somewhere. A source for our intuition is necessary to give objective experience content. But the thing-in-itself has, in Frege's terminology, only "sense," but no "reference." As an *ens rationis*, it is a purely conceptual entity. It cannot be quantified and measured by understanding, but nonetheless is postulated as necessary by "pure understanding" alone (Kant 1998, 362 [B310]), analogous to the "world" as one of reason's regulative ideas. The thing-in-itself is a "something = x, of which we know nothing at all, nor can we know anything in general (in accordance with the current constitution of our understanding)" (ibid., 348 [A250]). We know only that it ought to be thought. The concept denotes, as I said, nothing. It has no referent; there is no positive realm of experience consisting of truer objects. The concept is a "noumenon in the negative sense" since "it [the thing-in-itself] is not an object of our sensible intuition" (ibid., 360 [B307]). As a term that has at once sense but no reference/meaning, it marks the internal boundary of our phenomenal world of appearances and opens up the fantasy of a reality in a fullness that is as full (but also as indeterminate) as things-in-themselves could phantasmagorically be. In his book *Negative Dialectics*, Adorno gives a critical reevaluation of transcendental philosophy when, contra Kant, he affirms the "preponderance of the object" (Adorno 2004, 189). The latter underlines for Adorno an inner barrier that keeps the intrusive Kantian subject at an infinite distance toward all kinds of states of affairs. For Adorno, the distance can be a source of true salvation, for Kant, only a source of hope.

To put it in allegorical terms: according to Kant's metaphysics, in cognition, we move within the formal structure of a Klein bottle. Its form does not limit a content other than form itself. The content is the form folded into itself. Likewise for Kant. The form of cognition (characterized

by space and time, intuitions, categories, ideas) determines the content of cognition via the form itself. Phenomena do not demarcate themselves from noumena, since we can access the latter only in the form of a postulate. (There must be an X that passively confronts us. We must postulate a cause, even if, strictly speaking, the X cannot be a cause, since cause and effect are concepts of understanding and not of things-in-themselves.) The noumenal becomes the effect of a phenomenality directed toward itself and reflected in itself. The other of phenomena exists only as an internal limit of the phenomenal. Behind the concept of noumenon the negativity of phenomenon's self-limitation is hidden; that is, the noumenal realm has no positive content. Here we detect Kant's modern insight that the world of appearances can only be perceived against the background of its own non-identity. The world of appearances is infinitely separated from itself. It needs the postulate of a "world" as totality, which phantasmatically overcomes the eternal separation of appearances from themselves. But the demarcation between noumena and phenomena is, again, only one phenomenon among others.

As humans, our intuitions may differ. One person sees the garden table mentioned above from the left, the other from the right. And yet, unlike the insect, we easily agree on judgments about the table's color, form, height, and so on. The most diverse intuitions, in which objects are presented "to us [by the senses] as they appear," become objects "as they are" "in the thoroughgoing connection of appearances" (Kant 1998, 367 [A258]) as formal determinations of thought. They are homogenized into propositions through a semantic realm shared with others. This is a first insight of Kant's philosophy, presented here only in outline. There are objective experiences through demarcation from what is radically distinct within them: things-in-themselves.

As we have seen, Freud also unfolds a concept of the radically Other. His concern, though, is not the other as a "Something = x" (ibid., 348 [A250]) out of which the world of appearances emerges. Freud refers in the theoretical framework of the philosophy of psychoanalysis to "something = x" in the midst of the ego function at the origin of its emergence. We will come back to this.

Kant's solution of an (alleged) mediation between the rational school philosophy of his time (Christian Wolff, etc.), and the insights of Scottish skepticism (Hume) was rejected by his most prominent heirs: Maimon, Fichte, Schelling, Hölderlin, and Hegel. The philosophical price of his "synthesis" between rationalism ("thesis") and empiricism ("antithesis") was too high for them to pay. For them, and contrary to my own interpretation just mentioned, it consists in a two-world doctrine that resembles a new edition of Platonism for the modern era. A divine world of ideas in its being-in-itself stands disconnected from a "thoroughgoing connection of appearances" (ibid., 364 [A258]). Freedom cannot be proven theoretically and degrades to a postulate within the conceptual framework of practical reason. Likewise with God. How is He to be worshipped if his status is tantamount to a postulate? Can I bow to a fantasy that is brought forth as a postulate in the name of practical reason? This is another reason why Kant's successors saw the overcoming of Hume's skepticism by the philosopher of Königsberg as a failure.

In the twentieth century, Donald Davidson expresses a similar critique against his teacher W. V. O. Quine and the Kantian philosopher Peter Strawson (Davidson 1990). According to Davidson, neither of those thinkers overcomes Kant's error-prone distinction between the content-conditions and form-conditions of perception; that is, between content that the senses present to us (passively) and transcendental conditions that affect our judgment (actively). The result, Davidson argues, is a postmodern conceptual relativism associated with, among others, the late Richard Rorty, who switched from analytic philosophy at Pittsburgh to literary studies at Stanford. And just as, according to Davidson, Quine's philosophy of the "indeterminacy of translation" is guilty of ontological relativism because of his reinforcement of the form-content dichotomy in perception, so too Kant seemed guilty from the point of view of the idealists following in his footsteps. He was convicted of being an epistemological relativist and so, as a result, a skeptic.

Indeed, one can easily understand the accusation made by the first generation of post-Kantian philosophers. Let's just look at what an impoverished understanding of freedom man was allowed to live by according to Kant's (horrific?) anthropology. Freedom was denied the status of an empirical fact, with the consequence of its degradation to pure fancy: it is something we must (objectively) presuppose because (subjectively) we need it in our self-understanding. Kant's distinction between phenomena and noumena did not fare any better. It transformed truth into a figment of cognition with both entities, truth and knowledge, combined in a paradoxical structure of a missed encounter. Similar to Neo in *The Matrix*, humanity appeared to remain incarcerated in the prison house of virtuality. Access to God, freedom, and truth was, allegedly, blocked. On the other hand, the modern split subject of interpellation was founded in all its fragility. In its dependence on experience, history, and society, the Kantian subject becomes the eternal subject in question. As the only medium of truth left by the Kantian revolution, the burden of truth and responsibility on the subject increased exponentially.

3

Before we move on to Hegel, one last comment on Kant is necessary. It concerns the categories of understanding, called *Verstandesbegriffe*. Kant derives them from the judgmental structure of our thought in his so-called "transcendental deduction." The categories primarily have an epistemic function. This distinguishes them from Aristotle's list of categories, that determine, in judgments, facts in their metaphysical being-in-themselves. There is obviously in Aristotle no talk about "appearances" with regard to reason's limits of perception. This is another argument why Kant's categories have, strictly speaking, no ontological meaning. Through reason, a human being can postulate basic structures of his or her surrounding reality, but he/she cannot recognize these as understanding. Hegel will contradict this belief. Determinations of thought have an ontological function for him. After all, we use them to determine what an object is in its essence, for example, by means of a definition. That reality is not a static set of states of affairs, as in a spatiotemporal block universe, is the basic conviction of Hegel's process philosophy. In this philosophy, truth and knowledge fulfill an eschatological fate: to miss one another in favor of an ever more self-reflexive future of Spirit. Philosophy, as a fundamental science, is capable of this insight. It is "scientific knowledge of the truth" (Hegel 2010a, 14). Thus, Hegel's thinking stands, even more than Kant's, in the tradition of classical metaphysics. However, it does so exclusively under the condition that this metaphysics incorporates the Kantian revolution. "Through *thinking things over* the *truth comes to be known* and that what the objects truly are is brought before consciousness" (Hegel 2010a, 67, §26). To put it bluntly, one could say that Kantian appearances are reinterpreted in Hegel as "appearances in themselves," with things-in-themselves as that which makes appearances non-identical, open to future reevaluation. Their objectivity is assured. Everything that can be known and reasoned has objective properties. "Thought-determinations" are "*fundamental determinations of things*" (ibid., 68, §28)—at least if one takes into account Hegel's concept of negativity, which we will come to in a moment. An entity that corresponds to its concept is identical with the latter and is not degraded by "subjective conditions of thinking" (Kant 1998, 222 [B122]) to the status of appearances in distinction from things-in-themselves. With this conviction in mind, even Anselm's ontological proof of God, in its propositional form of a synthetic a priori judgment, would be an expression of an objective thought. After all, that which is true coincides with its concept.

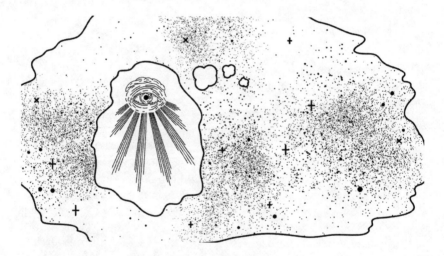

Anselm formulates an objective thought, God's existence, that does not lose objectivity through subjective conditions of thought. And are not Kant's own synthetic judgments a priori just that: expressions of objective thoughts by thought? With this background in mind, one may understand why Hegel's *Science of Logic* does not so much reveal synthetic a priori judgments in Kant's sense (which, as subjective conditions of thought, shape our judgments for the spatiotemporal realm of experience), but actually holds on to determinations of thought that bring thought and being into an objective (and not subjective) correlation of truth.

4

Hegel solves, on the one hand, the Kantian problem of appearances and, on the other, the problem of things-in-themselves. In contrast to Kant, he simply asserts that human beings as subjects are (always already) a subset of the realm of experience. The world of facts pulls us—or better: it calls us, interpellates us—into the historicity of its reasons, with the retrospective effect of our autonomy as rational agents being an effect of latency. We, as agents of Spirit, are "making *it* explicit" (Brandom 1998, my emphasis), with the "it" as that which needs subjects to be pulled out of multiple multiplicities. In other words, we make retrospectively explicit what reality from its very beginning was already all about. From this insight arises a mutual relation of subject and object in the genesis of reality's own becoming as Spirit and as called-out by Spirit.

So, the philosophical talk about objects and subjects does not cite an ontology of predetermined facts untouched by history, but underlines that objects and subjects only come into existence too late; that is, in their belated historical genesis of a constant missed encounter. For Hegel, the idea of reference between mind and matter detached from Spirit's own becoming in time is nonsensical. The latter, Spirit as becoming through receiving "the call" and answering it, is reality in its conceptual essence. Anton F. Koch, in the context of his Hegel-inspired hermeneutic realism, speaks analogously of a fundamental "readability of the world" (Koch 2016, 97ff.). If the concept of knowledge is supposed to have any meaning at all, the world is potentially a text to be metaphysically deciphered.

In contrast to Hegel, Kant does not reflect on the genesis of spirit as a social-historical entity. Kant presupposes pure reason alone as the only a priori condition of perception. He thus neglects how spirit's becoming has the recursive effect of unconsciously imposing ever-new a priori patterns of cognition in individual minds. A Kantian two-world doctrine, separating phenomena from noumena, thus seems unavoidable, with the Hegelian option of framing spirit as an emergent phenomenon of reflexive processes of cognition left out. Hegel's philosophy, by contrast, involves the insight that there is no neutral basis of knowledge outside of time—not even on the level of Kantian *Verstandesbegriffe*. There is no basis for a comparative assessment between objective states of affairs in their being-in-themselves on the one hand (i.e., Kant's *Ding an sich* as "the entirely undetermined thought of something in general"; Kant 1998, 349 [A253]) and the subjective representations of states of affairs on the other (Kant's *Erscheinungen*). Consciousness is division and fusion both for subjects and their objects. Consciousness cannot be neutral. It is time-conditioned, biased, prejudiced, and one-sided. Natural history and human history are the same medium of a process that recognizes, in the course of the evolution of conceptuality, its own status of being as a partial element (or subset) of reality on the way to its final destiny—which Hegel calls "absolute spirit" or "absolute idea."

Thinking thought, as a history-dependent unity of the form-condition of cognition and content-conditions of objects, shapes each new complementary relation between subjects and objects in time. These inferential conceptual relations are obviously very different in the seventeenth and the twentieth centuries. Human beings never face eternal states of affairs. They are the result of an evolutionary process of what Hegel calls both "Spirit" and the "concept." Sentient beings are, therefore, products of concepts and states of affairs because they are subsets of Spirit, which, as superset, repeatedly redefines its limits. This does not mean, conversely, that we live exclusively at Spirit's mercy. Spirit lives at the mercy of its supernumerary elements.

The moment Galileo Galilei "rolled balls of a weight chosen by himself down an inclined plane. . . . a light dawned on all those who study nature" (Kant 1998, 108–9 [Bxii]). The "revolution of the way of thinking" (ibid., Bxi) associated with Galileo did not change the object of investigation: the celestial bodies. The subject's epistemic position within reason's relation to newly discovered empirical states of affairs was changed. For Hegel, determinations of thought can historically recognize states of affairs objectively through the conditions of the possibility of objectivity imposed on them in an era- and time-specific manner. Thinking's determinations cannot step out of the brain to falsify from the outside of time and space the truth-values of facts. Does this mean that objectivity and truth are subjective? No. It means that objectivity in the temporal structure of consciousness simultaneously misses and presupposes the isomorphism between being and thinking.

Kant, too, develops a historical evolution for the improvement of human experience through time, but not with regard to ontological questions of epistemology. He mentions it in his 1784 essay "Idea for a Universal History with a Cosmopolitan Purpose," in the second section of *The Conflict of the Faculties* (1789), and in the teleology sections of the *Critique of the Power of Judgment* (1790). However, Kant does not apply this insight to formal conditions, that is, to epistemic categories of cognition. But even beyond that, especially in the *Critique of the Power of Judgment*, the idea of a goal-directed development within the natural order remains at the status of an "idea." This idea marks reason's self-referentiality; an idea's justification is its proclamation. It makes the reality surrounding us explainable in meaningful relations of purpose. Whether nature's or mankind's history can be attributed to an intrinsic and purposeful order (of morality and truth), however, is not possible to prove. According to Hegel, on the other hand, there is no doubt about it. To postulate only a regulative ideal of Spirit's progress is self-refuting. It ignores that Spirit in its attachment to time cannot interpret the performative gesture of its self-production in any way other than toward a progress in thinking and acting. Spirit's progress in time is not a figment of reason, but an empirical fact—the proof of which is manifest in history.

5

Hegel's critique of Kant is aimed particularly at the concept of the thing-in-itself. Even under the concession that Kant interpreted the term as a limit-concept, a limit to which no object in space and time can be assigned, it evokes the idea of a reality lurking behind our veil of perception. It is put forth as the backside of reality, giving the essential input to our five senses.

For Hegel, though, to postulate a conceptual beyond of this kind—even as a purely hypothetical idea of thought's limit—fails to recognize that in consciousness the "beyond" of reality is, so to speak, already an intrinsic part of consciousness's constant progress. For the same reason, the differentiation between phenomena and noumena is misleading. For Hegel, it is based on a misjudgment of the historical entanglement of thinking and being. There is no reality beyond its necessary complement with consciousness. What is real is real in and for thought.

In a similar way, it would be misleading for a spider in the animal kingdom—assuming spiders could philosophize—to ask whether its spider-world exists or not, or if there is a world that is truer than what the spider perceives as true. Simply put: there is no spider-world without spiders, as there is no objective world of facts without animals equipped with reason referring to them. And even if Hegel, in his philosophy of nature, missed out totally on the Darwinian idea of the evolution of species, he nevertheless gives us an evolutionary theory of thought. This insight is what his philosophy of the concept's becoming is about: the evolution of mind-with-matter through time, the entanglement of thinking and being within constant changes of conceptual roles. This entanglement must not be misunderstood as isomorphism, since only the missed encounter of thinking and being guarantees the progress of science.

I mentioned earlier that a similar argument has been made by Davidson against Strawson and Quine in various texts. Davidson attributes to both of them the fallacy of adopting Kant's dichotomy between form-conditions of knowledge and content-conditions of knowledge, and claims that this leads them astray to a relativistic understanding of "conceptual schemes" (Davidson 1990) with regard to a world beyond those schemes.

In this context, Hegel not only asserts that consciousness is conditioned by the external world as the locus of all possible experience within thought's (or consciousness's) evolution. He also states that consciousness is historically biased and one-sided by definition. Human beings are, allegorically speaking, part of reality, not opposed to it. We are changing subsets of supersets in which mind and matter co-depend on each other via an ontological gap of their non-identity. Or, to use a different image: sapient beings are species of a genus but, as such, are called to participate in the overcoming of what the genus stands for; that is, to redefine what the substance will be like, seen retrospectively (with horror?) from an open future. This guarantees the overcoming of consciousness's own measure of self-assertion, as it guarantees the progress of science through spirit's permanent transgression in an evolution of interpellations.

The retrospective condition of consciousness with regard to its experience in time can be elucidated with regard to our own historical formation. We may ask, for example: what was it like, back then, to be little Jonas or little Anna at the age of five or ten years? Can we yet remember our state of consciousness as an authentic experience of objectivity? If subjectivity and objectivity stick together like the two sides of a coin (with a hidden fissure in between), then one side affects the other necessarily. We may remember how hard it was for us to learn Latin vocabularies in high school. But, beyond that, can we retrospectively recall the level of self-consciousness back then, with its backside of objective states of affairs? This is impossible. Consciousness cannot subtract itself from itself.

What I want to get at with these hypothetical questions is the simple fact that in all stages of experience, we assumed back then, as we assume today, a more or less objective access to the reality surrounding us. Even if we say nowadays that we were uneducated back then at the age of twelve, we would not come to the same conclusion if we were by some miracle twelve years old again. In Hegel's understanding, we would have no *Begriff*, no concept, from which our twelve-years-old alter ego could judge itself with regard to what our consciousness incorporates as truth-apt today. There is literally no direct connection between me at the age of fifty-four and my identity at the age of twelve. The connection is a retrospective construction of my mind, always taking the present as the point of departure in time to give my experience a coherence and a direction to an open future.

At each stage of development that consciousness completes in its genesis, the individual mind of sapient beings is more or less certain of its objective grip on reality. Experiences of error may then intervene in a self-corrective way, but only to gain a new level of purported certainty. It is always this absolutely self-certain "I think" in its entanglement with an anti-individualistic social structure that recognizes, perceives, and judges states of affairs, whether at the age of six, ten, or twenty. At each stage, consciousness is usually certain of its objectivity. Only retrospectively does it recognize previous concepts of objectivity as both false and as the condition of the possibility of its progress. "This dialectical movement which consciousness exercises on itself and which affects both its knowledge and on its object, is precisely what is called experience" (Hegel 1977, 55, §86).

But then, one may ask, has the new object of science not always been the old one? This claim could be made, roughly speaking, by representatives of metaphysical realism, with Christopher Peacocke as one often-cited proponent (Peacocke 2019). How else could it be? Has not the heliocentric worldview always been true; that is, a fact discovered by intelligent humanoids and not created within the framework of consciousness's historical becoming?

Questions like these are misleading. They make us believe in an ahistorical point of view determining the objectivity of facts untouched by time. The world is taken as a space-time block-universe, similar to a loaf of bread. All possible states of affairs are already in place untouched by humans. It guarantees true propositions like a constant reservoir of facts to be contemplated by subjects. But this perspective is discarded by Hegel's philosophy of the concept's self-consumption and self-production. The truth of heliocentrism is the history of its conceptual becoming. This history is an objective part of heliocentrism's intrinsic property of being true. No wonder, then, that Hegel accuses Kant of assuming rigid categories of understanding that remain the same through time because they are (allegedly) timeless, separating a static consciousness with static conditions of experience from a static realm of things as they are in themselves. The interplay of form and content in historically conditioned processes of experience is not taken into account, according to Hegel's critique.

This discussion has recently received new arguments in a debate between Catherine Malabou and Günter Zöller. In contrast to Zöller's interpretation, Malabou rejects the view that Kant's famous table of categories is a static corset of a priori conditions of cognition (Malabou 2016, 40–42.). She claims instead that Kant knew about the "plasticity"—a term coined by her own philosophical work—of the human brain as a medium of process-philosophical redefinitions of what is the case. Be that as it may.

For my purpose, it is important to acknowledge, with Gerhard Gamm, that Hegel sees a theological motif shining through in Kant's philosophy, namely "the fear of the contamination of the absolute (the realm of the thing-in-itself). This absolute must not [in Kant's perspective] be tainted, as it were, by the cognitive schemes of finite human beings" (Gamm 1997, 95, my trans.). Hegel, by contrast, argues that nothing is contaminated here. Consciousness recognizes objective facts. They depend both onto-logically and epistemologically on consciousness. Take the simple fact of the concept "atom." Only its abstract form guarantees empirical content a line of demarcation. The former shapes the ontological access to reality, even if justifications never attain a final status of "justifications as they are in themselves."

6

Hegel's concept of negativity is of central importance in this context and for relating the philosophy of subjectivity in the tradition of psychoanal-ysis with German idealism. His concept stands in relation to Freud's in-terpretation of the human mind as an entity whose non-identity (or split identity) is an essential property of its reflexivity. And this is the reason why the long detour from Kant to Hegel presented in the sections of this lecture above was necessary. Hegel writes the following:

"The disparity which exists in consciousness between the 'I' and the substance [= totality of facts] which is its object is . . . the *negative* in general. This can be regarded as *the defect* of both [i.e., as a defect in the 'I' as the source of perception and as a defect in the object of reference], though it [the negative] is their soul, or that which moves them [i.e., the negative, which is both in the 'I' and in the substance (= totality of facts), moves both due to a lack of coincidence, or better: due to a constant missed encounter of knowledge and truth]. That is why some of the an-cients [pre-Socratics like Leucippus and Democritus] conceived the *void* as the principle of motion, for they rightly saw the moving principle as the *negative*, though they did not as yet grasp that the negative is the self [i.e., pre-Socratic philosophers already dealt with the negative as a property of being, but never as something that is essentially inscribed in the basic structure of the cosmos, so to speak, as an inner, ontological principle]. Now, although this negative appears at first as a disparity between the 'I' and its object, it is just as much the disparity of the substance with itself" (Hegel 1977, 21, §37).

We learn that the sum total of facts surrounding us is one in which an infinite lack of being is inscribed. Hegel gives this lack the name of "the negative." As a basic principle of being, the negative is the source of movement (*das Bewegende*), with us humans as embodiments of spirit maintaining and energizing this movement. We cannot complete it, due to a deficiency inherent in the object, so to speak, as well as in us, the subjects of knowledge. We cannot even recognize our place or role, vocation, or destiny in this process, as Hegel argues in the *Lectures on the Philosophy of World History* (Hegel 2011). Spirit takes hold of us, even against our own intentions. So, negativity concerns not only facts "out there" (= that which is the case), but ourselves, our missed encounters with our vocations, our false desires, and our ideological convictions. As humans, we constantly live "an einem anderen Schauplatz," at another scene (Freud citing Fechner, Freud 1981, vol. 4, 48). The dividing line between subject and object falls within our consciousness as the source of negativity. The dividing line is, abstractly speaking, "extension-equivalent" with the *Begriff* in progress through time, with us as both subsets and supersets in this process of becoming.

In short, the quotation given above contains at its core all that makes Hegel interesting for the Lacanian philosopher and representative of contemporary dialectical materialism Slavoj Žižek. He detects patterns of equivalence between Hegel's concept of spirit as a justificatory structure of what is in truth, struggling with its own lack, and Lacan's concepts of subjectivity as being split through the world of signifiers. The latter emerges from what resists psychological self-understanding and, in this respect, matches with Hegel's spirit as that which struggles to become coherent in time. In both cases, negativity incorporates properties of lack. It concerns the subject in its relation to the world of others, as well as, according to Hegel's interpretation, the subject-object dichotomy barred from becoming one. It is precisely this notion of negativity which Hegel calls "soul or the moving [*das Bewegende*]," and which continually undermines our determinations of facts. This insight led Lacan to call Hegel the "most sublime of hysterics" (Lacan 2007, 35). Hysterics find no rest. They try endlessly to catch up with their lack of identity. And indeed, Hegel locates *Geist* in this tension. *Geist*/Spirit "wins its truth only when, in utter dismemberment, it finds itself. It is this power, not as something positive, which closes its eyes to the negative . . . , on the contrary, Spirit is this power only by looking the negative in the face, and tarrying with it" (Hegel 1977, 19, §32).

But if spirit does not find rest, neither does the perceiving subject, the carrier of knowledge. The latter is in contradiction with itself and with the world. For this very reason, it is able to question everything, or rather, as soon as subjects begin to think, they are urged to question, via the objections of others, facts, to focus on contradictions in political and scientific discourses, and so on. World spirit proves to be a hegemonically disputed aggregate of modules of knowledge, which have to justify their truth claims in continuous feedback loops of judgments, commitments, entitlements, missions, and wars.

5

The Metaphysics of Contingency

(Lecture 6)

1

I pointed out in the last lecture that the thing-in-itself, postulated by Kant, apparently subtracts something from the object of knowledge. Its fullness (as thing-in-itself) is emptied in the act of an object's cognitive perception. Humans have rational, cognitive access to appearances as facts but not to things-in-themselves. As Žižek reveals in his reading of Hegel, an appearance is consequently the reduced form of an object. Its fullness is allegedly twofold. It consists of two properties: of being an appearance and of hiding a thing-in-itself. However, since the object of experience (for example, the desk in front of me) is only accessible to me as being an appearance, the objectivity of the desk in its being in itself is, allegedly, lost. But this causes a problem. Now the cognitive faculty of perception deprives us of what is factually true. A transcendental scheme mediates between mind and matter. In other words, the cognizing subject introduces between appearance and things-in-themselves the transcendental medium of cognition, thus building a semantic boundary to an objective Other, lurking within phenomena (without being part of their identity according to the rule of the law of identity).

For Kant, things-in-themselves remain unaffected by this addition of a transcendental scheme. This instigates Hegel's critique. Kant cultivates an excessive "tenderness for things [*Zärtlichkeit für die Dinge*]," since it would be "a pity . . . if they [the objects of experience] contradicted each other" (Hegel 1986, 359, my trans.). Genuine knowledge should, allegedly, eliminate contradictions and leave behind no epistemic remainder. Subjective additions inherent in cognition should be left behind and objectivity without contradiction should be accomplished. According to Hegel, however, contradictions cannot be removed from facts in which things as objects of experience in historical conditions receive their criteria of justification. For this reason, he emphasizes the insight, in contrast to Kant, that in "spirit (the highest) *is contradiction*" (my emphasis). Contradiction is "no harm" (ibid.) to knowledge, but part of knowledge.

Thus, for Hegel, the dichotomy between subject and object must be separated from Kant's static understanding of things-in-themselves as (allegedly) independent meta-entities of our epistemic acts. Hegel presents his arguments at the beginning of the *Phenomenology of Spirit*. He refers to the classical concept of substance (Greek: *ousia*) in the modern and Spinozist sense of the term, as, roughly speaking, the embodiment of something that "stands under or grounds things." Hegel shares with Spinoza the metaphysical conviction that the universe is substance itself, that is, the place of facts. It harbors no power that can oppose human cognition. This implies that being (as substance) is determinate and potentially available to a subject's knowledge. However, Hegel criticizes Spinoza's deductive concept of substance as "one indivisible totality; there is no determinateness which would not be contained in this absolute and be dissolved into it" (Hegel 2010b, 472). What this critique amounts to, in short, is that Spinoza's concept of substance lacks "immanent reflection" (Hegel 2010b, 474), which for Hegel can only be remedied by the idea of "subject" as that which differentiates substance from within through self-reflexivity. Thus, understanding substance correctly relies on grasping the structure of a self-relation (called "spirit") in which, to put it simply, identity (substance) and differences (subjects) co-depend and co-exclude themselves through time. In other words, substance is at odds with itself qua subject's "self-movement" (Hegel 1977, 13) and as such has to be conceived "equally as *Subject*" (Hegel 1977, 10, §17). The "subject" accidentalizes the essential property of substance and annihilates the concept's classical meaning. Substance now is no longer substance but, through being subject as well, accident, and *as accident*, substance. This is what Hegel's proposition that "everything depends on grasping and expressing the True, not only as *Substance* but equally as *Subject*" (Hegel 1977, 10) aims at. Substance is confronted with an Other of itself: "subject," as that which is in substance more than substance itself. A chiasmic exchange consisting in two auto-excluding meta-entities (substance vs. subject/accident/ mode) holds the Hegelian panpsychic universe together, but, at the same time, in a constant state of conflict. This precisely does not mean that the object of knowledge is "subjectivized" (as in Kant's philosophy), but that, as Žižek writes, "the act of subjective cognition . . . is contained in advance in its substantial 'object': the path to truth is part of truth" (Žižek 2008, 43, my trans.).

Žižek points out that behind the veil of perception, the Hegelian subject finds, figuratively speaking, only what it has brought with itself. Even Kant asserts this thesis at the very beginning of his first *Critique* (Kant 1998, 109 [Bxiii]). However, he does not develop the subject matter under dialectical premises, as Hegel does. This is another reason why Kant's two-world doctrine tends to protect "real reality" (= things-in-themselves) from the contingency of human knowledge, fallible and time-dependent as it is, but also from utilitarian (and immoral) maxims of action. Kant perhaps saw the danger of falling into (a postmodern?) relativism, due to the anthropocentric character of his metaphysics, with its subjective conditions of knowledge as pathways to objective truth. And indeed, this reproach is made repeatedly by metaphysical realists. They see Kant's first *Critique* as a foundational work of nineteenth- and twentieth-century constructivism. This accusation has been made prominently by Donald Davidson. Kant, he argues, prepared the way for modern conceptual relativism, with Rudolf Carnap and Willard V. O. Quine as two prominent representatives in the twentieth century. Kant's revolting distinction between content-conditions of forms and form-conditions of content in acts of both perception and justification carries all the guilt for misguided epistemologies.

A similar distrust can be found in the work of the Pittsburgh school, founded by Robert Brandom and John McDowell in their revival of German idealism inflected by analytic philosophy. Their readings of Kant and Hegel diverge sharply from those presented by representatives of a contemporary Left Hegelianism (Badiou, Žižek, Zupančič, Johnston, Menke, Finkelde, etc.). Unfortunately, we cannot address this issue here in more detail (see Finkelde 2021b).

Hegel formulates his separation from Kant in the statement that the fear of reason's error (*before* a cognitive investigation of its limits) is already "the error itself" (Hegel 1977, 47, §74). He asserts, with Kant on the one hand, that human cognition accesses appearances, but on the other, he rejects the idea of things-in-themselves as untouched by time. Truth emerges in processes of becoming within the genesis of a still-undetermined future of cognition, with justification evolving in the relation of human beings and their historical sites of experience. In such sites, human beings are interpellated time and again as torchbearers of what Hegel calls "the idea" or "the concept." Knowledge urges invocations in the name of truth, even when subject and object repeatedly miss one another, as the diagram below attempts to capture. It illustrates Hegel's dialectical teleology in time. The lower x-axis from left to right marks the timeline of historical events, from the Big Bang to the present. The y-axis represents the increase of spirit's self-reflexivity in its genesis, starting with the first and primitive forms of human consciousness that increasingly become more and more complex. The culmination of this process is Hegel's *Phenomenology of Spirit*, as the epitome of spirit's own self-illumination. Now, if one tried to integrate the famous monolith from Stanley Kubrick's *2001: A Space Odyssey* (1968) into the diagram, it

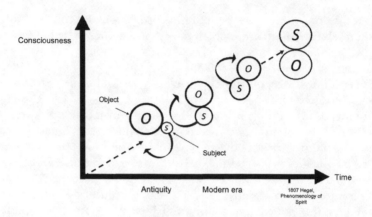

would indicate the transition between nature and culture. The band of apes that gathers around the monolith in a famous scene encounters a first enigmatic signifier. The monolith initiates, according to the film's art of suspense, the evolutionary history of mankind, and reappears at the end—as enigmatic as in the beginning—in front of the deathbed of the protagonist David Bowman. Apparently, millennia of human evolution have not been able to penetrate this object that knew too much. The monolith is as enigmatic for the astronaut Bowman as it was for the apes at the origin of consciousness and, in that sense, exemplifies Adorno's

talk of the "preponderance of the object" fittingly (Adorno 2004, 189). In the civilizations of antiquity, again in highly simplified terms, the object was seen as the sum of all metaphysical facts. It appears in prehistoric monuments; for example, a circle of oversized Sarsen stones. Here, the object is huge and the subject, as its counterpart, small. At this stage of the concept, humanity sees itself in radical dependence on natural forces, which are deified as objects of their worship. The thing, which, in its abundance, apparently knows too much, confronts consciousness as an instance of divine knowledge, force, and power. It is the shelter of a big Other who, like the gods of Olympus, can freely exercise power over all individuals on earth.

In the progress of self-consciousness, the subject experiences an enlargement in the relationship with the object. It conceptually penetrates the hard shell of states of affairs until divine and mysterious powers apparently diminish, without getting lost completely. Under this perspective of a teleological development of consciousness, belief in a world of things as they are in themselves is unnecessary. Realism with a capital R, which speaks of facts as being untouched by their historical patterns of justification, proves for Hegel to be untenable. Cognition and justification are part of a teleological progress within which error is a fully-fledged part of truth.

This proves the importance of Hegel's dictum that substance is to be understood "equally as *subject*." According to Žižek, this sentence must be read as an "infinite judgment" in the Kantian sense. For Žižek, it expresses Hegel's speculative thesis of evolving patterns of what exists in truth. The proposition is not to be understood as a simple assertion of identity (A = B) (see Žižek 2002, 119). Nor does it define truth conditions in the world of facts. It expresses, on the contrary, the metaphysical thesis of Hegel's teleological process metaphysics, in which substance (as the panpsychic totality of the universe in its becoming) is ever that which will have emerged via subjects in an inconclusive future. "'Subject' stands for the non-substantial agency of phenomenalization" (Žižek 2000a, 88). To understand the world of phenomena and historical contingencies in connection with the talk of substance as subject "means precisely that split, phenomenalization, and so forth, are inherent to the life of the Absolute itself" (ibid., 89). This thought is illustrated fittingly by the drawing by Eric Steinhart where processes of "mapping" knowledge between substance and subject bring to the foreground what the Hegelian concept incorporates retrospectively. The experiential journey of mind can—within the help of a different illustration—be even as terrifying as Ellen Ripley's walk through a laboratory of her genetically engineered prototypes in

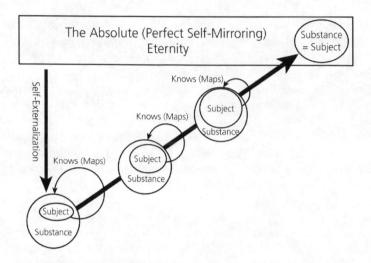

the fourth *Alien* movie. In a key scene, the heroine (played by Sigourney Weaver) enters a secret laboratory. In it, she discovers various failed clones of herself in meter-high test tubes like dead fetuses in an anthropological museum. The scene's importance lies in the moment of Ripley's self-recognition. Ripley comprehends that the monstrosities of herself as precursors of her identity are the condition of her self-reflexivity. The

scene opens up the abyss between Ripley and her clones as a slaughter bench-like pathway to identity. Consciousness proves to be a contingent embodiment of History's catastrophes. It is precisely this insight that Hegel confronts us with. His philosophy reveals a universe in a process of feedback loops of cognition that, despite a genesis filled with catastrophes, is nevertheless sacred and holy, and as such incessantly calls upon us to be answers with regard to ever higher causes. Cognition is on a historical mission, with new forms of knowledge provoking dialectical twists through paradigm shifts. In its execution, consciousness produces that which it recognizes and ejects, feeling an urge to overcome the past in the name of a better future. Or, to put it differently: the progress of knowledge is based on Ripley's experience of having to ascribe selfhood to monstrosities in test-tubes, of which she herself is the outcome.

In this context, Žižek emphasizes that Hegel presents the shift to synthesis from a thesis-antithesis dichotomy as a change of perspective. What is generally regarded as synthesis in Hegel—the conflict of mutually exclusive theses—is precisely not to be interpreted as reconciliation according to a clichéd understanding of *Aufhebung*, or sublimation. Synthesis does not mean that agents of thesis and agents of antithesis agree like contracting parties on a "tertium datur," a third alternative that satisfies all parties. As Žižek emphasizes, it is about a change of perspective that makes the conflict as conflict no longer capable of recognition. Žižek: "Hegel puts emphasis . . . on the fact that it is precisely the conflict that unites the opposite poles. The 'synthesis' which has been sought beyond the division is already realized by division itself" (Žižek 2008, 44, my trans.).

2

Let us summarize once more what has been stated so far. While Kant seeks to keep contingency out of his metaphysics, locating the relation of mind and world in front of a horizon of an aporia-free totality of meaning (the realm of purposes, the realm of things-in-themselves), Hegel, by contrast, recognizes that contingency must be identified retrospectively as a necessary ingredient of Being. This, however, compels us to understand the influence of retroactive explanations in more detail. To do this, let us refer to Kant's place in the history of philosophy in the aftermath of rationalism and empiricism. It is a common (and simplified) belief that he reconciles both currents of thought. Transcendental philosophy necessarily emerges out of two opposing philosophical traditions that preceded it. In this perspective, transcendental philosophy is the true heir of rationalism and empiricism. Through Kant we recognize that empiricism and rationalism are the necessary preconditions for the theory of "synthetic judgments a priori." Arguments from Wolff, Leibniz, and Descartes, through Locke and Hume seem to be necessarily connected to each other such that Kant emerges, with no place for chance in this equation. But what if Kant had never appeared in the history of philosophy? Could we imagine instead that the synthesis of empiricism and rationalism associated with his name would have been detected in the philosophy of Hume, for example by Fichte, Schelling, Hegel, or whomever? Could it not be possible to interpret Hume in a more Kantian way than Kantians did not see the need for, since Kant filled in the gap? Did Kantianism not distort Hume's empiricism for its own purposes of argument?

Žižek illustrates the interplay of necessity and contingency with reference to Napoleon I (Žižek 2002, 128–29). The latter's appearance on the stage of world-historic events is difficult to deny the status of a historical necessity, since the arrival of his leadership arose in the aftermath of the bloody course of the French Revolution. After the overthrow of Robespierre and the Jacobins in 1794 and the politically unstable government of the Directory, a political leader had to finally put an end to corruption and inefficiency. One could say that the political chaos provoked by the French Revolution needed someone like Napoleon I, just as the United States of America needed a president like Trump in 2016 to bring, allegedly, an end to the decline of U.S. supremacy caused by "the swamp" of left-leaning political elites in Washington, DC. On this description, necessity precedes contingency. According to Hegel, though, an interpretation of this chronological order fails to recognize the extent to which it only receives its imperative of necessity retrospectively from the future. Not until a (somehow) accidental emergence—for example, the emergence of a certain Immanuel Kant in Königsberg—is an order of events completed retroactively, which then leads to the sequence of events A, B, C, D, and E. However, C appears between B and D only when E has assumed its (E's) place in the sequence. The case is similar with Napoleon I. Through his entry on the political scene ten years after the beginning of the French Revolution, the events allegedly presupposing his seizure of power are interpreted retroactively as a teleological process to his arrival. And could one not say the same about World War II? Let us assume, with the science fiction author Philip K. Dick, that Nazi Germany had won the war in coalition with Japan and the fascist elites in Spain and Italy. Would this not change various judgments and, through the changed perspective of victory against American capitalism and Soviet Bolshevism, make Nazi crimes less problematic, more excusable? I do not want to claim that crimes like the Holocaust would have been dropped out of collective memory. Nevertheless, it can be assumed that the crimes would have been interpreted as collateral damage necessary to avert greater catastrophes for mankind.

Like all collateral damage, Nazi crimes might have been accepted as an unintentional by-product due to the "heat of the moment," the unexpected intensity of the war. Who can undo past injustices, such as the founding of the United States at the expense of indigenous peoples, especially under the condition of the United States's global supremacy? Such a transformation of war crimes to "crimes with a human face" from the winner's perspective shapes realpolitik to this day, since—to use Walter Benjamin's phrase—the winners of history establish the premises of what is to be judged as good and evil (Benjamin 1989). In this sense, the seizure of North American soil by European migrants cannot be interpreted as ethnic cleansing of indigenous populations. Ethnic cleansing of indigenous populations is the United States's condition of its being, just as Israel's continued occupation of the West Bank to this day is seen (by Western nations) as a condition of Israel's right to exist, with the consequence of implementing Palestine's nonexistence. In both cases, we perceive conditions of the possibility of a body-politics' self-understanding of what political reality is all about and why this reality is calling on citizens to defend a crime-filled past and a crime-filled present with the mental state of a good conscience. Collective acts of mourning in rituals of cultural memory do not escape the aporias mentioned, but confirm them.

For this reason, it can be expected that Israel will only erect monuments as a reminder of its apartheid policy when the last territories under the administration of the Palestinian Authority in the West Bank and the Gaza Strip become part of "Eretz Israel." The former good conscience at the time of land-theft in the name of God's chosen people will be mirrored in the good conscience of retrospectively mourning what had to be done to the Palestinians. The sorrow of all the injustices the Jewish people had to commit against the people of Palestine will be celebrated. Past injustice is left untouched, and yet symbolically elevated, within the framework of a collective sublimation. Facts have suddenly changed ontological properties, since a change of perspective has taken place collectively.

The examples mentioned express the impact of a retroactive performance discovered by Žižek in Hegel's philosophy. It affects, according to Lacan, the individual mind as well. Similar to Hegel's understanding of "world spirit's" retrospective progress, every mind of an individual orders the genesis of its becoming in new transcriptions of past events with regard to the present. What has happened in the past is hermeneutically open to be rewritten from the future, with the effect that the present can be symbolically changed as well. We will come to this topic later on.

A psychoanalytic treatment can help to initiate the mentioned perspectives change in situations in which individuals finally succeed in hermeneutically rewriting their symbolic status. The retroactive performance implies that a seemingly homogeneous chain of events could have happened differently. This indicates a rather shocking degree of contingency in "the order of the signifier" (Lacan), a contingency that the mind normally must suppress so as not to imperil its understanding of itself as autonomous. This concerns worldly matters with regard to paradigm shifts. All kinds of circumstances can appear retrospectively in a virtual space of seemingly infinite possibilities, transubstantiating them into necessary events from the present. This is why Žižek understands Hegel's dialectic as the "science of 'how-necessity-emerges-from-contingency" (Žižek 2008, 53, my trans.), since "necessity itself depends on contingency" (Žižek 1991a, 129). Modal categories of necessity and contingency are related to each other. The contingent gesture of determination is a performative speech act, as these are described by J. L. Austin. It does not depict, but rather creates, a fact. It can genealogically align a series of random events that precede it into a directed teleology.

Where exactly does the aforementioned change of perspective take place? This is not always as clear as one might think. The following drawing by M. C. Escher illustrates this fittingly. We see two species of animals

mutating through changing patterns of form that redefine their essence (= content). One animal turns into another as the content of another animal becomes its new condition of form. What was once a goose at the top of the illustration is now a fish at the bottom and vice versa. But, especially in the center of the drawing, the form of one entity conditions that of the other, without a clear hegemonic structure of dominance emerging between form and content. Therefore, when a goose is brought into view, the fish sinks back, and vice versa. Who can now proclaim what it means to exist, when the old form lies with the new content in a stalemate of heterogeneous indeterminacy? And doesn't an individual who opts for one fact, while excluding the other (like in front of an ambivalent gestalt image), inevitably cause misunderstanding, since history that remains open has not yet been hegemonized; that is, it has not yet stabilized its fact-making process in the name of the big Other? The Israel-Palestine conflict probably exemplifies this like no other. Here a stalemate has caused five decades of war and conflict with no progress in sight, no place of the new perspective directed from either the Nakba perspective or the Holocaust perspective. After all, numerous nations of the League of Arab States continue to believe that Israel is to blame for occupation and apartheid. In contrast, numerous states in Europe discover in the ongoing crisis only collateral damage to ward off an even greater evil, maybe even another holocaust. The Italian philosopher Antonio Gramsci calls an interregnum like this the realm of *fenomeni morbosi*, "morbid phenomena": in it, "the old is dying and the new is not yet born" (Gramsci 1977, 311, §34, my trans.).

Changing forms result in modifications of content, and changing content in return modifies the forms. A shape that originally produces a firmly defined meaning (a goose) gives way to a content that is subsequently united as a fish. The Israeli apartheid state (see Amnesty International 2022) may one day undergo such a transubstantiation and mutate into a true democracy, with Israelis and Palestinians remembering together the injustice done through occupation and segregation. From such a perspective, should it one day be adopted, I suppose "land theft," "displacement," and "ethnic cleansing" would no longer be named as such. It would contradict the experience of the new national zeitgeist incorporating a synthesis as its own form. Contents mutate, because what is interior accommodates itself to the outside factor of the new determination. And just as Escher's geese are suddenly transformed into fish, in the context of the 2010 Arab Spring, the former Egyptian president Hosni Mubarak suddenly transformed from an esteemed politician into a heavily criticized dictator. Formerly a guarantor of peace with Israel and of freedoms for a prosperous middle class, he mutated into a tyrant within a few hours due to tectonic changes in the political facts, leading to unexpected new background conditions. Suddenly, Western politicians were reluctant to appear at his side, even though years earlier they had courted Mubarak as a guarantor of peace in the Middle East. The examples given can be summarized in Žižek's statement that "what one seeks, one already has; what one strives for, is what is already realized" (Žižek 2008, 43, my trans.). Division has never existed. It was exclusively an effect of perspective (ibid., 44).

Part 3

The Human Being and the Symbolic Order

6

In the Mirror, the Image of my Enemy

(Lecture 7)

1

In the first two parts of this series of lectures, various arenas of structural negativity were presented. They concerned both relations of political norms within communities, which are unquestionably unstable in nature, and the mind's inner functioning. Judgments find their justification, or, if not, are revised. Subsequently, the human mind was reflected upon with reference to Freud, Lacan, and Kant. It became apparent to what extent the mind, like the hegemonic structure of socially administered fields of meaning, is organized around the repression of antagonisms and internal sites of contradiction. The mind proves to be confronted with conscious and unconscious contexts of justification. These invade and call upon us. After all, the individual enters a relation to herself and to her environment through the medium of an Other that never reveals itself in full transparency. For this reason, too, the individual does not simply stand neutrally in the midst of facts and states of affairs, but embodies a sometimes more, sometimes less, pronounced response to facts in a way that is analogous to a believer with regard to his religious worldview.

I tried to explain subsequently the extent to which Hegel, with his concepts of spirit and world-spirit, substantiates the thesis of consciousness's increasing complexity in the history of mankind. He unfolds a pre-Darwinian theory of evolution, not with reference to animal species, but to evolving patterns of justification of what is *in truth*. Spirit progresses through experiences of negativity and transgression, following a teleological purpose to increasingly become what it always had been. Spirit is not an unmediated substance, but one "to which negation and mediation are essential" (Hegel 1977, 61, §99).

The philosophy of psychoanalysis has a similar perspective on man's subjectivity as a recursive loop of self-reflexive cognitive acts in which the relation to the world is always submitted to conscious and unconscious processes of reevaluation. The gaps in meaning that generate difference within normative orders are therefore in a necessary interrelation with gaps affecting the individual mind. For this reason, the following block of lectures will focus more precisely on Lacan's philosophy of psychoanalysis and its epistemological potentials. The central object of consideration will be, among other topics, Lacan's theory of the "mirror stage." Before that, however, it should be recalled that psychoanalysis, similar to epistemology, is dedicated to the subject matter of truth. So-called "adaequatio" and "holistic" theories of meaning examine under what conditions our judgments are veridical, that is, truthful in their relation to facts and states of affairs. Truth is then, for example, understood as a "correspondence" between a judgment and a fact, or—"holistically"—as a justification in the context of other justifications.

The question of truth in psychoanalysis has nothing in common with these concepts. It is neither concerned with propositional truth in judgments, nor with the determination of the theoretical roles of concepts in semantic theories. Instead, it focuses on what a subject should know about oneself in order to relate to oneself in coordinates of interpellation. This is illustrated by the following oft-cited joke that Žižek mentions in one of his publications.

2

A man who thinks he is a grain of wheat is admitted to a psychiatric clinic. The doctor on duty does her best to convince the patient that he is not a grain of wheat. Unfortunately, he comes back shortly after his release shaking with fear. He has encountered a chicken and is afraid that it might pick him up and eat him. The doctor, annoyed, reacts and says, "'You know very well that you are not a grain of seed but a man.' 'Of course, I know,' replies the patient, 'but does the chicken?'" (Žižek 2006, 351).

What this joke illustrates is the fact that the patient unconsciously ascribes to the outside world—in this case: to the chicken—a knowledge about his true ego function which he cannot reasonably reconcile with respect to the way he sees and understands himself. The chicken literally knows too much about the patient. The doctor brings the patient to the reason-guided comprehension of not being a grain of wheat. However, the panic attack in the encounter with the chicken immediately invalidates this rational knowledge. This kind of knowledge cannot hegemonize the symptom that occupies the mind and pulls its strings. Freud's patient Emma, discussed in his *Project for a Scientific Psychology*, suffers from a similar experience. She cannot give reasons for the anxiety she experiences when stepping into a department store alone (Freud 1981, vol. 1, 353–56). Freud finally discloses a prepubescent event in which the woman proved to be a victim of sexual assault. It was actualized by her mind years later as traumatic. The neurotic angst of not entering department stores unaccompanied proves to be—like the panic attack of the man in the chicken joke—the compromise that Emma's psyche produced to resolve the conflict as well as possible. Her symptom is a resolution to a mental deadlock.

The man in the chicken joke has not yet realized that his tic has the structure of a symptom. He does not know that there is another locus of knowledge that harbors multiple symptoms untouched by the intellect. The chicken in the joke is, analogous to department stores in Emma's case, the objectified form of a congestion of "energy-quanta" that are not directly accessible. As such, both stories represent the extent to which a subject stands eccentrically in relation to something within him- or herself that is more than he or she can give justification for.

The chicken joke is insightful because it points to truths that we cannot directly encounter through reasoned argument alone. These truths are held back by a doppelgänger. Freud calls it "the unconscious," and Lacan, paradoxically, "the subject of the unconscious," to underline an agency without an agent. But this double within us is interwoven with something else: the socially overdetermined external world, which, as we saw in Hegel, is endowed (and endows us) with its diverse and conflicting layers of truth, interpellations, meanings, and justifications. It calls upon us in the name of God, Shiva, truth, progress, etc., and commits us to the status of being a living response to an always (or often) bigger cause. This is another reason why analyst and analysand do not usually look one another in the eye during a session. The session is not a dialogue. It is a conversation among three: the analysand (who does not understand why he or she suffers), the analyst (who supposedly can uncover what the analysand's mind is unable to think), and the unconscious (which embodies a non-knowing knowledge, in part conveyed by social memes). Or, in the terms of the chicken joke: the psychoanalytic session is a conversation between the analysand, the analyst, and the chicken as the spokesperson of the unconscious.

But how does it come about that we have this unconscious at all? Lacan gives an explanation with the following line of argument: If I try to become certain of myself, of my existence and identity, I am forced to have my existence recognized by an Other. Consequently, this Other becomes the master of my being. Recognition is mediated by a place where I am *not*, but which is, at the same time, the only gateway to myself.

Hence, subjectivity is inscribed in a paradox. The ego is dependent on *what it is not* to relate to itself *as a self* that it can never truly be. But this is good news, as every human being is not a fixed entity bound to fixed states of affairs.

Here is a brief anecdote that fits this context. Years ago, I had a conversation with a colleague of mine who complained about Lacan's concept of "the big Other." My colleague said that it was inadequate insofar as the talk of *the* big Other personalizes a socioeconomic superstructure that is anything but personal. Ergo, there is no big Other. Claiming that there is one falsely incarnates a social bond, analyzed by sociologists and social theorists (not by theologians) as a metaphysical entity. I was puzzled that a colleague of mine who, as a Jesuit, believes in God, could not understand Lacan's emphasis on *the* big Other and Lacan's rejection of equating it with an anonymous social superstructure we are part of. With his concept of the big Other, Lacan does not explicitly refer to the God of a certain religious confession—obviously. But to a devout Christian who, like my colleague, really believes in this big Other in its metaphysical form of essentially being a subject, it should be obvious what is at stake here: the insight that we, as subjects, are called and under the spell of interpellation—namely to answer or to be answers of what facts, mediated by the big Other, call on us to be, no matter if I am a Buddhist, a Marxist, or an eliminative naturalist. And this call is always mediated by persons with certain facial expressions, gazes, symptoms, and enjoyment.

The famous "I want you" poster made by James Montgomery for the U.S. Army in 1917, with Uncle Sam pointing to potential recruits on the streets, is an emblematic example of this big Other. Every society needs certain faces like this one at its center, gazes to call upon us in structures of transference. No society, however ideologically shaped, wants citizens with ant-like characteristics, simply doing their jobs without the desire to have some kind of civic purpose. A body politic wants bearers of a mission that is metaphysically oriented toward the good, the true, the one, and the beautiful—the so-called scholastic *transcendentals*. Even Habermasian discourse-ethics is evidence of this desire. It postulates reasonable citizens with eschatological, or metaphysical, properties. And the big Other in all its personal forms—perhaps exemplified in the face of Habermas himself—is the only way that an interpellation, the call for a mission, can potentially find its addressee.

The Other is the larger frame of reference of human identity, but not on its own. It must always embody itself concretely in persons (kings, party leaders, a Führer, charismatic personalities) who have their own unconscious and trigger their very personal processes of transference. A distressed mind in particular knows this: Why am I facing this terrible fate? What have I done to deserve a life like this? Why me? Who is looking at me? In the same way, one can ask such a question before the judge in the process of one's divorce. Why does the law, personified in this judge, want to destroy my personal life? Žižek refers in this context to the love between mother and child as a relationship of interpellation in which the child seeks to be the desired object that the mother wants to see in it. And so, for example, the child, "in order to demonstrate how well-behaved he is," is ready "to fulfill his mother's demand." He finishes "the plate . . . without dirtying his hands and the table" (Žižek 1993, 72). The desire of the subject, and the pleasure and desire to please the mother, are channeled. "Pleasure is 'barred,'" as Žižek writes. It is "prohibited, in its immediacy, i.e., insofar as it involves taking a direct satisfaction in the object; pleasure is permitted only in the function of complying with the Other's demand" (ibid.). Lacan's philosophy of split subjectivity is based on this kind of demand as one cause of an evolving unconscious. Another cause is analyzed in a kind of myth that Lacan called the "mirror stage" (Lacan 2006c). Because of its prominence, I will dwell on the theory only in passing.

3

What is the mirror stage about? It is about the birth of the ego function through an act of a constitutive misrecognition. Lacan's guiding thesis is based on discoveries that anthropologists in the nineteenth century had already presented. According to these, children from about 6 to 18 months of age do not remain indifferent to their reflection in a mirror, as do, for example, chimpanzees. Instead, they show great interest in their image. This may go so far as to accompany it with a gesture of jubilation. Lacan adopts this observation as the starting point of a general theory of split subjectivity (which he later relativizes), in which misrecognition is inscribed in the self-reflexivity of a human being. Indeed, the infant's identification with its mirror image has a paradoxical character, since that which identifies itself as self in the mirror does not exist prior to the act of identification and misrecognition. The paradox can only be resolved in the sense that identity is not recognized, but performatively produced through *what it is not* (A = Not-A). There is no clear identity ascription of I = I, but rather exclusively of x = I, if by "x" one understands a variable that is not yet bound by self-reflexivity into a clear coordinate system of objects, properties, and their relations. This kind of binding can lead to the realization that many objects are indeed objects, but some are

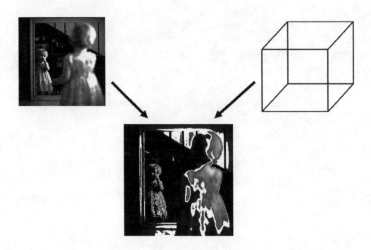

subjects with incomplete statuses of identity. Individuation arises upon a projective surface where one's own *gestalt* appears among other objects—the child's bed, the ceiling, the closet, the mother, and so on.

Lacan claims that the infant's gaze phantasmatically fills a gap in its phenomenal world of experience and lures itself, from the deficient situation of not yet being a self, onto a path with no return. The mirror image is literally the entrance to a path to nowhere. As a result, the child becomes fundamentally alienated. But, as we will see, this is good news. A real mirror is not necessary. Toddlers can recognize their gestalt in the form of children of their own age, and thus initiate the misrecognition.

A clear distinction between the I (ego) and the other has not yet taken place, due to the lack of a clearly defined ego-function. Without yet being an ego, the infant registers itself as a gestalt among others with clear contours. This unity, however, precedes the embodied experience of being dominated by partial objects and partial drives. The child does not yet experience itself as a unity of its motor system, but rather as animated by autonomous body parts that carry their own somatic programs. Or, to put it differently: identity is constituted by the filling of a gap that the mirror image simultaneously tears open and closes. Metaphorically speaking, the imagined wholeness in the mirror pushes the *corps morcelé* ("fragmented body," Lacan 2006c, 78) into a mold, resulting in a unified "imago" (ibid., 79) as that which the child tries, from now on, to catch up with. This is what the following illustration is meant to show, with the acknowledgment that the child depicted is not of the age that is crucial for the mirror stage. In its state of helplessness, the child envisions itself,

or better, anticipates itself, in the mirror as a unified gestalt. It fails to coincide with the level of experience of its not-yet-integrated body parts. Often parents are present in these situations, either in the background or because they themselves hold the infant in their arms in front of the mirror. In this sense, they verify and authenticate the act of perception with their presence and with their words.

Lacan sees in the mirror image, in which the child seems to lose itself, the quintessence of the ancient Narcissus myth coming to life. The child is lured into a useful illusion of its completeness. It identifies with something that is at once itself and yet not identical with itself. A double alienation takes place: (1) an alienation of the child's gaze through the adoption of the gaze of others (e.g., parents), and (2) an alienation of its being, that is, an alienation between what it feels and what it sees. The illusion of self-identity is articulated at the expense of embodied experiences. What the child sees is not in line with what it feels. Hence, subjectivity emerges as a twofold unity, a split unity that never comes to itself, since an alien gaze from the outside is clandestinely internalized as one's own desire and gestalt-to-be. Think again of Žižek's words: the desire of the child and the joy and desire to please the mother's desire are channeled. Entering the state of internalization of the gaze of the Other shapes both the creative drama of identity and the drama that every culture carries with itself. Lacan: "The moment at which the mirror stage comes to an end . . . the whole of human knowledge [tips] into being mediated by the other's desire" (ibid., 79).

Lacan mentions the term "competition" in the process of identity-formation because in order to become myself, I always have to see myself from the place of the Other. Thus, my ego is part of a competitive community, which children experience already at the age of one, when suddenly a sibling is born. The newcomer disturbs the symbiotic relationship of love with the parents. When child A looks enviously at his little sister B because she is sucking on his mother's breast, it is not because the child has a concept of "his" or "hers," of envy, or of the law of identity, and so on, but because he recognizes that there is an other in his place stealing his enjoyment. The sister becomes the medium of experience of one's own lack, the lack of not being at mother's breast. When child A sees his sister enjoying a cuddle with his mother, he sees his own exclusion and perceives this as a physical crisis. This crisis originates in A only because little sister B takes his place and splits him through A's being not-B.

Lacan's theory of identity as competition can likewise be detected in national or international beauty contests. They are cultural accomplishments of narcissistic self-love, in which the singular body of a woman is pushed to live up to the expectations of others, producing women who look astonishingly alike. For this reason, Lacan does not hold back from declaring the mirror stage to be an allegory of a fundamental destructive force at the heart of human identity. He writes: "destructive and even death instincts" thematize "the obvious relationship between narcissistic libido and the alienating *I* function, and the aggressiveness deriving therefrom in all relations with others, however charitable" (ibid., 79, trans. changed).

David Hume, in his critique of Descartes's concept of a thinking substance, illustrates that the latter cannot be more than the inner stream of perception (Hume 1985, 299–310). Consciousness is time-dependent. It is a stream not of someone perceiving, but of many perceptions, producing the illusion of one. The sum of these perceptions has no claim to be more than its parts. If the stream of perception is gone, so, too, is the ego. Or, in other words: the stream of perception does not take place on the stage of the ego, but the stream of perception *is* the ego. Hence, consciousness is a one-way street and cannot bring itself before itself as an object of experience. The gestalt that the child sees in the mirror is likewise no object, but an imaginary and idealized projection on what it is not. In it, aspects of interpellation are at work, including in the form of pure autopoiesis. After all, in the gesture of jubilation, the child virtually welcomes itself through the affirmation of a third party, the parent(s). According to Lacan, the subject will from now on attempt, in ever new endeavors, to bring its identity into congruence with the ideal mediated by the mirror. In doing so, it is fundamentally dependent on processes of transference in which the unconscious desires of others are central.

Lacan also emphasizes that the "fragmented body" as a primordial experience of ourselves will continue to haunt us. It haunts us because the ideal image or bottleneck of our ego function cannot accommodate all that the *corps morcelé* contained before the organism allowed itself to be captured by its gestalt (and the invocations hidden therein). For this reason, Lacan, following Melanie Klein, sees in infants' fantasies of dismemberment the compensatory resurgence of those somatic identities that could not be entirely taken into the ego function. But an ego function needed to be adopted to finally be a full member of society. Lacan's insights are applicable to the many homicidal fantasies of our Netflix and Amazon Prime entertainment culture. They sedate us in the evening after a trivial daily routine in the office, on the assembly line, or at the cash register. The brutality of fiction consoles those parts in us seeking revenge for their lack of identity, their lack of full enjoyment. Lacan speaks here of "images of castration, emasculation, mutilation, dismemberment, dislocation, evisceration, devouring, and bursting open of the body" (Lacan 2006f, 85), which show up in dreams, among other things.

Violence has been done to us in order to enter, as subjects, the shared space of giving and asking for reasons. This space is not sacred and harmonious but, due to its lack, the embodiment of injustice (see Rancière 2015)—though also of order. No wonder that it can become a breeding ground for acts of violence, from the homicidal atrocities of police to mass shootings at schools and universities—especially in the United States. The 1999 film *Fight Club* illustrates this. It captures the escape from the aforementioned structures of submission. Fraternities unite in eruptive acts of brawling in an era of increasing liberal-democratic pleasure-control. The violence purportedly done to men by

civilization under democratic conditions is reversed in a compensatory way. Now beating is allowed again and the hidden violence of the democratic culture is inverted into the raw violence of man against man within a secretly shared state of nature. Beating and being beaten turn out to be acts of liberation.

7

Lacan's Graph of Interpellation

(Lecture 8)

1

In the film *The Life of David Gale* (2013), Kevin Spacey plays a professor who, in one of his lectures, mentions Lacan's "graph of desire" and begins asking the following questions: "What is it that you fantasize about? World peace? . . . Do you fantasize about international fame? Do you fantasize about winning a Pulitzer Prize?" It is worth asking more questions of this sort: Do you write diaries in the hope that they will one day be published? Do you want to become the most important woman philosopher after Hannah Arendt? Or maybe become a genius musician?

Lacan was fascinated by the human mind's production of fantasies. It can produce extreme forms of hallucination, especially among the mentally ill (recall the fate of Daniel Paul Schreber). But it can also make everyday life soothingly coherent for the healthy. It covers over the "horror of the real"—the traumatic chaos of unrestricted events, contradictions, and disturbing incidents in the realities surrounding us in daily life—and marks an underlying motif of our personality, since fantasies express patterns of desire, that is, the kind of pleasure or displeasure with which we embody our solipsistic way of being a response to reality, since the conditions of facts and states of affairs surrounding us never rest in a neutral space of the factual. They are, among other things, the result of historically administered, economic, and culture-influenced fantasy formations. These formations must be administered through procedures of fantasy management (see Finkelde 2016, 2020b, 2023). Every nation's, every institution's grip on reality is strengthened by certain ideals, historical events, and their associated forms of subjectivity.

As I mentioned in the preceding lecture, the fantasies we have of ourselves are often abundantly positive. I assume that we all have an inflated positive self-image of ourselves. As the center of our world, we are usually a good center. Even here, fantasies are not primarily reality-based, but excessive. According to Lacan, they have to be. For the moment we actually transform our fantasies into reality, we require new ones. We are familiar with such experiences. Especially as children, we fantasize about owning a toy that, soon after our possession, has used up its potential to make us happy (via fantasy-formation). Then we are once again at a zero point, from which we create the next object of desire with the help of our imagination. In individual cases, a mental disorder can develop when we are no longer able to form fantasies built around virtual pleasures. Depression after creative performances of high intensity are manifestations of this dynamic. The world appears empty and without promise. The object of desire, appropriated after an excessive act of creation, puts the mind in a misalignment of its fine-tuned homeostasis, since its imagination does not yet know how to purposefully direct itself toward something new. But Lacan takes his thesis even further. He claims as well that the exaggerated character of our fantasies reveals that we do not even want to reach the place of our fantasies. Only the radical remoteness of that place of our happiness secures us lasting desire. Desire infinity and life becomes bearable—one could say this with regard to Kant's concept of the Kingdom of Ends. The ambition of reaching this infinity allows one to get out of bed every day, but without actually reaching what we strive for.

This kind of dialectic of desire is aptly summed up in a short story by Robert Sheckley (1928–2005) entitled "The Store of the Worlds" (see Žižek 1991b, 7–8). The protagonist, Mr. Wayne, lives a conformist life as a family man in a typical American suburb. He is intrigued by a desire: to visit the mysterious old Tompkins, who is famous for giving his clients insight into their most hidden desires. No one who has visited him has been disappointed. But there is always something edging in between Wayne's desire and the realization of actually visiting Tompkins: hectic days at the office, vacations with the family, a renovation of the apartment, and so on and so on. Years go by with ever-new obstacles and constraints of everyday life . . . until Wayne suddenly wakes up. He is amazed to recognize Tompkins at his side. He gives the magician the small payment agreed upon before he makes his way to a homeless shelter, walking through a landscape of ruins. Only now does the reader realize that Wayne's innermost desire was revealed: the desire for a trivial life with a family in an American suburb. But this life, in reverse, is by no means without desire. It too is marked by an insatiable lack. In Žižek's words: "The realization of desire does not consist in its being 'fulfilled,' 'fully satisfied,' it coincides rather with the reproduction of desire as such, with its circular movement. Wayne 'realized his desire' precisely by transposing himself, in a hallucination, into a state that enabled him to postpone indefinitely his desire's full satisfaction" (ibid., 7).

What does Sheckley's short story tell us? It illustrates the importance of our mind's dependence on desire that paradoxically finds pleasure in non-fulfillment of that desire. The novel I hope to write one day motivates me to not lose faith in it. I keep telling my girlfriend about its brilliance but the act of speaking postpones, through the production of more desire, the confrontation with the trouble of actually writing and possibly failing at it. The desire for my novel leads to the postponement of its fulfillment. This postponement generates gratification and desire on its own. In other words, the story of old Tompkins illustrates the extent to which we build our world around patterns of lack and their cultivation. Lacan was fascinated by the mind's production of fantasies not only as a protective shield to ward off negative experience, but also with regard to its hyperbolic nature, its excessive exaggerations. Fantasies fill in gaps of what resists explicability, but they likewise invigorate our desire through what is unattainable. It is fantasies that constitute the subject as the animal that desires the impossible.

Why do we long for megalomaniac stories of success and reputation? Why can the longing to become a prominent pop singer become so pressing that it turns a career, even at the peak of its success, into hell, causing suicide? A central and, at first, simple-sounding explanation goes back to a motif from the mirror stage: recognition. In order to be, we must be recognized and called out. The so-called graph of desire (Lacan 2006d) illustrates this idea from a different perspective. As a central building block in Lacan's theological epistemology, it is presented here in three of four stages.

2

The first stage of the graph of desire shows the extent to which desire is related to the world of signifiers. We see two lines: Lacan calls the first line $S \rightarrow S'$ the "signifying chain" (ibid., 681). What is this? Roughly speaking, it is an inferentially linked network of sign-mediated concepts that are interconnected in clusters. They generate meaning (political, scientific, artistic, etc.) through difference, inferential justifications, and dogmatic assertions. Signifiers orient us in dealing with our surrounding reality, mediated by their semantic roles. They open up hegemonically structured hierarchies of values, norms, and practices, and give the individual the possibility to read and to be read symbolically. Chains of signifiers are not simply linear, as the illustration suggests. Due to the polyvalence of words and concepts of different grammatical and semantic functions, they are vertically and circularly organized as well.

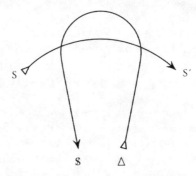

It is worth mentioning that chains of signifiers do not mirror facts "in the world," but enable people to communicate about facts via justifications. This succeeds because in chains of signifiers we unfold worlds of meaningful connections according to different patterns of thought (economic, ecological, artistic, epistemological, etc.). Signifiers do not reflect a preexisting world, but enable facts to be veridical or falsifiable in chains of reasoning. Modifying a famous quote from Donald Davidson, one might therefore say, "chains of signifiers are true or false, but they represent nothing" (Davidson speaking of "beliefs," 2001, 46). In this sense, the tree in the park is always divided between the individual object and the concept that eliminates the particularity of the single tree through its universal tree-form. What is particular is determined by its subsumption under a universal. And concepts are universals. Sensing, perceiving, desiring, acting, and thinking determine something *as something*. Without the potential material of what Anton F. Koch calls the "readability of the world" (Koch 2016), we would be unable to perceive a fact *as a fact*. No Kantian "intuition" would be accessible to us since, following McDowell, the human's capacity for sensing is pre-structured by its conceptual capacities (McDowell 1994, 9). Animals and humans are not only divided by the capacity of language, they are separated by different intuitions as well. Luckily, sapient beings can read the tree in the park as a tree. The tree can even be taken out of the park as a signifier and integrated, for example, into this lecture or into the flag of Lebanon.

In the graph, the chain of signifiers runs from left to right, since we cannot go back in time. The vector direction of the first line expresses a chronological structure. Every discourse proceeds in time. The second vector ($\Delta \rightarrow \$$) expresses the dependence of the human organism on the signifiers of others, or the big Other. They give rise to worlds of experience from clusters of meanings. Hence, we have the emblem of an organism in need of help in the lower right of the graph (Δ), which—

against the direction of vector one—converts into a split subject ($) by its suffusion through chains of signifiers. Only the retrospective passage through the chain of signifiers changes a sentient being into a sapient one. The latter evolves counter to the direction of time *in time*. It becomes what it retrospectively has always been—seen from the future. The subject's very reflexivity is mediated by an Other of itself pushing the desire to be one into infinity. This desire can never truly be satisfied due to the differential structure of chains of signifiers.

Lacan illustrates this line of argument more precisely with reference to the "diachronic function" in a sentence "insofar as a sentence closes its signification only with its last term, each term being anticipated in the construction constituted by the other terms and, inversely, sealing their meaning by its retroactive effect" (2006d, 682). In the articulation of a truthful thought—a proposition—we *aim*, as one aims at the center of a target. Whether the target's bull's-eye has been hit, however, becomes apparent only at the end of the sentence. When a speaker begins to speak, she crosses the intersection on the right of the graph. The meaning of her sentence, however, is only established in the act of articulation when it crisscrosses intersection point two (on the left in the graph) as well. The sentence can only be meaningful if it crosses both intersection points. Meaning needs articulation, but not every articulation is meaningful. Let us take the example of an oral exam in philosophy. The student, who is supposed to give the correct answer to a question, starts to speak (right intersection). He or she gets lost in a jungle of interconnected ratiocinations and misses the "central station" of meaning (i.e., the left intersection). Now the sentence can neither be wrong nor right, only meaningless. Only the second intersection point retroactively confirms the very beginning of the thought (the first intersection point), if it conveys a thought at all.

According to Gottlob Frege, thoughts carry truth values, which express an objective fact. While Frege, in his affinity for Platonism, postulates for this purpose a meta-language within a "third realm" where "thoughts are neither things in the external world nor ideas" (Frege 1984, 363)—a realm that functions like a storage room for singular instantiations of propositions beyond the world, as in an eternal realm of objective and timeless coherence—Lacan rejects, like Hegel, any belief in a meta-language. Chains of signifiers are nominalistically grounded in the practices of speaking beings.

3

Lacan's recourse to linguistics elucidates the structure of retrospectivity for his understanding of desire. Therefore, in what follows, we must apply the example of retrospective meaning-formation to the unfolding of subjectivity. We saw that the human organism in its early childhood is in a constant state of need. It is not able to bring recognition and meaning to itself. To do so, the entrance into a relationship with others (as shareholders of signifiers, interpellations, and fantasies) is necessary in the subject's orientation toward satisfaction. The individual experiences a miraculous transubstantiation. The status of sentience is left behind and the status of sapience comes to the fore. Now the individual is linguistically split through being infused with chains of signifiers. It becomes what it always was, a subject of metaphysical meaning and of metaphysical needs, since chains of signifiers are, by definition, structures of needs. In short, the second vector must cross the first in reverse order of direction.

The needy organism enters language segments—vector one. It is trained in dealing with meaning and value in such a way that the need *normatively conforms to the pattern of signification.* As in the case of linguistics, the second intersection point (on the left in the graph) is crucial. From now on symbolic satisfaction is only possible within chains of signifiers, but only in passing, due to the latter's differential structure. Satisfaction wears off. It fades away and makes room for more desire. What Lacan calls the "symbolic order" is the inferential system in which clusters of subsets and supersets define meanings antagonistically but also hierarchically.

Intersection two (on the left side of the graph) stops the sliding of meaning, which would otherwise be unrestricted. It literally marks the Oedipal law (or cut). It makes identity possible under the rule of the law of identity. If everyone would be allowed to say anything, communication, recognition, and a shared space of experience would not exist at all. An example of this comes from my time in college. A mentally distressed fellow student in one of my seminars did not stop talking once he started to speak. At first the audience was polite, then annoyed, and finally aware that something was not right. The student had to be repeatedly interrupted by the professor. In a certain sense, he had the problem of reaching the second point of intersection in his production of meaning. He was constantly under the pressure of not having expressed his thoughts with precision, producing more words to be again filled with more words. His mind lacked what Lacan calls in another context the "paternal metaphor." It marks the internalized norm of the Law (of the father) as the rule of the law of identity to block an infinite discourse for the sake of order, not of justice. A similar neurotic behavior can plague PhD students

who cannot complete their dissertations. Not being able to stop becomes
a torture: with the growing abundance of what is written, the number of
differences to be clarified increases as well.

4

The prominent fate of Hellen Keller illustrates the existential significance
of the entry into chains of signifiers described above. Suffering from both
deafness and blindness due to an illness in early childhood, from the
nineteenth month of her life on, Keller lived in a proto-world due to a very
limited access via her senses. The inability to learn to speak held her mind
in the prison house of what Hegel calls the mental state of "sensuous
certainty" in the first chapter of the *Phenomenology of Spirit*. Rudimentary
acts of cognition fall without any semantic structure (with Lacan: without
any chain of signifiers) into a world without limits. Deictic references can
bring things to the fore: here, now, there, and so on. But the place of the
"here" changes permanently for Keller. For at one time "'Here' is, e.g. the
tree," then again "a house instead" (Hegel 1977, 60–61, §98). It is the same
with time. "Now is night." But this truth becomes "stale" within hours and
minutes, as Hegel writes (ibid., 60, §95). Suddenly, the now is "the day,"
no longer "night."

This deictic world of narrow experiential boundaries receives its
first crack when Keller is trained by her tutor, Anne Sullivan, in braille.
Letters are pushed through finger patterns into her hands. Keller now literally traverses the intersection point of the right (not left!) in the graph
of desire, though she still does not know enough about a signifier's role in
a web of other signifiers for the purpose of producing meaning. One day,
however, this is the insight she receives. She crosses the bar between signifier and signified. When her teacher Sullivan writes the word "w-a-t-e-r"
in her hand at the same moment when the flow of water touches Keller's
skin, the second point of intersection in the graph (later called $s(A)$ by
Lacan) is crossed. "She dropped the mug and stood as one transfixed. . . .
She spelled 'water' several times. . . . All the way back to the house she
was highly excited, and learned the name of every object she touched. . . .
Everything must have a name now" (quoted from Cassirer 1944, 34).

This story illustrates the coincidence of grasping what a signifier
is with the simultaneous desire to extend the chain it is part of. Keller
immediately wants to know more words in braille. She is overcome by
an enthusiasm of denotation. But why? Why doesn't she say to herself:
"Okay, the word *water* is enough for me for today; tomorrow I'll learn

another one"? The answer is obvious. Keller realizes that the signifier she identified opens up, as the zero point of meaning, an infinite number of new meanings. "Water" becomes "the word in the beginning" (John 1:1). She literally grasps with one signifier a node of a fish net. When she pulls on it, multiple worlds of facts and states of affairs come along. This process knows no end, because "nothing can count as a reason for holding a belief except another belief" (Davidson 2001a, 141). Or, to use Frege's terminology, Keller has come to understand that a singular word has validity only in a phrase, with more words and meanings in play to grasp what the individual denotation is about. The semantic comprehension of "water" does not establish an ontology of single entities floating disconnected next to each other. It establishes facts. They are nested in the context of more facts in the midst of other facts.

Facts can be expressed in true propositions; for example, the fact that "the liquid stuff in the hands of me, Helen Keller, is water." Or, using Alfred Tarski's theory of truth: "The proposition 'water is the stuff from the water pump' is true if and only if the stuff from the water pump is water." Keller captures this insight in crossing the second intersection of the chains of signifiers. The tutor, Anne Sullivan, is here literally the supply reservoir of signifiers. The fact that in a famous scene of *The Miracle Worker* (1962) the signifiers "father" and "mother" are immediately named by Sullivan underscores the exclusive binding of meaning through hierarchical orders.

This fits with Lacan's description of a similar awakening in 1961. This time, though, it concerned Lacan himself. He was visiting the archaeological museum of Saint-Germain en Laye and immersed himself in the contemplation of exhibition cases in which various Stone Age hunting devices with small notches on them were on display. Suddenly he was struck by the insight that the individual strokes or scrapes are to be understood as primordial signifiers. A first interruption within the state of nature is unearthed in the form of a rudimentary sign, signaling the prototype of an abstract entity, a signifier. "How can I describe to you the feeling I felt when—leaning over one of these glass cases—I saw on a thin rib bone, obviously the rib of a mammal, . . . a series of small strokes: first two, then a small pause, and then five, and then it starts again. Then I said to myself . . . that's why your daughter is not mute [sic], that's why your daughter is your daughter, because if we were mute, she wouldn't be your daughter." Lacan continues: "Obviously, there is a certain advantage in this [he means here the markings or signifiers: they have an evolutionary advantage], even if one lives in a world very similar to that of a universal madhouse. . . . These strokes . . . appear . . . several thousand years after people knew how to make objects of realistic accuracy. But compared to these art objects of exactness we find here . . . the trace of something that clearly belongs to the signifier" (Lacan n.d., "L'Identification," session of 6.12.1961).

As Lacan points out to his audience, humans had the ability to articulate a kind of single-thing ontology with artifacts thousands of years before the appearance of the strokes mentioned. Carved objects "of realistic accuracy" and cave paintings articulate, roughly speaking, an artifact-to-object relation. They have representational properties, yet they do not constitute signifiers. What fascinates Lacan about the strokes is their pure abstraction. They articulate difference detached from a primitive image-to-object ontology with regard to the world surrounding the humanoids in this era of human history. The invention of the so-called transcendental subject, with its very special mind-world relation, rests on this difference. It is now infinitely outsourced in ever more differences, as depicted in a famous Hindu cosmology from the fifth century: first on elephants, then on a turtle, then a snake, which in turn floats again in another medium.

A silhouette of a bear depicted on the wall of a cave does not stand for the conceptual property of being "as hungry as a bear." But the strokes Lacan contemplates in the museum stand for the "killing" of an animal, which the stroke itself has literally nothing to do with. This pure and similarity-defying difference (1 stroke = 1 killing) marks for Lacan the birth of the signifier, starting with numbers as abstract entities. Animals understand signs ("sit!" "drop it!" etc.), not signifiers. While there are experiments with primates, I haven't yet seen a primate in a library reading and writing.

A cat can give me a sign without difficulty: it paws at its feeding bowl to express the desire to eat. However, she cannot hint at the bowl to tell me that her hunger is as big as the bowl is wide. She would take a universal (the concept hunger as exemplified in the bowl) into practice and identify it with the depth of a dish, not only transforming the dish into a signifier of hunger but also into a signifier of her hunger's quality. Were the cat able to give signs like this, I could enter immediately into a primitive exchange with her about all kinds of facts, through interpretive gestures. She would have the same experience as Helen Keller and enter chains of signifiers instantaneously. It is from here that Lacan's interest in metaphor is to be understood. Through metaphor, an entity is identified via another entity and establishes a reference that cannot be vouchsafed by the world itself, only by subjects. Metaphors are cuts in the texture of materiality, proving that there is more in matter than matter itself.

If, as Lacan supposes, each stroke stands for the killing of an animal, the totality of five strokes is its sum. As signifiers, the strokes stand for the "killing of the thing" (Lacan 2006e, 262). With the evolutionary appearance of chains of signifiers, man steps out of the world as unity and enters the world of appearances, interpellations, and enigmatic signifiers. In chains of signifiers, things are separate from themselves because identity cannot be disconnected from difference. Lacan says this explicitly: "It is the signifier that makes a cut [in the texture of reality]. It is he who introduces difference as such into the real [into the indeterminacy of reality before its transubstantiation as signifier]." "A signifier differs from a sign first of all . . . in that signifiers first manifest only the presence of difference as such and nothing else" (Lacan n.d., *L'Identification*, session of 6.12.1961).

It is the signifier that cuts into the texture of reality in order for appearances to emerge as an effect of difference. Likewise with Keller: the world as fantasized totality is legible insofar as everything refers to something else, calling on me, the subject, to read and act upon what has meaning. Under these circumstances, the sky can stand for the paradise I long for and a tree's silhouette on a flag for a nation I must die for in uniform. Signifiers have no natural ties with things, but things become objectively accessible through them, with differences producing interpellations and justifications at the same time. What is signified moves beneath the chain of signifiers. Meaning (substance) does not reside "in" the world, just as, according to Quine, the essence of a rabbit lies not in the rabbit, nor the essence of water in the formula "H_2O." Meaning lies in the form of semantics whose form fills the content. Or more abstractly with Hegel: substance is subject, that is, substance is what it is and will be in the future through subjects and their semantic conditions of objectification.

5

While the first stage of the graph of desire illustrates the pattern of the split subject with the retrospective effect of speech and its truth value, the second stage focuses in detail on the inner cohesion of subjectivity. This is why the split subject ($) moves on vector one back to the place of (Δ). A new "matheme" I(A) is introduced, which, as an ego ideal, indicates the destination of subjectivation. It marks a symbolic ideal which the subject has to approximate through incorporating patterns of the order of the signifier as patterns of the subject's own second nature. This is the precondition to become an agent of meaning, sense, entitlements, and valid judgments. These patterns are the pillars of interpersonal facts among symbolic animals.

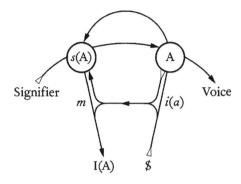

Lacan locates the big Other (A = "L'Autre") on the right side of the vector. Its place embodies the "treasure trove of signifiers," *le trésor du significant* (Lacan 2006d, 693). For Helen Keller it was occupied by her tutor Anne Sullivan. She, and not Keller's parents, incarnates both the treasure of the signifier and the limits of meaning. Truth can be multiple, but not every truth is permitted.

The word "voice" in the illustration at the end of vector I remains rather enigmatic. It refers to the power of language on the level of its mediality. Babies in the womb hear the voice (as partial object) of their parents in various forms. Strictly speaking, this voice has no meaning, but it carries validity nevertheless, for example as consolation, an outburst of anger, a whisper, soothing talk, and so on. Voices can have an effect on us, not as a medium of a code, but in their pure materiality. Adolf Hitler's voice is a good example: during a 1938 public talk in Hesse, he himself appeared to be carried away by his voice's pure form of materiality. As partial object, the voice can, according to Lacan, neither be clearly assigned to the mind nor to the body of the speaker. This is brought into view by Charlie Chaplin in *The Great Dictator* (1940). The Chaplin/Hitler-*Deutsch* is a croaking and barking. Its message does not have to correspond to the content of the words; it has validity on the level of its form, not on the basis of its semantics. It provokes political effects even without being understood. In his book *A Voice and Nothing More*, Mladen Dolar (2006) refers to the spectral, or ghostly, properties of the voice as a medium of itself. It belongs to the psychoanalytic category of so-called partial objects. As I said, the voice can be assigned neither to the mind as an instance of rational reasoning—for its mediality says, like a symptom, more than the content transmitted—nor can it be exclusively assigned to the body as a medium of practices, drives, and affects. As Derrida's reading of Husserl reveals, the voice as phenomenon incorporates the fantasy of self-presence of the thinking subject (Derrida 2003). In Kant, it carries

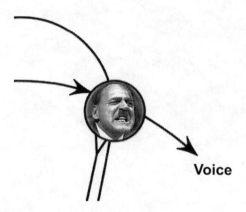

Voice

a horrific spectral dimension. Kant mentions the voice of the moral law "that makes the boldest evildoer tremble and forces him to hide from its sight" (Kant 1999, 204). The wicked subject is compelled to duck away by an inner command that points to what in the subject is more than the subject itself.

Let us come back to the graph of desire. At the site of A (the big Other), "the signifier [. . . is] constituted on the basis of a synchronic and countable collection in which none of the elements is sustained except through its opposition to each of the others" (Lacan 2006d, 682). It is to be distinguished from the intersection s(A). The latter marks "what may be called the punctuation, in which signification ends as a finished product" (ibid.). One could also say: the vector between s(A) and A is the symbolic royal court of A. The current king of England, Charles III, as A (big Other), would be meaningless without the House of Windsor and its "royal court" composed of thousands of individuals that are part of the extended household of a monarch. The House of Windsor and its court is the hegemonic authority that interpellates a human body to be truly the king of England. Accordingly, the process of subjectivation looks like this: the so-called split subject $ (bottom right of the diagram) crosses the symbolic order of the big Other (A) in such a way that, at the end of this process, it has internalized the idealizations that have acted on it from A and its semantic field of authority (s(A)-A). At the end of this process of civilization, the subject has, in assuming its identity (for example as king of England), unconsciously enabled the binding structure of signifiers to become part of its second nature. In doing so, the subject represses the circumstance of its forced choice according to the premises of A and the symbolic royal court of A's authority, s(A)-A. It accepts the role sometimes more, sometimes less, self-consciously and self-reflexively.

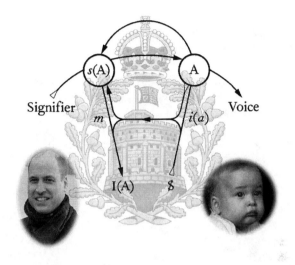

To illustrate the ordinariness and frequency of this process of sub-jectivation, one can take the fate of Prince William as an example. We may consider his symbolic life as the duke of Cambridge to stand em-blematically for all of us. How does he become who he is supposed to be? Prince William, Duke of Cambridge, becomes himself in the very same moment when he complies with the House of Windsor's demand that he *be* Prince William, I(A). This has to be accomplished in such a way that his imagination of himself as Prince William, i(a), unconsciously complies with this demand to really be Prince William (m = *moi*) in the personal union of a biological body and its symbolic mandate. This example is obviously an ideal-typical simplification since, according to Lacan, the un-conscious is a repository of resistance to the symbolic and no individual falls into unity with his forced choice without remainder. The ego-ideal, I(A), in its symbolic mediation, leads the individual to place him or her-self as the ideal ego in a mirror image-like relationship. But, as we see in the case of Prince Harry, success is not guaranteed. The result is an image that "becomes fixed . . . from the point where the subject fixates as ego-ideal" (Lacan 2006d, 685). An imaginary identification of the little prince becomes symbolic identification. With the other various arrows in the drawing, Lacan underlines an endless cycle of ever new identification.

It is important to keep in mind that the place of the Other (A) within the chain of signifiers is necessarily unstable. Here Lacan shows himself to be an ontological relativist like Rudolf Carnap and Willard V. O. Quine. The latter suggests with regard to questions concerning the "inscruta-bility of reference" and the "indeterminacy translation" that when we translate meanings from other languages into our own, we rely on a kind of "manual," or set of guidelines, to map words and concepts from one language to another and finally to the world. But Quine focuses on our native languages as well, highlighting that even within our own language we face challenges in pinning down exact meanings and references. This suggests that the problems of meaning and reference are not just issues of translation between languages but are inherent in language itself (see Quine 1969). Lacan shares this insight. Meaning is neither to be found in master-signifiers alone (the House of Windsor) nor in the English king, nor in the world's being-in-itself. It unfolds in chains of signifiers with respect to the enigma of reference between mind and matter in the various translation manuals with which we humans seek to understand each other, the world, and our symbolic mandate within.

The big Other can never be self-sufficient and unchanging because the chain of signifiers that stabilizes its normativity has no anchor point in a sufficient ground of facts. Mind and world correlate around a point of impossibility, which, in turn, theologically interpellates us through epistemic remainders that no justification can coalesce to what Quine calls "bound variables." For this very reason, the current king of England, Charles III, may one day suffer a fate similar to that of Charles I. Neither one of them is immune from critics of their symbolic roles; or, to say it with Quine, they cannot be shielded from people who see no possibility of entering into a process of understanding the incompatible ontologies that separate them, where in one case the translation manual has an entry for the word "royal = being a king by God's grace" and the other does not. Being a king or queen is not a natural kind. And whether natural kinds are "natural" is already a question of interpreting what the term "nature" stands for. There is no natural order of being that forces me to ascribe to kings and popes the mode of existence in my translation manual. The big Other is indeed powerful with regard to the individual British citizen, for "he" (as king) can subjugate, kill, torture, praise, promote, marry, ordain him or her, and so on. But this does not mean that the big Other is omnipotent.

What is decisive for the process of subjectivation is the fact that the subject is separated from its self-identity. Similar to the various traumas described above (Emma, etc.), subjectivity cannot come to rest. But this holds true for the big Other as well. He cannot close off the field of his hegemonic authority, since no political system can ultimately justify the conditions of its reasons. Every normative system is necessarily eccentric to itself as its boundaries, which are determined by differences with regard to an Other.

6

Some remarks on the lower section of the graph: I(A) stands, as mentioned, for the ego ideal. The process of subjectivation by interpellation has succeeded when we accept the ideals that society emits behind our backs. Now William is truly prince of Wales. Unlike his ancestor King George VI, depicted in the film *The King's Speech*, he has no problem expressing himself in speech as a medium of his presence. The former's stuttering, by contrast, put the symbolic body of a nation in danger in the 1940s, when confronted with the challenge of Adolf Hitler's hysterical performances. The restoration of King George's symbolic body is the subject of the film.

Prince William is not playing the theatrical role of a prince. He *is* his role. The vector i(a) anticipates the idealization in the fantasized self-image of little Prince William. He wants to be what his family suggests he already was from the beginning. Unlike his brother Harry, for whom various invocations seem to have missed the unconscious as it was supposed to function, William wants to be a good heir to the throne. The subject sees himself through the eyes of the Other and confirms an inner division. How does the Other want me to be seen? What is my duty? What is it that I am called to do? In order for the subject to confirm his identity, he has to deal with the "imaginary other." The matheme i(a) marks this imaginary other (Isn't he a big boy!): m = the imaginary ego (my self-image: yes, I am a big boy; right.).

According to Lacan's philosophy of subjectivity, the subject not only submits to the big Other, it also unconsciously sets the institution of the big Other as the condition of the possibility of the subject's own autonomy. Resulting from the transcendental necessity of forced choice, from the assumption of the legitimacy of my being interpellated, I as a subject, in anticipatory obedience, always presuppose this authority first. But this very presupposition is one that I cannot recognize as such. The forced choice is obvious, but it cannot be accepted from the individual mind's practices of living. In this sense, Žižek argues that the condition of the subject is its own misrecognition: "esse est non-percipi" (Žižek 1989, 68). To exist is not to recognize, but to *misrecognize*, oneself.

It is important to emphasize that this process of submission never completely succeeds. Something structurally resists this process: the unconscious. It flocculates out of the process of shaping the ego function as the other within the ego. This is so, because the unconscious arises only through the process of subjectivation. Humans encounter one another in the space of giving and asking for reasons with masks on their faces, like actors on stage. They are literally "dramatis personae," wearers of masks. The masks they wear bring about the unconscious as the epistemic remainder of each and every subject. There is no unconsciousness without the mask as its condition, simply because our so-called second nature generates the first nature retrospectively. So, strictly seen, only mask-bearers, sapient beings, can have an unconscious. Animals are spared the split of identity. They lack theatrical roles. Were we therefore to take off our masks, we would not only lose our theatrical role. We would, in front of a mirror, find ourselves face-to-face with the face of an animal and see, literally, nothing but matter.

For the sake of clarity, the decisive coordinates of the graph of desire are presented here in the form of short definitions:

1. $ = the split subject [Who am I? *Che vuoi?* What do you want me to do?].
2. A = *L'Autre*, the big Other (guarantor of signifiers, the symbolic order, language) [As yet you are nothing, so listen, and listen even if you don't yet understand anything].
3. s(A) = the signifier of the Other. Here, meaning is denoted through semantic structures and conceptual roles. The subject is woven into fields of sense under the supremacy of multiple master-signifiers. [This is where your metaphysical fulfillment is granted: father, God, freedom, democracy, the leader]. Meaning is constituted retrospectively as a finite product of a proposition under the arc from A to s(A).
4. i(a) = the self-imagined ego mediated by A [You are a big boy, just like daddy].
5. m (French *moi*) = my imagined ego. [That's right, I'm a big boy].
6. I(A) = ideal ego [I am now like dad, mom, my big sister, my philosophy professor, my leader wanted me to be. My ideal self corresponds to what dad, mom, etc. have always seen in me. I have made it. I am really Prince William, Duke of Cambridge].

One can transform the pattern of forced choice, which is presented here in broad strokes, into individual jokes, which express it with a touch of irony. The following ones came to mind for me:

—I feel called to be a Jesuit.
—No wonder, your mother always wanted that.
—Hm, right. What good fortune!

—

—I'm going to vote. It's important for democracy!

—Right, because democracy says you should vote because it's important for democracy. Maybe that's why you are going to vote?

—Well, yes. Is this a problem for you?

—

—I could not bear the life of a Muslim. What a moronic image of God.

—Yes, and you are quite lucky! You are not a Muslim, but a Christian. You've never heard of Islam and you know nothing about it.

—Absolutely. Thank God!

7

Finally, let us consider the last stage of the graph presented here: the vector $ – d – S\lozenge a. It starts from $, the split subject, and arrives at S\lozenge a, the matheme for Lacan's concept of phantasm. Of central importance is the idea that the subject's entry into the domain of the symbolic order can always be conceived as a traumatic event, which, as such, must be phantasmatically soothed and appeased. Lacan expresses this in the formula of the question "Che vuoi?" He takes this question from a novella by Jacques Cazotte, a pioneer of eighteenth-century fantastic fiction, entitled *Le Diable amoureux* (1772). In one of the novel's scenes, the hero Don Alvaro

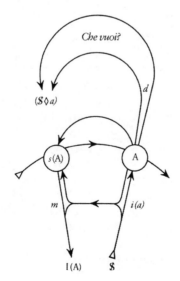

tries to summon the devil. As he succeeds, the devil shows up in the form
of a camel and reveals himself with the question, "Che vuoi?" ("What do
you want?"). The question perpetuates itself, however, as the devil falls in
love with Don Alvaro and seeks to be all that Alvaro could wish him to
be, so that his love is finally returned. Lacan alludes here to an irritating
dimension of ourselves—becoming dependent on the desires of others.
We know this experience from situations of being in love. What is it that
you want me to be in order for you to finally love me? Do I have to be more
intelligent, more beautiful, more successful? Should I dye my hair? Even
the devil is no master of the riddle of desire of the other. For this reason,
when confronted with his desire for another's desire, he loses his temper.
"What do you want?"

However, as Žižek, following Lacan, repeatedly indicates, the subject
addresses the question not only to a beloved person, but to the big Other
in all its guises. The individual seeks a place of recognition in society. But,
as we saw in Kafka, what is thrown at the subject is not always a clear assignment. Sometimes it can be a meaningless proposition, a tautological
phrase like the well-known identification of God in the second book of
Moses: "I am who I am" (Exodus 3:14). As answer, it begs the question: But
who are you? And why is this important? The obscure authority emerges
with sometimes more, sometimes less clarity.

Central, however, is its autopoietic circularity. "I am who I am" mirrors the law of identity: for all a: a = a. The leader demands allegiance. Why? Because he is the leader (for all a: a = a). Why should I obey the nation? Because I am part of it. Why should I defend democracy? Because there is nothing more beautiful than the freedom of the democratic rule of law. But what is this freedom in concrete terms, when I suffer a lack of justice and live a precarious life? Well—no one said democracy was perfect!

Another example of the big Other and its obscure political authority struck me in 2015. The attack on the French satirical magazine *Charlie Hebdo* had just taken place in Paris, with almost all members of the editorial staff shot dead by Islamic assassins. In the wake of it, a famous demonstration was organized and attended by a large number of European politicians and leaders. But why should this big Other on the streets expressing its right to demonstrate peacefully, this big Other who gathered in Paris expressing its conviction that "I, the civilized world, am the authority; you shall have no other god than liberal democracy," be an example of Lacan's "Che vuoi?"

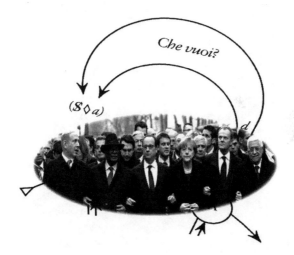

Why is this big Other still obscure in this unambivalent situation of an injustice that cannot be relativized? The obscurity came into view in the moment when two main agents in the conflict between Islamic violence and Western violence placed themselves under the same master-signifier on the day of the demonstration, January 11, 2015; namely, the Israeli prime minister Benjamin Netanyahu and the president of the Palestinian National Authority, Mahmoud Abbas. Both are—I think this is fair to say—sworn enemies, each using violent means to oppose the violence of ends of the other. But what exactly is it that unites the two in such a way as to put themselves in a "chain of equivalence" (Ernesto Laclau) with other politicians in Europe? What is the message that the big Other in Paris is calling out with the widely circulated photo of the demonstration? "No more assassinations"? But what if the assassination is an act of liberation against the terror of Western state violence in the Middle East? And what if the terror of state violence is an act of liberation against unpredictable assassins? What does the big Other in Paris stand for, if two political agents, who perceive each other as terrorists, can place themselves under the same hollow political gesture? May we not feel inclined, at this moment, to ask the question "Che vuoi"? *What do you want? What do you, you politicians in the name of democracy, want politics to be when the demonstration is apparently an expression of a political stalemate, at best?* Žižek was, as far as I know, the only one to criticize the emptiness of the political gesture of the demonstrators and the solidarity rally as a surreal product of fantasy. In an interview with the German newspaper *Die Tageszeitung* he said: "The pathos of an all-embracing solidarity that exploded after the Paris killings ended on January 11 in the hypocritical spectacle of politicians from around the world holding hands. The true *Charlie Hebdo* gesture would have been to put on the cover of last Wednesday's issue a cartoon mocking this event: Netanyahu and Abbas or Lavrov and Cameron and other couples passionately embracing and kissing while sharpening knives behind their backs" (Žižek 2015, my trans.).

I mention this example to illustrate that the democratic big Other also speaks in riddles, even in today's allegedly "post-metaphysical" (Habermas) times. What does the German government want? It propagates freedom of speech and collaborates with regimes of injustice and occupation, regimes like China, Saudi Arabia, and Israel. What is its measure of values? Why are sanctions imposed on Iran but not on Israel, whose "system of apartheid" (Amnesty International 2022) is sufficiently documented? Why does the government criticize working conditions in China but not the fact that there are seven times more people in prisons in the United States than in any other Western democracy, not to mention the number of Black Americans behind bars? Should Germany not implement economic sanctions against the United States, too, as it does with regard to Russia?

Questions like these underline the fact that the big Other resembles the elfin figure discussed by Kierkegaard, which is hollow on the inside. The big Other necessarily speaks in riddles, pure and simple, because it is hollow by definition. It lacks a metalanguage to absorb without remainder the totality of conflicting facts inherent in its clusters of administered reasons and collective fantasies. That is why Lacan's concept of phantasm is needed, both for the individual subject and for the political state apparatus. With the help of human imagination, it fills various gaps and vacancies which arise both in states of affairs and in enigmatic interpellations. Phantasms help the mind to ward off what Lacan calls the Real—that which cannot be represented. We require phantasms because the big Other cannot succeed in closing off the discursive field of its authority. This is why the photograph of the politicians in Paris is purely phantasmatic: it iconographically calls its citizens to a certain form of being a response (in this case, to terror) and, at the same moment, phantasmatically wards off the terrible antagonism of an everyday political reality in which Palestinians and Israelis confront each other amidst a history of European colonialism. The photograph is thus a pure fantasy not because it was taken in a side street and evokes only the appearance of a real demonstration of prime ministers among their peoples, but because it postulates a place beyond the field of political conflict that those present in the picture *prevent* in their real political agendas. After all, deadly enemies are in the very midst of the demonstration and, to speak again with Quine, each articulates what violence they consider legitimate in the struggle against the other according to their own translation manuals. What then does the demonstration in Paris accomplish? The phantasmatic filling of a gap in the face of a traumatic catastrophe. The phantasm appeases the split in the symbolic that has become obvious. Through the phantasm, the subject answers questions that it sees as yet unanswered and unfulfilled in the big Other.

This is another reason why Lacan underlines the inconclusiveness of subjectivation with regard to the third stage of the graph. The question of the desire of the Other ("d" for *désir*) nests itself in self-reflexivity. This insight leads us back to Jean Laplanche. He interprets desire with regard to situations of seduction between child and adult that always remain enigmatic. The enigma of the Other is a sign "that signals. A sign offered to the infant by the adult" (Laplanche 2005, 78). In the process of transmitting enigmatic messages, a counter-semantics, to which the world of adults remains opaque, sets down its roots in the mind. It is a primal seduction scene to which the child must relate in a structure of retrospectivity. "What does he want from me?" (Lacan 2006d, 690). A process of translation that has always lost its origin in opacity shapes the subject's negative stance to what is real. Lacan: "The ego is only completed by being articulated not as the I of discourse, but as a metonymy of its signification" (Lacan 1991c, 184).

Lacan, as we saw, adorns this process with the formula "Che vuoi?" Žižek translates it the following way: "At the level of your utterance you're saying this, but what do you want to tell me with it, through it?" (Žižek 1989, 111). Interpellation, in its opacity, creates cognitive stress. It is moderated through the phantasm (S◊a). With the help of this phantasm, we therefore learn to desire, insofar as we seek to answer the desire of the other. Phantasm soothes the hysterical disposition of subjectivity. The object small a depicted in the graphic cannot be grasped and (in Quineian vocabulary) transformed into a "bound variable." It functions as a lost object in the middle of the subject and as such grounds an insatiable longing. It is not a concrete object, but, meta-psychologically speaking, the "object's function [is located] in desire" (Lacan 2019, 373). The phantasm covers the deficiency in the Other, which, in turn, has an effect on the subject as well. Desire "adjusts to fantasy . . . like the ego does in relation to the body image" (Lacan 2006d, 691). According to Žižek, it marks the function of every ideology: it ascribes an inner coherence of "so it is" to everyday reality, which remains overdetermined and unstable. For this reason, the function of phantasm protects the mind against the Lacanian Real as a traumatic experience of chaos. "Fantasy mediates between the formal symbolic structure and the positivity of the objects we encounter in reality" (Žižek 1997, 9).

8

Let us summarize once more what the analysis presented so far has led us to recognize. It is the thesis already sketched in the prologue, that is, that we humans enter a world of facts only if we internalize diverse metaphysical background assumptions into our unconscious, so that we are an answer to a reality that is characterized by a missing link. This happens through symbolic forms within the framework of ideological subjectivation-processes. The acts of interpellation emitted by educators and institutions of symbolic authority are quintessential. They push the human mind in the mental state of giving answers to a call. In processes of transference, callings shape the organism in such a way that an unconscious emerges in the riddle of the other's demand and in the riddle of the disciplinary powers of established orders, the big Other. This unconscious is the—ultimately hidden—third element in the dichotomy between mind and world, word and object. Since each genealogical process of subjectivation is never capable of subjectivizing everything in the organism, the unconscious flocculates as residue out of the processes mentioned. As such, it resists any equivalence with the universal law of identity. Precisely for this reason, however, it effects the tension between mind and world behind the protective screen of reasons, justi-fications, and meanings. Reasons are the railways of universal concepts, unable to grasp the particular without identity. But this is exactly what the unconscious is: an entity without identity. The unconscious can be recognized, to speak with Freud, in psychopathologies of everyday life as something undetermined by its effects. It is not an entity and yet has identity—in Freudian slips, symptoms, dreams, and so on. It is constantly at work behind our ego-function. From there, it shapes the specific form of our disorientation, through which our mind-world relationship misses its mark—and yet *this very form of its misencounter* concerns us most in life.

8

Infinite Desire

(Lecture 9)

1

In the course of this series of lectures, we have focused repeatedly on the fact that subjectivity orbits a lack of being that is inscribed into it. We will analyze this in more detail with the help of Lacan's theory of desire and repeatedly refer back to the previous lecture. There, I tried to show, with reference to the graph of desire, to what extent subjectivity is constituted at intersections of multiple norms and occasions of interpellation. The fate of Prince William was cited as an example and blueprint for every individual's destiny. The genealogy of this sovereign identity presupposes not only the acquisition of language, the capability of "giving and asking for reasons" and of distinguishing between "commitments" and "entitlements," but also a performative process by which one embodies an answer to a call. Prince William is not hiding in a costume equipped with the symbolic investiture of the House of Windsor. He is the living form of his costume and role. The latter is in unity with his biological body. Insignia sent out in appeals are absorbed, with the effect that the prince recognizes himself in them as in a mirror. Lacan calls this process "forced choice" (also known under his catchphrase: "Your money or your life!" If I choose money, I lose both). Marx, for his part, expresses this idea in an analogous examination comparing the form of a commodity with the universal form of humanity. In *Das Kapital* he writes: "In a certain sense, a man is in the same situation as a commodity. As he neither enters into the world in possession of a mirror, nor as a Fichtean philosopher who can say 'I am I,' a man first sees and recognizes himself in another man. Peter only relates to himself as a man through his relation to another man, Paul, in whom he recognizes his likeness. With this, however, Paul also becomes from head to toe, in his physical form as Paul, the form of appearance of the species man for Peter" (Marx 1982, 144, footnote). Peter becomes the genus *Mensch*, "man" or "mankind," through the formal reflection of himself in Paul. The proximity to Lacan's concept of forced choice is palpable.

According to Lacan, however, the subject can never be completely absorbed in the second nature imposed on her or him. This is impossible. It is impossible because something in the subject resists such transubstantiation. One effect is that the unconscious emerges as the part that has no part of what the genus "man" stands for. This is why it is "necessary to find the subject as a lost object" (Lacan 1970, 189).

The mask of being a person is proverbially put on the individual through socialization. But, like a Trojan horse, it allows an Other to emerge beneath the mask. Animals are excluded from this experience. They are epistemically too poor to endure processes of forced choice and the emergence of an unconscious structured "like language, French or English, etc." (ibid., 198). Subjectivity marks "the introduction of a loss in reality, yet nothing can introduce that, since by status reality is as full as possible" (ibid., 193). Kant denoted this loss as things-in-themselves, which can only have meaning for epistemic beings such as us humans. He interconnects this loss with the lack in the subject as well, since the latter is nothing but "I, or He, or It (the thing), which thinks" (Kant 1998, 414 [A346/B404]). The thing-in-itself as *Vorstellungsrepräsentanz* (a Freudian, not a Kantian term) inserts a gap in phenomena, which in turn cannot be found as a phenomenon among phenomena.

So the formal constraints on our access to reality are never fully intelligible. Our understanding can never recognize the place of our present here and now in its historical courses of experience. The photo I snap with my cell phone today does not depict the same thing I will be contemplating twenty years from now. The formal place of its reception changes its content. Suddenly we recognize the scandal of our former hairstyle or laugh at our former clothing, which, while basic at the time, is subtracted in the present experience of the photo. Kant expresses, as I mentioned, this fundamental loss with the formula of "things-in-themselves." We recognize the reality surrounding us only in accordance with our historically variable apparatus of perception. For this very reason, things-in-themselves are inscribed in every act of cognition of appearances as that which opposes the latter's self-identity. And this experience already pops up in the simple contemplation of a photograph not being identical with itself through time. Or to put it differently: in every appearance, as in a negative-space drawing, the subtraction of things themselves is always already a partial element of appearances, but cannot be determined as such. The reality surrounding us is necessarily smaller than the quantity of its parts. But only a subject can make this loss a subject matter; a chimpanzee cannot. Countless subsets and their mereological sums, which open power sets, withdraw the self-presence of our surrounding reality. And this is good news, not bad.

This does not imply that there is something *beyond* reality. What we perceive as beyond or as an "other" in reality is the unconscious subtraction which has the effect that things exist at all—be they abstract, "middle-sized," macro- or microscopic. This is the result emanating from things-in-themselves as non-sensible conditions of the sensible and intelligible. For this reason, the loss in reality indicated by Lacan emerges as soon as we refer to facts and states of affairs. What is the case must always be subtracted from its imperceptible subsets and from its future, proving that states of affairs are never what they appear to be. Animals are, as I said, excluded from this intertwinement of presence and absence in our practices of living and our judgments about facts. But this is not because they lack sapiential, or linguistic, properties, but because they are—to put it bluntly—too much in contact with things-themselves that, by definition, have no future nor epistemic leftovers. Their direct and unmediated reference protects them from the gap between appearances and things-in-themselves and makes them unreceptive to symbolic interpellations. Sentient beings are not supposed to be an answer to reality, sapient beings are.

The subject matter of the aforementioned paradoxical twist of presence and absence, expressed in Lacan's proposition that the "subject is the introduction of a loss in reality" (Lacan 1970, 193), plays a central role in my following remarks. It can help us understand why human desire must be essentially unsatisfiable. This discovery is far from being a discovery of Lacan. But psychoanalysis as a transcendental philosophy has special concepts with which to interpret desire in its structural immanence.

2

First of all, let us take a step back. If, in the relation of mind and world, the reality surrounding us arises from a historically conditioned and genealogically generated interaction of subjects with subjects about objects, facts, and circumstances expressed in propositions, then the deficiency-structure of subjectivity has to be an integral part in the generation of knowledge. This insight was, as we saw, put forward in Hegel's concept of Spirit's dialectical evolution. But Lacan's concept of the mirror stage plays into this argument as well. Let us recall my seventh lecture. Despite the noncoincidence between the infant's haptic incapacities, its lack of coordination, and so on, it anticipates itself in the mirror image as an ideal unity. Misperception is granted, and non-coincidence between the envisioned gestalt and the experience as "corps morcelé" is pushed to the background. Lacan does not only say that the child misrecognizes itself. He also claims that the child perceives itself as an object among other objects. Whereas the child's perception of the world before the mirror stage was unmediated, in the wake of the mirror stage it is now determined by a new pattern. From now on, the individual experiences a new epistemic access to the lifeworld through its evolving ego function. The desire of the Other is now subliminally contained in the dichotomy of mind and world. The fate of Prince William has illustrated this. Subjectivity cannot enter into a relationship of self-reflection without the transference of messages of educational authorities.

Lacan now claims that it is precisely at this step, that is, at this epistemic rupture where the child steps into its "second" nature mediated by others, that something is withdrawn from the child's perception in the true sense of the word: allegedly an uncorrupted and unmediated perspective on reality as it is in itself. This reality, though, is a fantasy-product of subjectivation. It is fantasied as the true place to be or the true place to strive for. By bringing the ego function into effect, perception fantasizes that the subject, prior to its becoming, was not alienated, but one. (Recall in this context the fort-da game Freud mentions in *Beyond the Pleasure Principle*.)

Yet, how can that be? How can an entity that becomes itself in the process of subjectivation already be an entity prior to its becoming? The entity in question can neither be a subject yet (because it emerges through subjectivation, with the mirror stage as one important stage of many), nor can it be nothing (because something is emerging as a subject from somewhere.) Herein lies one of the poignant aspects of the mirror-stage theory: the subject emerges from a pre-subjective stage, which negates itself in an act of its overcoming and thereby negatively reifies itself as that which can no longer be caught up with.

One could now tell a fairy tale about how things-in-themselves are accessible to the unmediated view of a child prior to its subjectivation via the mirror stage. After all, the child has not yet entered into the sinful descent of the division of mind and world that is expressed, for example, in judgments.

Hölderlin, as we saw, speaks of such a division of being with regard to judgments in his posthumously published text *Urteil und Sein* (*Judgment and Being*) from 1795. The expression of facts in propositions is conceived by him as an act of tearing apart the metaphysical unity of being in order for a predicate to be truthfully reconnected later on within a true proposition. But this division, or *Ur*-division, is only possible, according to Hölderlin, because it is supposedly based on an indivisible ground of Being that guarantees the word-object relation as per se truthful. And, truly, every judgment we make proves this metaphysical hope in the very act of speaking. I distinguish between a sentence's subject and its predicate, and connect both with the help of the copula. A universal property (a color, form, location, etc.) is, for example, attached to a particular entity. I can say "The book is on the shelf" and unite subject and predicate in the proposition with the aim of expressing a fact. But the book on the shelf at IKEA suddenly turns out to be a dummy and not a book. My judgment has missed the fact. But then, my goodness, can the original unity of being be defended at all? Do our judgments align themselves with things-in-themselves, or only with appearances that are underminable by epistemic errors and defined loosely by incomplete chains of judgments? At the very least, one can argue with Donald Davidson that the majority of our beliefs must correspond truthfully to the facts surrounding us, otherwise any claim to knowledge undermines its own conditions and plays into the hands of skepticism (Davidson 2001a).

3

Due to the inability of a months-old toddler to assess facts through judgments, his or her experience is not yet built up in clusters of concepts and meta-conceptual reflections about these. This is why one could tell the aforementioned fairy tale—the extent to which infants linger in a paradise of things-in-themselves. Learning concepts, linguistically and practically, expels infants from this paradise. It renders them inhabitants of two worlds: inhabitants of a biological body, with first-nature properties, and inhabitants of a social body, with second-nature properties. The latter is composed of abstract entities that Gottlob Frege locates in his so-called "third realm" of truthful thoughts. These are, for Frege, eternal, as only God can be, and they allegedly guarantee the coherence of Being's totality, though this totality is, for humans, forever postponed into the future. No wonder that loss is part of the world of experience for symbolic beings. Loss haunts us in science, politics, and art—but also in our dreams. This is one reason why Lacan links the subject's loss of reality to its semantic capacities. This loss is misperceived by the human mind at the moment of its epistemological subversion, for example in the mirror stage, as something that it had once possessed and which is now gone forever. But what is lost is an epistemological phantasm retrospectively hypothesized by subjectivity itself. In other words, the aforementioned loss (of things-in-themselves), or the distance to the realm of truthful and eternal "thoughts" (Frege), is the retrospective collateral damage in the evolution of a sapient being. Among other things, this evolution is reflected in the mind's unconscious longing for its true self, an ego prior to the ego. Or, to put it another way: the development of the ego function harms us in such a way that this harm keeps us caught in the structured repetition of attempting its reversal. This may explain why films like *Blade Runner* give so much pleasure to an international audience. Here, the heroines and heroes animated by an artificial intelligence wrestle with our own fate—with the question of how one can become oneself in the midst of what one is not.

It is true that animals know desires too. They are directed toward natural objects according to instincts and drives: food, mating, and so on. But these desires are different in kind, not in degree. Animals inhabit an ecological niche according to biological instincts of experience, not according to symbolic forms of adaptation. Humans, though, while likewise inhabiting ecological niches, inhabit the phantasmatic dimension of a social world. We are not only dependent on the instincts and conditions of survival built into us by nature. Our survival conditions have increased exponentially through the power of thought's negativity. Human desire is therefore mediated by the aforementioned deficiency inherent in symbolic forms. Lacan: "Desire is a relation of being to lack. This lack is the lack of being properly speaking" (Lacan 1991, 223).

Kant was one of the first in eighteenth-century philosophy to point out that objects of experience are phenomena only with regard to an inherent lack. Human desire as lack of being is not lack of this or that, but lack of lack itself, a lack through which phenomena exist. As a result, our desire knows no standstill, no end. How could it, since that which is desired only structurally marks the place from which desire emerged. This is the basis of the strategy of any form of advertising: "Desire!" "Want more Wants!" Human desire is in fact an unnatural desire in this sense, a crazy desire, because our eccentricity implies that it cannot and shall not be satisfied. The infinity of signifiers stands for the infinity of all the things I can desire: the next iPhone, the next car, the next watch.

4

Lacan invented a short formula for this desire: object small a or "objet petit a." The letter small "a" refers to the first letter of the French word "autre." It expresses the essential connection to the big Other, since it embodies both the phantasmatic illusion of pure satisfaction and the impossibility of really being able to incorporate pleasure through objects of consumption. Accordingly, object small a resembles a bone stuck in the throat of my desire that is impossible to swallow and to digest. Due to the inability of an animal to draw the square root of nine, or state a simple predication, it is not in touch with object small a. As a consequence, the animal cannot develop an unconscious like humans do. If it wants a carrot, for example, it still never desires it in the human sense of the word: wanting it in the name of wanting more wants. The free market economy of modern capitalism is so productive precisely because it makes use of the infinite metonymy of desire. As such, it generates the undeniably positive side effect of increasing the gross national product through ongoing consumer transactions, though obviously with the negative side effect of its ecological toll.

Lacan consequently thinks with "object small a" an object that is neither to be found on the side of the subject, nor on the side of the external world. In a certain sense, object small a belongs to both sides and to neither. It is part of me, but it is also part of all others. Object small a is, as Lacan says in *The Four Basic Concepts of Psychoanalysis*, "a small part of the subject that detaches itself from him while still remaining his" (Lacan 1981, 62). It is something that is intimately owned by me but can nevertheless simultaneously emerge outside of me as that which my desire is lacking. Mental states of depression can be understood, among other things, as psychological disorders in which object small a seems almost ungraspable. Our desires have weakened. We must learn to give them a new direction, to desire something else that will tie us back to the horizon of opportunities. This is another reason why object small a is the psychoanalytic object par excellence.

Part 4

Ideology as Ontology

9

Sublime Objects

(Lecture 10)

1

Lacan's theory of interpellation was presented in lecture eight to illustrate that subjectivity cannot simply be integrated into inferential clusters of norms and concepts according to the rule of the law of identity. Subjects are confronted with over- and under-determinations of the clusters of meaning surrounding them, in which objects of all kinds are negotiated (abstract, middle-sized, physical, political, artistic, etc.). A well-defined part-whole relation is thwarted and renders the mind-matter nexus heteronomous. Specifically, our dreams are evidence of this heteronomy. They would not exist, at least in the way they affect us human beings, if we were absorbed in symbolic forms the way animals are absorbed by their ecological niche. Jokes, symptoms, and slips are prominent evidence of this contentious bond of mind and world. They reveal unconscious activities in the midst of consciousness's grip on states of affairs.

Even though subjectivity is always in part a recursive effect of preceding forms of interpellation and justification—as I tried to illustrate with the example of Prince William—individuals are never entirely absorbed in the chains of signifiers and their feedback loops. Both the lack within social structures of justification (Lacan's big Other) and the necessary lack within ourselves are responsible for this. Moreover, I suggested that forms of interpellation reaching the child can carry traumatic moments of varying degrees of intensity through diverse instances of symbolic authority. Lacan brings this to the strange question "Che vuoi?"—What do you want? It reverberates in all kinds of questions regarding one's mandate. What do my parents want me to be? What is my vocation before God? What does the Jewish Talmud ask me to discover in it? In what community of destiny am I placed such that I am called a naturalist, a judge, a capitalist, or a Buddhist?

This last question became apparent to me during a trip to China. I was at a conference in Hangzhou, where one of the most important Buddhist monasteries of China is located. Children were observing their parents bowing in front of huge statues and copied their gestures, engaging in similar movements. The parents probably did not know what they were doing exactly, nor why; what matters is that their gestures participate in the ritual actions of others. Something that remains enigmatic even to the parents is, in turn, enigmatically transmitted to their kids. A child may think that the venerated statues are superheroes and tentatively fill in a justificatory gap with fantasy. But as I said, I doubt that even the parents knew why they were doing what they did. They need not know, so long as the ritual of bowing is performed as a reverence to another dimension of reality by the community of other believers similar to people going to church, to the mosque, or the synagogue.

Žižek applies Lacan's insights into the enigmatic nature of meaning to the context of political philosophy. For we may feel the same way about the picture of the German chancellor on the wall as the parents just described feel about the Buddha statues. This subject matter is discussed in Žižek's theory of "sublime objects of ideology." These structure existing discourses in the political arena of controversy in such a way that normative centers of gravity help to decide which chains of reasoning (or sets of propositions) organize, in advance, the space of reasons as both basic and reasonable. A brief insight into parliamentary debates of the German Bundestag proves that the "force of the better argument" (Habermas) is not of much importance. Differences in political opinions presented by the ruling party and the opposition are not overcome through better reasons, but through the majority in parliament. But how can it be at all possible to defend the supremacy of a certain rationale about facts in a debate on values and norms, if the better argument does not necessarily help to win the battle?

This can be accomplished when an argument in political discourse makes the claim to be elevated above the many because it (apparently) claims to be meaningful across all political differences. Or, to put it another way: since the struggle of discourses in the arena of politics (with parties like the SPD—Social Democrats, CDU—Christian Democrats, Greens, AfD—Alternative for Germany, and so on . . .) cannot be resolved, strictly speaking, within discourse itself, there is a need for a place outside of the arena of speech. This place out of place within the power struggle for the better argument has the birthright of dominating all other discourses. And according to Žižek, this is one of the structural effects that sublime objects of ideology have the force to accomplish. They elevate one discourse, as sublime, above the many.

A concrete example can be found with regard to the Green Party. Here, the sublime object of ideology is inscribed in the party's proper name. "Green" obviously places emphasis on a special attachment to nature. It expresses, purely and simply, the recognition that nature has to be protected since it is the crucial resource for present and future generations. But, as trivial as this sounds, the concept of nature is at once over- and under-determined. After all, why shouldn't a storage facility for nuclear waste be as much a part of nature to be protected as the zoo in Berlin or a tract of forest in the Amazon? "Nature" is obviously a very anthropocentric concept in this political context. It is that which ensures the survival of humanity. So, it is no wonder that no party program of the Greens mentions the wish to reduce the number of people on planet Earth for the sake of the survival of orcas in the Pacific. Perhaps you see what I am getting at. The universal property "green" is, for political purposes, both under-determined and overdetermined. Therein lies its political force. Every political party needs nature for its survival. As an external place of the political sphere, nature's validity as a universal concept cannot be questioned.

A very similar ideological effect characterizes the concept of individual "freedom" in the party program of the Liberals. No doubt freedom is more important than nature. After all, who wants to live in an eco-dictatorship that protects orcas at the expense of humans? Individuals do not live for the sake of the survival of insects. Freedom is part of the essence of humanity, even if it comes at the expense of frogs.

National-conservative parties, in turn, will understand the nation and the *Volksgemeinschaft* as the unifying bond that holds society together. Exemplary here is the American catchphrase in presidential speeches when "the American people" is evoked, and even summoned, as a homogeneous block of people. Here a general term, "the American people," is used that only pretends to denote an object, since the thing it refers to is a priori politically divided. On the other hand, no political discourse can do without hollow talk like this one. After all, political emancipation is only possible, according to Ernesto Laclau, by splitting politics in the name of noble lies (Laclau 2013) to open up the political as such. It crisscrosses the rule of the law of identity and subverts hierarchies of order. There is no politics without raising questions of justice, truth, and emancipation. They transform other justices, truths, and emancipations into collateral damage.

Now, what do the aforementioned concepts ("nature," "freedom," "the American people," etc.) have in common? They try to hegemonize the space of politics from an external place by means of a signifier that is simultaneously empty of content and overdetermined. Every political struggle therefore has to be "ideological" when, with the help of sublime objects of ideology, it decides (1) which political parties are defined through their inferential relations to other parties (concepts and convictions), and (2) which of them has the privilege to pre-structure these relations in order to be the only medium for giving other parties their proper place. Since there is no politics without political agents, there is no politics without ideology.

In recent years, we saw how established parties in the German Bundestag started to struggle for hegemony in confrontation with the right-wing party Alternative für Deutschland (Alternative for Germany; AfD), founded in 2013. The political conflict concerned the question of whether that party was compatible with democracy at all. Because every newcomer in an established web of norms and values faces intimidation, the fate of the AfD was no different. The party's electoral success opened up a gap in the people's established form of representation and put pressure on an old regime that pushed back. As a rule, the established parties are structurally blind with regard to the legitimacy of any newcomer. However, the AfD's success was confirmed by the Federal Office for the Protection of the Constitution. This does not imply, however, that the other parties must back down. They can continue to attempt to delegitimize the AfD's right to be part of the democratic legacy of the Bundestag. In this case, the sublime object of ideology would be the distribution of an image of the Federal Republic of Germany as "anti-AfD territory," since it would a priori reject right-wing nationalist ideas. According to this ideological narrative, the AfD would be an illegitimate party that sits in the Bundestag only by virtue of some kind of social mistake or gaffe.

As in a cartoon, we can imagine the conflict of and for political hegemony as a dispute in an indigenous village. The representatives of political parties literally carry various totem-poles with them to dictate where the center of the village should be located, whether around the concept of "nature," "freedom," "nation," and so on. For this is exactly what, to put it simply, sublime objects of ideology strive for: to invent a meta-norm in the very midst of political differences which forces all other discourses into a direct or indirect dependence. But why, exactly? Well, because the totem-pole as master-signifier is putting a hyper-differential center of authority into effect empirically. Divergent normative claims must from now on be subordinated to it. The master-signifier incorporates hegemonic authority and defines from its central position what is "right-wing," "left-wing," "extremist," "common," and so on. The center resembles an area of sanctity because it claims to keep extremes at bay as the other of its own. At the same time, the political center makes its own extremist power gesture, to define what is extreme, invisible.

The structural force of master-signifiers can pop up everywhere. Recently it did so within German cultural politics. The subject matter concerned a dispute over the filling of a conductor's position in an orchestra. In the fiercely contested battle over whether the position should be filled by a woman according to principles of gender equality, the conflict was suddenly decided at the moment when the male opponent was of Jewish descent. A new master-signifier, the conductor's Jewish identity, hegemonized the struggle and left the female candidate and her feminist supporters deprived of her structural advantage. The Jewish candidate was, of course, not lacking in competence. His international reputation was outstanding. But neither competence nor gender identity were the defining criteria anymore. A new signifier surpassed classical differences: in this case, the question of gender-equality in elite institutions was pushed into the back.

Let's summarize what has been said so far. The task of master-signifiers ("green," "freedom," "the nation") in political discourse is to maintain a maximum of fictitious idealizations in order to keep the trauma of an impossible society at a minimum. Numerous authors, from Ernesto Laclau, Didier Fassin, and Chantal Mouffe to Jacques Rancière and Oliver Marchart, have addressed this issue. If Žižek explicitly refers to the Kantian concept of the sublime in this context (Žižek 1989, 202–7), the reason is that for him, the aforementioned master-signifiers in the ideological field produce, as "empty signifiers," an effect similar to the Kantian sublime. They seek to overwhelm us emotionally, just as, according to Kant, the sublime does in contrast to the beautiful. When Barack Obama speaks of "the American people," we are moved because this term can invoke infinite associations of meaning: from the deceased heroes on D-Day storming the beaches of Normandy, to the victims of terror and violence on September 11, 2001. The subject thus faces the aforementioned sublime objects of ideology in a peculiar tension. This tension marks an excessive demand ("too muchness," Santner), which paradoxically can also be tied precisely to the master-signifier's emptiness and overdetermination.

2

Master-signifiers such as "nature," "freedom," "the American people"— but also propositions shaping occidental history such as "We the People of the United States of America . . ." or "Human dignity is inviolable"— phantasmagorically pre-invent what they claim to depict: a fact that, as a self-evident norm, seems to ground the area of politics, and actually precedes it as a postulate. The "People of the United States" exist—similarly to Yahweh's self-identification ("I am who I am," Exodus 3:14)—in and through the performative act of self-proclamation. A phantasmagorical event, the invention of a norm, determines the form and content determination of what it means to exist. It supplants the contingent moment from which the normative claim is pronounced. Nothing precedes the self-imagination of the United States and the sublime objects of ideology it rests upon. Rather, legality opens up through an illegitimate foundation. Diverse meta-narratives from politics stage imaginary pre-inventions of what it means to be an entity with identity. From monarchy to democracy, they claim an unquestionable ground for their justifications, even under so-called "post-foundational" conditions (see Marchart 2013). But Kant can also be mentioned here because in his theoretical philosophy he gives a vivid example of such a supplementary master-signifier's erasure of its own stipulation when he talks of "things-in-themselves." They give phenomenal reality its principle of sufficient reason, even if this paradoxical concept potentially shatters Kant's entire transcendental edifice. Self-transcendence of form and content through the content-positing of the form-gesture can be crucial in both justifications mentioned, be they political or theoretical. Kant's thing-in-itself is the source of intuitions (*Anschauungen*) as well as the residuum of the postulates of reason. As "ens rationis," it embodies a paradoxical structure already observed by Friedrich H. Jacobi. This structure is both included and excluded in Kant's epistemological framework. Within transcendental philosophy, the thing-in-itself exists outside the theory's limits; outside the theory's limits, it is located at the center of phenomena and concerns both our theoretical knowledge and our practical action. Sublime objects of ideology, entangled with fantasies, exhibit an analogous structure. Or, to use the wording of Bertrand Russell's famous set-theoretical paradox: Kant's thing-in-itself is (somehow) a partial element of reality, insofar as the realm of experience is caught up in it as in an indeterminate set of all sets, but just in the area of experience it (this set of all sets) is not allowed to exist, since this very existence would undermine transcendental philosophy's distinction between noumena and phenomena. Phenomena emerge as appearances from the thing-in-itself, but the thing-in-itself— although it must be part of the world of appearances—cannot be a part of it. This antinomian structure threw Jacobi into a strong confusion, since he "could neither enter the Kantian system without the thing-in-itself, nor remain in the theory with the thing-in-itself" (Jacobi 2019, 109, my trans.).

Through his theory of the so-called three registers (the symbolic, the imaginary, and the real), Lacan shows how, in the course of community formation, excessive fantasies must spread in collective networks. And Kant's thing-in-itself is an excessive fantasy. Fantasies form the glue that allows for cohesion; they do so especially through surplus signification, processes of mutual transference, and secret transgression. Émile Durkheim had similar theoretical intuitions. In his later works, he outlines a social ontology of the difference between the profane and the sacred in religious rituals (Durkheim 1995). Representations of collective ideas and ideals are periodically renewed in rites of communal excess. They transcend everyday life to revitalize communal bonds.

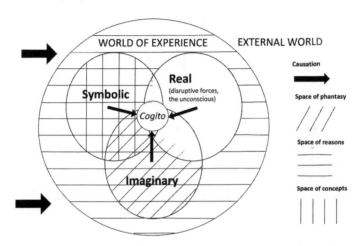

Jeremy Bentham, one of the founding fathers of utilitarianism, demonstrated the influence that fantasies have in social networks in his *Theory of Fictions* (Bentham 2001, 141–50), which Lacan comments on repeatedly in his seminars (Lacan 1992, 187, 228; 1981, 163). Nothing corresponds to fantasies beyond the reality they open up. They do not refer to any facts except when these facts are products of fantasies themselves. As such, fantasies cannot only evoke a transcendent surplus in the space of giving and asking for reasons, but are always already themselves the surplus. Jean-Paul Sartre calls fantasies and fictions "irrealities" in his *The Imaginary* (Sartre 2004, 190). They embody the aforementioned supplementary structure that is characterized by a paradoxical inclusion and exclusion. An elemental structure and structural elements both open up a space that is pre-invented, although the pre-invention can only claim its validity retroactively. The elemental structure becomes factual and experiential only after the positing of the structural element (our example above was Kant's thing-in-itself). It already implies a figure of latency within its foundation. For Sartre, this property of the imagination as the source of fantasies has the advantage of being able to always start anew against the realm of facts with the help of what can be imagined. Therefore, "essential poverty,"

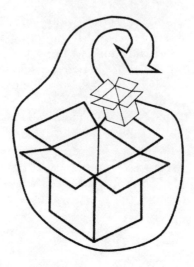

fact-denial, under-determination, and a tendency to schematized generality in the imagined/imaginary is, according to Sartre, not interpretable as imagination's lack, but as its gain (Sartre 2004, 133; Finkelde 2022).

One task of politics is therefore to establish, with the help of fantasies as simultaneously elemental structures and structural elements, the space that is to be pre-invented. The polity and its fantasies must be continuously cultivated and managed with affective and vital forces. However, it can be equally all-decisive to challenge the polity phantasmatically during times of crisis, when the ideological structures destabilize—and thereby to purposefully overtax the polity with fantasies. This can go so far as to restage the foundation of the community from a constitutive and even downright obscene fantasy that deliberately provokes a division of the society *in favor of the community*. The difference here between society and community goes back to the difference between politics and the political, a key distinction in social and political philosophy in the works of Nancy (1981), Rancière (1990), and Mouffe (2005), among others.

Politics here means the "art of the possible" that is administered by society. The latter distinguishes itself from community, the driving force of the political, which can demand the seemingly impossible as a force of dissent and opposition. The realm of the social imaginary, then, is disrupted in the name of community (against society) by a "radical imaginary" (Castoriadis 1987, 128). But in the disruption, community is also refounded, as in a religious conversion. Cornelius Castoriadis, the Lacanian philosopher and social critic, invented the concept of the "radical imaginary" as the "elementary and irreducible capacity of invoking images" (ibid., 127). The radical imaginary sets itself apart from the "actual imaginary" that has become ossified in social institutions and cannot transgress the limits of hegemonically determined formulations of political differences. The radical imaginary contains the power of scission. As an embodiment of human freedom, to question limits of all sorts, it may not refer to anything but itself. Therefore, the following remarks focus especially on fantasies that, similar to Kant's concept of the thing-in-itself, evoke self-insertion and self-exclusion at the same time: scission and auto-creation. Of interest is an encounter with an Other in the supposedly own, which can exclusively be phantasmatic and yet—as Lacan says—retrospectively "also constitutes reality itself" (Lacan 2013, 26). Or, in other words: it is about phantasmagorical elemental structures that initially become factually experienceable only after the positing of the phantasmatic structural element.

3

To illustrate this argument, we can consider the much commented-on Nazi phantasmagoria of a Jewish world conspiracy in Germany in the 1930s or of the propagation of an Aryan race. Both fantasies succeeded, to put it simply, in concealing various inherent antagonisms in German society during and after the failure of the Weimar Republic (see Confino 2014). They unified non-Jewish Germans and displaced internal social contradictions with the help of a sublime object of identity: the Aryan race. The latter now essentially defined what is "one's own" within the community. Henceforth, a new fantasy framework determined from 1935 onwards that citizens in central Europe of Jewish origin were excluded from certain rights. (On the relation of National Socialism and fantasy, see Kakel 2013; Hutton 2005; Žižek 1997, 69–77.) Heidegger's 1933 *Rektoratsrede* in Freiburg, "The Self-Assertion of the German University," may be an outstanding example of community-founding fantasies in socially unstable times. Heidegger enacts the call (or the interpellation) for a new, collective enjoyment that begins to unite through imaginations to a common will, a common destiny, in a time that presses for decision (Heidegger 1993). Even his colleague and postwar critic Karl Jaspers was impressed. Heidegger forces the belief (evoking a collective and potentially illicit enjoyment) that German society, under the leadership of chosen philosophers and with the help of the National Socialists, could join a new philosophical awakening in the name of a pre-Socratic, post-Enlightenment renaissance. With the help of National Socialism's fantasies, the challenges of modernity (massification, industrialization, bureaucratization) can, allegedly, now be met. This is to underline that with fantasies, mechanisms can be set in motion that blur the aporias immanent to society through a collective enjoyment of what it means to be "we . . . we who we are." And National Socialism did this exemplarily. Heidegger himself underlines that communal phantasmagorical elements have the force to subvert an outdated mind-world relation. They open up new metaphysical ways of being in the world. Fantasy evolves into reality.

When aporias in the social fabric of a society abound, the discursive realm of political debate is in peril. Antagonisms emerge which had previously been suppressed by narratives and fantasies which shaped the space of reasons via enjoyment as a political factor (Žižek 1997, 11–16). Now, in certain situations, it is precisely this (sometimes arbitrary) exclusion and inclusion (from ancestral civil rights, for example) that, as a condition of revival, grounds the new community and its new enjoyment against the outdated society. It connects groups of people in sublime fantasies that make the phantasmatically invented "own" palpable in its difference from what is alien. An obscene enjoyment now unites the community in the form of a pleasure-by-transgression of previously established traditions and as an evocation of a new sublime object of identity as one's own. The transgression of certain traditions unites those affected as though there were a secret "code of honor" in order to, literally, blot out social contradictions with the help of a new fantasy (see Žižek 1997, 7).

Žižek speaks, in a similar context of analysis, of the obscene backside of the law. It bursts onto the scene at the moment when the seemingly neutral-enlightened law (the law of Weimar) is perceived by individual groups of the population as close to failure. The ruling law appears, for example, too weak and "too good to be true." In situations like these, fantasies enter voids that have been opened by formal symbolic structures but can no longer be closed by them. The "secret code of honor" consists now in the transgression of the ruling doxa and in a shared will to radicality against the (threatened) law, though *in the name of law*. As such, excessive fantasies embody the antinomian structure I mentioned above with reference to Russell. As "otherness and as a constant origin of otherness" (Castoriadis 1988, 369), these fantasies simultaneously generate a performative inclusion and exclusion which can be traced, with limitations, to Castoriadis's notion of the "radical imaginary" as a medium of "form[ing] the creation of 'images'" (ibid., 369). These radical and excessive fantasies uncover a newness in which those who mutually transmit the fantasies among their peers retrospectively recognize themselves. Those who fantasize create an area of their reality and place themselves in it.

4

Lacan emphasizes in his 1966–67 seminar "Logic of the Phantasm" that fantasies are extimate (as opposed to intimate). They are socially constructed phenomena (Lacan n.d., "Logique du fantasme"). As such, they form the boundary between subject/individual and object/community and, analogous to Kant's schematism as presented in the *Critique of Pure Reason*, enable humans to perceive reality in terms of shared patterns of imaginations. Fantasies have social properties like money and marriage, two institutions of social interaction. They are, as entities, primarily owned by groups, secondarily by individuals. Acting toward a world is dependent on an autopoietic frame of reality that is within the object mediated by the community and, subsequently, within the subject (see also Finkelde 2018). Fantasies form the matrix of cultural and often non-cognitive valences that unconsciously precede the individual's and community's discursive understanding of shared certainties that are normative for life in that community. Thus, it is important to understand how structures of enjoyment can concretely unite communities through collaborative and overdetermined fantasies.

The task of every body politic is to regularly update the moment of suturing (or knitting) a "people's body," as depicted allegorically by Abraham Bosse in his famous frontispiece of Thomas Hobbes's *Leviathan*. This is what I have tried to make clear with the example of Heidegger's *Rektoratsrede*. It evokes a sublime dimension of excessive surplus in the own, the German people, and gives the body politic a new content through a new calling. And this can and must happen time and again, even when an apparent abundance of fantasies on which the polity rests is already in place.

The aim is to cite a primordial act in the name of a re-foundation of community. As a paradoxical element, this act links the chains of signifiers in the ideological field of community (which always tends to destabilization) in a new way. Just as there is the phenomenon of material fatigue, which describes the advancing process of damage in a material, there is also fantasy fatigue. Fantasies corrode. In times of political crisis, they burst open like joints in the body of political society and accelerate the dissolution of clusters of signifiers. Consequently, the aforementioned excesses of fantasy are a phantasmagorically staged breaking-out from the pure formal conditions of what it means to be a body politic—especially in times of crisis. And particularly in Germany, the phantasmagorical concept of constitutional patriotism ("Verfassungspatriotismus") coined by Habermas, among others, is a good example of such a formal condition. It was normatively given in distinction to an ethnic understanding of the state in the attempt to "overcome fascism in the long run" (Habermas 1990, my trans.).

Strictly speaking, there can never be enough fantasies about what the polity rests upon, or rather what shape its sublime body will take tomorrow and in the future. There is simply too much lack and surplus among what fantasies depict. And especially in times of crisis, the mission of politics can be, as discussed above, to reconstitute or re-create society anew by extreme forms of imaginary universalization through division. Fantasies prove to be particularly effective when—against the formality of, for example, "constitutional patriotism"—they incarnate a secret transgression and evoke surplus enjoyment.

These remarks may illustrate the extent to which a master-signifier expresses its authority to give structure in relation to other elements in an inferential field of meaning through an act of inversion. We encounter this inversion everywhere in performative speech acts which naturalize an entity in the name of, for example, "the American people," "freedom," "nature," and so on. Even in philosophy, this is very common: the naturalization of aporetic concepts as part of performative speech-acts maintained by the industry of academia. A philosopher may not always be able to recognize how much meaning and truth lies at the bottom of her field of research, precisely because the theoretical network she had to dig herself into can be so overdetermined, with so many incoherent and contradictory concepts, that only a handful of experts are capable of a vague synthesis. But she may think that it is exactly this that makes the endeavor sublime and inspiring. This kind of overdetermination can then lead her to spend her whole life with a special kind of "nonsense." Her book may then be built on eight central concepts that ground the coherence of her thesis. But at least four of these concepts may be so overdetermined that five of the colleagues who can understand her book at all have such conflicting interpretations that, as in the domino effect, the entire thesis falters. A theory can be supported by noble lies transmitted in concepts that were believed ten years ago, but then suddenly suffer the loss of faith of their believers.

And indeed, we experience such processes all the time. In this context, I should briefly mention the indignation of Daniel Dennett with regard to his eternal adversary in the area of the philosophy of mind, David Chalmers, when the latter admitted at a conference that he had actually no idea what he was referring to while promoting the so-called "hard problem of consciousness." Dennett attended the same conference and saw himself suddenly vindicated by Chalmers himself. When he began his talk after that of Chalmers, he could not resist expressing his deep frustration at having always known that the "hard problem of consciousness" was an empty signifier, a lure, a noble lie that held philosophers worldwide in suspense due to a cleverly launched overdetermination. The nonexistent hard problem of consciousness was responsible, according to Dennett, for the publication of countless articles and books in the area of philosophy of mind, which were consequently void in their content. As Dennett has repeatedly stated in interviews, he can only view the academic output of his opponents as a "waste of talent."

10

Fantasy Maintenance and Transgression

(Lecture 11)

1

Lacan emphasizes that the symbol has no "sensuous evidence in human reality," but that, subsequently, this very reality can find its "confirmation [in the symbolic]" (Lacan 2013, 26). In this sense, following Lacan—but also numerous other authors such as Benedict Anderson, Chiara Bottici, and Raymond Geuss—the social imaginary is always already determined by a paradoxical structure of self-insertion and self-exclusion. It creates a space out of itself, in which it is a sub-element and can find its reality confirmed on the basis of the performative power of its determinations. The social imaginary embodies the force to create and maintain the virtuality of reality. We are familiar with this force from everyday political life, when politicians utter propositions such as "Yes, we can" (Obama), or "Make America great again" (Trump), or "We can do this" (Merkel). These words refer to facts that emerge performatively. Such foundational gestures, which can differ greatly in their radicality, must be repeatedly injected into the space of the political. Why? Because a purely formal ideal, cleansed of any form of obscene fantasy transgression, may be not as powerful in bonding the community.

The social imaginary is not a translation of something physically material into an imaginary and/or symbolic. It is our—that is, mankind's—unique mode of being and, as Castoriadis emphasizes, this makes "representation" a possibility. It does so, however, not via the "representation of something," but by representation "*out of nothing*" (Castoriadis 1987, 283). The psyche is "a *forming*, which exists in and through *what* it forms and *how* it forms: it is *Bildung* and *Einbildung*—formation and imagination" (ibid.). The spiritual essence of man, expressing itself in images, imaginations, ideas, and so on, has neither immediate access to "reality," nor any interest in "reality" (Castoriadis 1997, 151). For Castoriadis, there is no consciousness in individuals that does not always already arise as eccentric and in symbolically shared forms. Castoriadis thus also denies that the grammar of being is to be interpreted as "being determined" (Castoriadis 1994, 148).

In the United States in the years 2016–17, it was possible to experience, in exemplary fashion, the performative power of excessive fantasies in combination with sublime objects of ideology. Various fantasy formations, with which representatives of the Republican Party set themselves apart from representatives of the Democratic Party, were clashing in the struggle over a contested vision of the country's future. The Republicans in particular proclaimed a radical will to divide the nation into left-wing liberals and right-wing conservatives. They generated, in exemplary fashion, a secret and obscene code of honor. This code was to be handed out to the electorate as a joy in the transgression of the established normative order so as to create a community in opposition to a society that had, allegedly, become compromised by laws that are too good to be true. Many of Donald Trump's fiercely contested propositions embody this call for transgression on behalf of an obscene underside of the normative order. For it was astonishingly rare that his abstruse and often self-contradictory pronouncements were criticized by his supporters. His words had no need to be located in the ancestral realm of "giving and asking for reasons" (Robert Brandom). Rather, his supporters saw (and still see) him as embodying a will to break with prevailing reasons. They can quite rightly regard substantive contradictions as secondary if they are convinced of the need to save the community from society. New fantasies about the United States are distributed in order to correct the alleged aberrations of left-liberal politics. Through scission, and in their universality, these fantasies provoke both inclusion and exclusion. Those who share these fantasies—about the danger of illegal immigrants, about the "swamp" in Washington, about the international supremacy of the United States, and so on—belong "to us." As such, this new community knows well that facts acquire a different valence in the familiar everyday language of politics.

Far more important than the hotly contested question of how many people gathered outside the west front of the Capitol for Donald Trump's inaugural address on January 20, 2017, is whether the United States can return to its former greatness by, for example, building a wall with Mexico or curtailing minority rights (such as those demanded by the LGBTQ movement). The status of a phantasmagorical examination of illegal immigrants at the border with Mexico is crucial in this context in the channeling of political pleasures. For how should one be able to rule out the possibility that criminals mingle with illegal immigrants crossing the border from Mexico to the United States? Only those who share that fantasy as being a fact can be "with us," whether or not the fantasy is verified by facts. One also sees similar strategies of excessive fantasy management on the part of the Democratic Party. The interest of the Democrats in maintaining the belief in Trump's collusion with the Russian government until 2020 shows to what extent a shared fantasy of "Russian collusion" united this community as well.

What the politics of sublime objects of ideology accomplishes is this: managing the pre-invention of a sublime body through the creation of a paradoxical phantasm, that of illegal and violent criminals, for example. The latter is included and excluded in the empirical realm that it opens. The goal is the re-foundation of the/a community through excessive fantasies in order to ward off aporias in the ideological structures of society. An illegal primal act of the foundation of the community is cited. Or, to put it another way, politics enacts an "own" or "proper" that precedes the constituted community. It uses, in an expression of Roberto Esposito, a "semantics of proprium" (Esposito 2010, 2). Through this semantics, an imaginary unity is invoked. Crucially, this invocation and evocation of a "proprium" rests on a form of division, a constitutive antagonism that first articulates a palpable universalism. In this sense, it is not a matter of random fantasies, but of paradoxical ones that pre-invent the space of community through a moment of constitutive division. Retrospectively, this place will then have emerged in its legitimacy.

2

In propositions aimed at splitting the society with the help of excessive fantasies, it is often no longer possible to make clear judgments about the status of facts: if they are exaggerated but true, or fabricated and false. This is illustrated by the aforementioned reference to the fiercely contested wall at the U.S. border with Mexico in the years from 2016 to 2020. Are the aforementioned violent criminals the wall is supposed to keep out a fantasy or not? This can only be judged retrospectively, that is, after having adopted or rejected the fantasy, since a sub-element of violent criminals among illegal immigrants cannot be excluded. The way this partial element is interpreted is decisive. And yet, in the same question of interpreting a fact, fantasy already plays a role. To put it pointedly and radically: an authority capable of determining the empirical fact (before the fantasy of criminals sets in) does not exist prior to the adoption or rejection of the fantasy. This is precisely what makes the issue a vehicle of division and open to both community-building and society-demolition. For now, accepting the fantasies of immigrant perpetrators of violence or rejecting them as a polemical-populist gesture of speech is a matter of faith. In the first case, the faithful are "one of us," while in the second case, they are not. The excessive imagination is the measure of the space of reasons. It is a hidden condition of political rationality.

By speaking of fantasies that include and exclude themselves, I refer to an often unconscious, illicit enjoyment of discarding normative claims for the sake of an unwritten, allegedly imperiled law. The rejection of established and also internationally recognized legal traditions then only unites the new community, to the disadvantage of society. In the United States, this became evident in the summer of 2018 in the "fight" against illegal immigration with reference to the separation of minors from their parents. This policy was deliberately promoted as transgressive and as a violation of rights—even while the White House published statements to the contrary. (In the summer of 2018, the U.S. administration pursued a "zero tolerance" policy toward illegal immigrants trying to enter the United States through Mexico. From April 2018 into 2019, this involved separating minor children from their parents and placing them in separate refugee centers.) In the case of the family separation policy, the political leadership ostensibly demonstrated assertiveness against the law *in the name of the law*. The obscenity of indulging in fantasies can reunite the polity into a transgressive entity and help bridge inherent aporias. If this can be accomplished, then in certain cases, the transgression of traditional legal culture, as characterized by the family separation policy mentioned above, cannot be perceived as obscene. This obscenity first brings the people in question to a sequence of interferences of communal desires and reasons. It makes palpable what it means to be a new "we."

In several publications I have tried to show how for Hannah Arendt, this process was exemplified in the early (and still ongoing) ethnocratic policy of the state of Israel, which, as the historian Benny Morris professed, could not have consolidated itself without ethnic cleansing (see Finkelde 2018). But as noted, the transgressive fantasies cite foundational gestures of political narratives and are therefore paradoxical. They stage an inclusion by an exclusion, and whoever is then willing to accept the fantasies (regardless of questions of empirical verification) is part of the community against society. The community's enjoyment of an obscene "we" is structurally inviolable because it is an axiomatic condition.

11

Longing for Leadership

The Time of Haste

(Lecture 12)

1

Theoretical questions about the limits of human knowledge, as well as practical questions concerning justifications of our deeds, cannot be detached from analyses of the emergence of the unconscious. It concerns both the individual human being in confrontation with enigmatic signifiers and political states of affairs through inter-generational processes of transference. What is real is, among other things, only real via unconsciously transferred a priori patterns of interpellations. These evoke all kinds of historically generated fantasies of norms and values (truth, equality, the good, freedom, etc.) and, through them, extract facts out of innumerable multiplicities into clusters of experience. This is why philosophers from Martin Heidegger through Walter Benjamin to Michel Foucault and Christoph Menke, to name just a few, give all sorts of genealogies to show—like in a psychoanalytic session—mistaken background conditions of what it means to exist for laws, norms, moral values, institutions, and so on. Heidegger's talk of the oblivion of being (*Seinsvergessenheit*) is just that: his very idiosyncratic plea to relate to facts in the neglected tradition of Heraclitean metaphysics, among others. Benjamin, for his part, urges his readers to perceive the "poverty of experience," *Erfahrungsarmut*, dating back to the Enlightenment (Benjamin 1999, 731). Foucault lays bare what is "historical a priori" (Foucault 1989), and Christoph Menke's genealogy of "subjective rights" presents the conceptual roots of the neoliberal egotism of our era (Menke 2020) and finds them in ancient Rome and in London of the modern era. In all these cases we are confronted with hidden, repressed, ideologically informed, and therefore unacknowledged, aspects of the conditions of knowledge. As far as the latter are concerned, interpellations of "sublime objects of ideology" have always spread their authority. Areas of experience establish themselves in processes of transference and misrecognition, and psycho-theological moments in turn play into them time and again. Contemporary epistemologies are little concerned with these issues.

Precisely for this reason, however, even concepts such as "commitments," "entitlements," and "trust," which are currently debated by adherents of the Pittsburgh school, founded by Robert Brandom and John McDowell, are not of much help. Enigmatic signifiers and patterns of interpellation are altogether neglected by them. This is a pity, because patterns like these precede the space of reasons. Enigmatic signifiers open socially mediated spaces of experience in educational processes. This is one of the reasons why the insights presented so far in these lectures with regard to the importance of processes of transference will be expanded in this lecture. It will be discussed in terms of the motif of the subject's dependence on a master, which invariably triggers certain puzzlements or irritations in the evolution of a sapient organism.

This topic was already touched upon in lecture eight. I mentioned the influence of the House of Windsor on a newborn human body of a future prince, as well as the force of interpellation of the king of England upon his devoted servants. However, the extent to which ambivalent shifts of love to hate play a role has not yet been commented upon. I will do this in what follows.

In relationships of allegiance, love and hate have an indisputable influence on the mind-world relationship. After all, the instability of politically or scientifically administered spaces of experience has its origin in structures of subjugation and interpellation that can never be well-ordered. Just recall how many philosophers have felt deceived by philosophical traditions they followed for years, by their teachers exposed as frauds, in academic communities blinded by "Continental" or "analytic" ideologies. This can lead someone to respond to the once-beloved professor, teacher, or king only with hatred. Perhaps a sudden slide into the precariat caused the former love for the head of the Anglican Church to tip over into disgust for the richest of the rich. An up-to-date, unacknowledged lack of legitimacy in the sublime medium of interpellation may suddenly appear. Then, within a few days, and under partly contingent circumstances, an inversion of love for the leader may turn into hatred of him. The center of sublime greatness transubstantiates into the offspring of that which must be overcome at all costs.

The patterns of change from love to hate in structures of subjectification became clear to me when considering sects and cults with their religious beliefs typically regarded as heretical. This topic appears prominently in psychoanalytic circles as well, especially among Lacanians. But the actual catalyst for the following analysis was the disturbing fate of the American sect called the Peoples Temple. It gained grim notoriety through an act of mass suicide in the late 1970s. I will refer to the fate of this sect today in order to study, with Lacan, the paradoxical relationship between love and hate in processes of transference, which, obviously, applies to *all* political communities. It is no unique feature of sects and cults alone.

The Peoples Temple was founded by cult leader Jim Jones in Indiana in the mid-1950s and, after many years of expansion in California, finally settled in the South American country of Guyana. Decisive for the focus of my investigation is a farewell party given in honor of a guest from the United States, Congressman Leo Ryan. He traveled to Guyana on November 15, 1978, with a delegation of staff and journalists as part of an investigation. Numerous negative reports had surfaced about the lack of transparency in the finances of the Peoples Temple, as well as allegations against their cult leader of abusive behaviors dating back to their time in California. These accusations were investigated by Ryan and his staff during the visit to Guyana. However, the American could not confirm the allegations. Jones was relieved and on the evening of November 17, before Ryan's departure, gave a dinner in honor of the congressman. As mentioned before, the fragility of the mind-world relationship can be illustrated here, since mental states of love and hate have an effect in excluding and including states of affairs as they, the mental states, decide basic features in the relation of word and object.

The gathering was lively and gleeful. Original footage of the evening, featured in Stanley Nelson's 2006 documentary *Jonestown: The Life and Death of Peoples Temple*, leaves little doubt. Congressman Ryan talked with a microphone in hand about the very honest conversations he had with supporters of the movement.

Separately, though, individual members slipped messages to Ryan's delegation expressing a desire to fly back with them to the United States. The congressman assured the defectors of his support and promised that they could leave Jonestown's jurisdiction under the protection of his authority.

Jim Jones and his supporters were approached by journalists about the letters smuggled into the hands of the delegation. As if in a chain reaction, a few hours after the events, a culture of allegiance that had previously been experienced as committed collapsed (see Reiterman/Jacobs 1982, 445–570). A collective panic broke out, not only among the cult members who wanted to leave on the senator's plane back to the United States, but especially among Jones and his followers. They became extremely violent, as if they had to protect the ideal of a utopian community and the sudden drop of conviction in their leadership by means of a collective catastrophe. It unfolded at the Port Kaituma airport in Guyana. Shortly before the departure of the American delegation, the congressman and several of his companions were shot there. A few hours later, the members of the sect committed a collective suicide on Jones's orders, killing more than 900 people. Jones's final words were: "We committed an act of revolutionary suicide protesting the conditions of an inhuman world" (quoted in Chidester 1988, 138).

Even if the aforementioned documentary film by Stanley Nelson does not explain why a cheerful celebration could suddenly tip over into its opposite and cause a catastrophe for Ryan and the Peoples Temple, a potential answer is obvious. It is likely that commitments to Jones among individual cult members had been fragile for some time, possibly even feigned. Fear of violent repression and the lack of alternatives had probably increased doubts about the cult's leadership and organizational style.

Many of the members probably only pretended to still be convinced of the message of their leader, while secretly thinking about escaping. Some of them seized the moment when the window of opportunity opened with the visit of the American delegation.

This is certainly the most obvious explanation to understand the abrupt change of conviction. However, this interpretation underestimates that, as subjects, our consciousness operates via layers of vague and robust beliefs and convictions regarding the surrounding lifeworld of values and norms. Not all mental states of our most basic beliefs may be equally robust with regard to the justifications they are built on. As discussed, ideologies depend on producing an unconscious structure of allegiance with the firm conviction that "this is how the circumstances really are." How deeply this unconscious structure penetrates our practices and thoughts is never fully intelligible from the perspective of ideology, but neither from the perspective of the individual him- or herself. For this reason, it may be a contingent moment that suddenly causes hidden or unconscious thoughts and doubts in an individual's mind to come to the forefront over robust beliefs (like in a gestalt switch), releasing an inherent panic and desire for abrupt change. Tranquility turns into haste on behalf of a conviction only vaguely felt, which might never have risen from the pre- or unconscious into consciousness (of the individual as well as of the community) due to my being integrated into collective mental patterns with others. Especially in moments when others suddenly reveal their doubts, a truth can emerge in my mind which, in its latency, was always already suspected, but taken into account *as a fact* too late. The sect's violence toward the defectors can be related to such a sudden emergence of doubt within "relations of reciprocity" (Lacan 2006b, 170) that turn love in allegiance into hatred of traitors and of an "inhuman world" (Jones).

At least, this is the thesis I want to develop in more detail below. The main reason for this is that the fate of Jones's followers in the final hours of the Peoples Temple is similar to Lacan's prisoner sophism introduced in his text "Logical Time and the Assertion of Anticipated Certainty" (Lacan 2006b). What is it about? In the text, Lacan analyzes the temporal time structure of "haste" (ibid., 171) as something that subjectivity cannot overcome due to interpersonal "relations of reciprocity" (ibid., 170) with others. Haste is construed as subject-constituting and distinct from the intuition of an "*objective time*" (ibid., 171). It arises, in highly simplified terms, from the uncertainty with which others look at me due to their need to reassure themselves, their identity, while I look at them for similar reasons. That this fits patterns of one's eccentricity, which pertain to the mirror stage and the graph of desire, is obvious.

2

Lacan's text presents a thought experiment involving three prisoners and five identification tags—three white and two black. None of the three prisoners knows which color tag he wears on his back. Since each prisoner lacks the knowledge of his own identification tag, he must deduce his identity from observing both the markings on the backs of the other two prisoners and their reactions to what they see on him. Speaking is not allowed. The situation is dilemmatic precisely because all prisoners—who, in order to be released, must correctly identify which color plate identifies them—have only white identifications attached. Consequently, no one can quickly deduce a clear inference of the color of their own tag from the observation of the others (for example, of two black tags).

Lacan then outlines three sequential stages in the inferential process of reflection that the prisoners follow. In the first stage, "the instant of the glance," each prisoner quickly observes that the others are wearing white tags. However, this observation does not immediately allow them to determine their own color, as they could have if they had seen two black tags. As a result, they remain motionless and move on to the second stage, "the time for comprehending." At this stage, each prisoner starts to reason and reflect on the situation. They consider that if their own tag were black, then the other two prisoners would each see one white tag and one black tag. The prisoners then reflect on the fact that if they themselves had a black tag, the other two prisoners would have already deduced their own tags to be white (because they would see one black and one white tag, knowing that at least one tag must be white). Since the other prisoners are not moving, each prisoner realizes that the others must be reasoning similarly. This reflection leads them to understand that they, too, must have a white tag, since all prisoners remain undecided. The "moment of concluding" sets in slowly. Now the prisoners will move toward the door at the same time. However, when each sees the others getting ready to leave, they must question whether the others have based their conclusion on seeing one white tag and one black tag. Through the hesitation of all, the individual prisoner realizes that no one has yet succeeded in a clear deduction. Observing each other's hesitation allows them to consider that they are all hesitating for the same reason. This idea is confirmed when they each make a second tentative step toward the door, followed by a second pause. "The very return of the movement of comprehending, before which the temporal instance that objectively sustains it has vacillated, continues on in the subject in reflection. This instance reemerges for him therein in the subjective mode *of a time of lag-*

ging behind the others in that very movement, logically presenting itself as the urgency of the *moment of concluding*" (ibid., 168). Once they mutually realize this insight because of mutual hesitations, only haste or urgency remains. Lacan emphasizes here that the moment of concluding is not merely the result of logical deduction; rather, it involves an element of anticipation, haste, and subjectivity.

If we widen the narrow circle of the sophism, we can see what Lacan is concerned with in the text. He underlines that subjects assert certainty, often in the face of uncertainty, thus committing themselves to a course of action or belief. This moment is where the subject's identity is most profoundly shaped, as the decision taken reflects and solidifies the subject's position within the symbolic order. In other words, Lacan unfolds this sophism to interpret the deficiency structure of identity in a mirror stage that is in analogous interrelation to the gaze of others. Glances go back and forth between subjects within "suspended motions in the process" (ibid., 165), but not so much with the intention of deciphering the identity of others, but in order to grasp in the glances of others one's own identity in distinction from the reactions my eyes have on them.

Since, as stated, each of the three prisoners must observe what the others are doing in parallel with the logical exclusion of alternatives in order to know which color tags are on their backs, glances and reactions cause inferences about one's own identity. In this way, the self-relationship is bound up in reciprocal reflection in the gazes of others. What does the individual attempt to do in order to be able to determine himself? In the stalemate described in the sophism, it is an ad hoc attribution of identity in the sight of the insecurity of others. Haste, then, is called for "not because of some dramatic contingency, the seriousness of the stakes, or the competitiveness of the game," but because of "the urgency of the logical movement that the subject *precipitates* his judgment and his departure" (ibid., 169).

This constellation is not unlike the situation at the festivity in honor of the American congressman Leo Ryan. Here, individuals are united, some of whom have lost the conviction of their identity status. Are they prisoners of a madman or free followers of a prophet? Some may ask this and feel dependent on the gazes and gestures of others, to find an answer, who in turn gaze back at them. Similarly, one can imagine the situation in the last days before the downfall of the German Democratic Republic (East Germany), when members of the state security force look into each other's eyes in the corridors of their office building, trying to recognize in the looks of others whether or not they remain faithful to the Party, the big Other. Here as well, open discussion is obviously not allowed. But doesn't the individual in such a situation look all the more insecure in her own convictions to those who may look at her in turn for clarification of their own convictions? Just as in the prisoner's sophism, the cult members obviously could not simply discuss the status of their identity with regard to Jones and his closest allies. Or, to put it in Brandom's vocabulary: "commitments," "entitlements," and "trust" remain in the limbo of their conditions of application and, in a situation like this, are no longer effective in unconscious conditions of transference. As in Lacan's narrative, in which all communication between the prisoners is forbidden by the prison guard, social control in the Peoples Temple made the open discussion of doubts likewise impossible. The individual subject then directs his gaze to the Other, that is, he desires to learn who the Other is, in order to learn who he or she is. And when one learns that no clarification of identity can be deduced (are we prisoners? are we free? are we victims of abuse?), must one not seize the chance to escape with the U.S. delegation into freedom, however vague that freedom may yet be? If I and the others do not know if we are either imprisoned or free, with this insight becoming obvious only in the hesitant postponement of identity in view of others, then—as in Lacan's sophism—the leap into haste may, for some, be the only choice. We know this kind of haste from revolutionary upheavals in which no guarantee is given as to whether individual actions are justified or illegal.

Is the uprising of Palestinians on the borders of Gaza, as happened repeatedly in 2018–19, an illegal act by terrorists or a liberation action against an occupying power? Who risks breaking the prevailing narrative if the answer is so obvious? Even European politicians may fear reprisals in this very specific political context because of an opinion perceived by the big Other as impermissible or, more commonly, as antisemitic: to call out the occupation as a crime or to mention the Nakba as historical fact. In 2023, a teacher in the United States had a similar kind of experience, when a new Iowa law barred educators from teaching that the "United States of America and the state of Iowa are fundamentally or systematically racist or sexist." The teacher sought clarification as to whether he could state as fact (not as merely his opinion) that "Slavery in the U.S. was wrong." His supervisor was reluctant to give an answer. "I really need to delve into it," she said, according to an article in the *Washington Post*, "to see [if that] is . . . part of what we can or cannot say" (Natanson 2023).

The fear of not knowing how, exactly, the big Other—in this case the political majority—thinks, leads to the suppression of one's own convictions for fear of democratic repression, sometimes without acknowledging the repression itself. Later generations may then no longer have a clue about the unconscious structure in place—suppressing widespread opinions—and, as a result, cannot understand the collective structure of blind obedience (with regard to Israel, for example) that perpetuates injustice. The consequence of the predicament just described—think again of Lacan's prisoner's dilemma—can only be in part a rational act, since even the prisoners of Jonestown may have a fifty-fifty chance of being either traitors or disciples, prisoners or free agents. The haste of some to escape may then provoke a violent aggression in those who reacted too late, and at the same time evoke a love for the betrayed leader of their cult. However, one can imagine that at least some who remained behind must have come to the realization that they had betrayed their most intimate convictions.

12

Betrayal in Times of Overdetermination

(Lecture 13)

1

Independently of the aforementioned cult-like discipleship that stimulates extreme forms of love and hate through a leader's deficient and ambivalent status of his or her entitlement, there obviously exist many other deficient conditions of knowledge that people have to cope with. Not only with regard to their leaders. They affect us as individuals and condition our patterns of mutual misjudgments and misrecognitions. Already in everyday life we experience continuously how we stand in modally vague, rather than modally robust judgments, in relation to facts. Judgments are partial elements of inferential justifications. Often they cannot be deduced and guaranteed by one person alone, without the help of experts of all kinds. This proves to be a basic condition of experience, since human beings living in webs of supernumerary information processes can only build social relations through unacknowledged forms of passive or "interpassive" (Pfaller 2017) structures of transference. We are rational beings due to being excluded from all kinds of properties of all kinds of things. This can cause multiple conflicts for the individual human being reaching out toward facts, as well as for political communities where one sees another as blinded by some kind of "dogmatic slumber."

In epistemology, this topic is discussed especially between so-called "externalists" and "internalists." The former, to put it simply, hold an understanding of knowledge as justified true belief, according to which our beliefs are embedded in inferential metastructures of reasons and thus rest on the cognitions of others that are not necessarily accessible to us (BonJour 2010). Individuals simply cannot justify, in everyday deliberations, every kind of belief with the same competence as those who are the sources of the beliefs they adopted as their own. For example, someone may know that "mass attracts mass" and that "water is H_2O" and yet not be able to scientifically justify either proposition in more detail, physically or chemically. With respect to numerous other facts concerning questions of economy and politics, individuals judge all too often under the auspices of a big Other, taking beliefs of others as their own, without the ability to effectively guarantee, in any detail, the justification or derivation thereof. Thus, I personally know with 100 percent certainty that "mass attracts mass," but I could not justify at all *why* mass actually attracts mass.

By contrast, "internalists" hold that a person's beliefs can only be epistemically grounded if the beliefs are "*cognitively accessible* to that person" or "*internal* to his cognitive perspective" (BonJour 2010, 364). And while so-called internalists—again, in very reductive terms—can grant no one a claim to knowledge without the corresponding capacity for justification, externalists assume that there is no alternative to outsourced beliefs that both stabilize and destabilize our knowledge. The concept of knowledge would dissolve or be opposed to our basic understandings of what we claim to know (without justification) in everyday life. I mention this to illustrate the extent to which many of our judgments, resting on unquestioned processes of transference, in some cases feature more non-knowledge than knowledge, since only expert groups could inferentially give reasons for what we know. Hilary Putnam speaks prominently in this context of a "division of linguistic labor," without which a complex society could not get along (Putnam 1975, 144).

This reference to epistemological debates of the 1970s and 1980s is connected to the fate of the Peoples Temple insofar as it illustrates how we humans are necessarily under-determined at many levels, even that of the simplest judgments about facts and states of affairs. As such, we are always in the situation of passively adopting the inferences of others as our own. This enhances the impact that enigmatic signifiers have in varied patterns of interpellation that we have discussed in the previous lectures. At the same time, it explains how internal contradictions in interconnected chains of reasons can arise abruptly within communities and undermine a mind-world relationship believed to be well-grounded in collective and phantasmatically managed webs of beliefs. Beliefs and practices can abruptly appear hollow, unfounded, and self-contradictory.

An apt example of an abrupt and unexpected disagreement between a mastermind and his disciple concerns a conflict between Daniel Dennett and Sam Harris, which I will mention here only in passing. The two famous naturalists and proponents of an eliminative materialism appeared together as pioneering critics of religion in 2004–09, together with Christopher Hitchens and Richard Dawkins. But suddenly they found themselves standing in opposing camps when the question of free will divided their materialist stances. Harris could not understand why a mastermind like Dennett, who had ascended as the spokesman of a revitalized physicalism with his book on *Darwin's Dangerous Ideas* (1995), could still cling to a folk psychological understanding of free will (Harris 2014). In other words, his mentor proved to be just as dogmatic about the question of free will as believers are, according to Dennett, with regard to their unquestionable creeds of faith. This was intolerable for Sam Harris. Dennett undermined an entire project of naturalism by giving folk psychology its due with regard to free will.

The reason why Dennett stuck to this position is not entirely comprehensible. He probably saw no alternative, free of paradox, to maintaining faith in the individual autonomy and responsibility needed to retain the rule of the law of identity in both society and science. Regardless of this anecdote, it is likely that cults, sects, and religious communities are nevertheless more susceptible to radical alternations in changing and opposing beliefs, because the structures of their norms and values are not as modally robust as those in the natural sciences. But as the dispute between Dennett and Harris makes clear, the hard sciences are not immune to this outcome.

2

Freud analyzed the forces of interpellation just mentioned in *Group Psychology*, which is why he conceives a crowd of people as "a number of individuals who have put one and the same object in the place of their ego ideal and have consequently identified themselves with one another in their ego" (Freud 1981, vol. 18, 109). He exposes two emotional bondings in mass psychology that originate in familial environments: identification and object-cathexis. They are transmitted to the field of mass psychology, making the crowd a family of a higher order. A crowd of people literally reconstitutes the family situation and maintains its unity through the fact that all strive for the same goals, of which the leader as paternal authority is the embodiment. This may explain in particular why justifications that sustain their force of bonding through paternal authority can break away abruptly and trigger a change from love to hate. Philosophy is also not immune to these alternations between love and hate. This can be confirmed by countless polemics between various schools of thought from antiquity to the present. Think of Nietzsche's polemics against Plato, or of Heidegger's polemics against his once venerated teacher Edmund Husserl. In several letters, he complains about Husserl's stupidity; according to Heidegger, Husserl has nothing to offer but an incomprehensible and outdated phenomenology which Heidegger vaunts himself to have overcome (see Heidegger 1990, 42). But one can also think of the much commented analytic-Continental divide still in vogue today as one of many lines of conflict in which the disputants perceive their philosophical foes not as debate partners, but as fools.

In the area of Lacanian theory, this kind of conflict against a paternal authority is exemplified nicely by the academic life of Dylan Evans. In a 2005 article entitled "From Lacan to Darwin," the author of the much-cited *Lacanian Dictionary* describes his departure from Lacan's philosophy toward naturalism as a path from darkness into the light of the natural sciences.

Evans's judgment, presented as it is with the bivalent categories of right versus wrong or good versus bad, is striking. He cannot ascribe to Lacanian theory, which undoubtedly produced and still produces sect-like discipleships (this much may be granted), the smallest share in the path of enlightenment. It embodies for him only a "poor understanding of science." For this reason, it is "very sad" (Evans 2005, 55) that scholars in the humanities remain in a state of delusion that Evans deems himself to have overcome. One is surprised to read these words, since Evans himself is credited with having presented central concepts of Lacan's philosophy in his dictionary for an international audience. Since 2005, though, a connection between science and Lacanian theory is no longer evident for Evans. And while Lacan was once seen as a source of meaningful knowledge of concepts, he is now exposed as a charlatan.

In conclusion, it should be emphasized that patterns of discipleship of the kind that characterize sects (religious and philosophical) are not to be condemned across the board. Often, forms of sect-like allegiances emerge with emancipatory intentions in opposition to the dominant ideological convictions inherent in modern societies. They should not be

underestimated as only networks of false belief, from which every rational being must run away. The Hulu series *The Path* expresses this insight aptly. Contrary to the first impression of a purely negative view of abusive relationships among cult members, it unfolds an irresistible tension in that a member critical of the cult experiences his own spiritual calling by leaving the cult in order to subsequently found it anew.

Part 5

Enjoyment as an Ontological Factor

13

Jouissance

(Lecture 14)

1

The following and last series of lectures addresses a concept that is central to Lacan's philosophy: the concept of enjoyment, or *jouissance*. With its help, Lacan illustrates not only how enjoyment plays a central role in the way subjects integrate their symbolic bodies into collective forms of pleasure, but how, in certain situations, we can fall out as "abjects" in the social world around us, that is, as objects of disdain and contempt. The term "abject" originates in Julia Kristeva's philosophy to denote objects in a liminal state of transition, resisting a clear part-whole distinction and therefore sometimes inflicting experiences ranging from aversion to horror. Let's go step by step and start by approaching the concept of jouissance.

In the broad literature on Lacan, the concept of jouissance is often interpreted as an idiosyncratic form of enjoyment (Braunstein 2003; Chiesa 2015; Miller 2000). It embodies a pleasure-and-pain economy and opposes the homeostasis principle presented in Freud's multiple comments on the *Lustprinzip* within the philosophy of psychoanalysis. In *Mourning and Melancholia* (1917), Freud mentions the "self-tormenting . . . which is without doubt enjoyable" (Freud 1994, vol. 16, 12), and in *Beyond the Pleasure Principle* (1920) he detects how a life-consuming enjoyment of trauma patients, through not letting go of "the situation of the [traumatic] accident" (Freud 1994, vol. 18, 12), gives them something more in return.

Lacan follows Freud and, in the course of his development of the concept, speaks specifically of surplus enjoyment: a paradoxical pleasure that involves a certain type of suffering with violent consequences that threaten the mind and the body. Jouissance, he says, can be a "path towards death" (Lacan 2007, 18), since "without a transgression there is no access to jouissance" (Lacan 1992, 177). "Transgression in the direction of jouissance only takes place if it is supported by the oppositional principle, by the forms of the Law" (ibid.). As such, jouissance is social, as Matthew Sharpe makes clear: It "presupposes the existence . . . of the 'other' . . . of a community's system and Laws, since it is what insists when a subject approaches too directly what this Law has named as prohibitively 'off limits'" (Sharpe 2004, 110). Jacques-Alain Miller's oft-cited essay on the "Six Paradigms of Jouissance" in Lacan's oeuvre is one of the most concise elaborations of the concept's development from the early to the later seminars, if one does not see his periodization of the concept as reducing the latter's multiplicity of facets (Miller 2000). He shows how Lacan, at different stages of his work, links jouissance to his so-called "three registers"—the symbolic, the imaginary and the real—into which subjectivity is woven, libidinally and normatively, like in a threefold braid. In so doing, Miller underlines that jouissance can be narcissistic, as captured in an imaginary dyad of ego and alter ego; but it can also be symbolic, insofar as jouissance emanates from demand (*Seminar V*); and it can touch upon the real as that which cannot be represented. Here, the human being enjoys, at the cost of his own well-being, an experience that is beyond norms and imaginations. And this enjoyment *is* his well-being, even if his well-being is exactly what is lost.

Lacan uses the term "jouissance" for the first time in his *Seminar I* of 1953–54, adopting Alexandre Kojève's interpretation of Hegel's master-slave relation (Lacan 1988b, 170, 222–26). He shifts it toward sexual connotations after 1956. François Perrier and David Macay have proven the importance of Georges Bataille in the notion's expansion, though Lacan himself only rarely mentions Bataille by name (Macey 1988, 204–5). Now the erotic, as a potential realm of violence, becomes important. It brings jouissance closer to the border of death, with excess as an essential, rather than accidental, property. Miller describes this shift as one where jouissance, as a special form of enjoyment, is no longer to be found exclusively in two of Lacan's "three registers" in which subjectivity is libidinally and normatively "hung up." Now it becomes "impossible jouissance" (Miller's third paradigm), with an essential reference to Lacan's third register, "the real," as that which makes any symbolic and imaginary interpretation on what subjectivity is about impossible in its core. This means that especially in *Seminar VII*, jouissance becomes for the first time a prominent concept by "pushing the signification to its limit" (Miller 2000, 6). Lacan now talks explicitly of surplus enjoyment. He refers to Freud's "das Ding" and Kant's fascination with "the Law" that, through unfulfillable injunctions, overburdens the subject by definition (Lacan 1992, 315–16). Jouissance stands for the eroticization and transgression of limits. It becomes a transgressive quality, and Lacan's main concern is how it overflows the mind with pleasure by overstepping existing moral and legal norms.

In the lecture "Psychoanalysis and Medicine" Lacan writes: "What I call jouissance—in the sense in which the body experiences itself—*is always in the nature of a tension*, of a forcing, of a spending, even of an exploit. Unquestionably, jouissance starts in the moment when pain begins to appear, and we know that it is only at this level of pain that a whole dimension of the organism, which would otherwise remain veiled, can be experienced" (Lacan 1967, 47, my trans.).

2

The following comments now focus especially on what Miller calls "impossible jouissance" (Miller 2000, 19). The goal is not so much to repeat Miller's insights, which have been taken up and elaborated by others, but to broaden his reading of jouissance as surplus enjoyment and as transgression of the Law (in the name of Law) with regard to Lacan's concept of "forced choice"; that is, the unconscious submission that an individual must endure in the genealogy of its ego-function. Lacan posits his theory of "forced choice" especially, but not exclusively, in *Seminar XI*. The purpose of this investigation is to better understand jouissance as a libidinal source that can push the human being to reset her or his conditions of living by crisscrossing the so-called symbolic order (embodied by what Lacan calls the "big Other").

Someone can live a fulfilling life and be happy at all levels of what modern society has to offer, and yet may not resist a very specific form of jouissance—to risk all in favor of a small and obscene deviation from the ordinary—for example, through a WhatsApp message to a minor showing oneself half-naked (as will be presented later with regard to the political fate of Anthony Weiner), through cocaine use, or through a photo of a preteen Thai girl which is hidden in a drawer. The life of such an individual becomes condensed as symbolic in confrontation with this minor and sinful deviation from the conventional (the nude photo from Thailand, the drugs, etc.), which is, paradoxically, effective only by its capacity to potentially destroy the symbolic universe of the individual. The seemingly "slight deviation" (Epicurus), which, following Kristeva, I will combine with a theory of "abjection" in the following, may, as a traumatic and overly intense encounter with an other, influence the subject's ability to accept the full ontological weight of her or his experience of the world. Lacan's notion of jouissance helps us understand this kind of transgression, which an individual mind might have to risk as a reenactment of what Lacan calls the "forced choice" of subjectivity.

As such, this lecture seeks to show that within Lacan's concept of "impossible jouissance" (in his middle period) a "jouissance of enigmatic

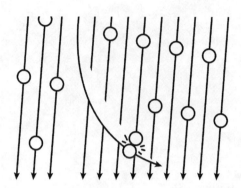

vengeance" can also be found. Thus, it helps to interpret jouissance not exclusively as a clinical concept but also as an ontological one. Subjectivity not only experiences itself as getting stuck time and again in relations to all kinds of objects with their demands, attraction, and negativity. Subjectivity can, in addition, literally transform itself into an "abject" of the world with the goal of recalibrating the world as the subject meets it from the position of its (sinful-autistic) singularity.

In contrast to Kristeva's often-cited use of the concept "abjection," the concept's intension as presented here does not refer to something that both "disturbs identity, system, or order" and "does not respect borders, positions, [or] rules" (Kristeva 1982, 4). On the contrary, here abjection is interpreted as a form through which to realize one's existence by touching upon what cannot be represented, that is, the real. This property of jouissance (*passage à l'acte*) as acting-out will be elucidated in the following as enigmatic vengeance with regard to two examples (one from fiction, one from politics). It is paradoxical, since the subjects in question gain surplus enjoyment not only through questioning, but even by potentially destroying their own conditions of symbolic life. Jouissance is therefore described as an erotic and sinful force of an individual's psyche to question the foundations of its own reality through transforming her- or himself into an abject of the world.

This argument will be demonstrated with regard to two individuals: the first is taken from a work of fiction, the movie *The Thin Red Line* (1998) directed by Terrence Malick, in which, similarly to Ernst Jünger's essay *Copse 125* (1925), a colonel finds an unconditional ground of existence in risking his life and the lives of others in a senseless uphill battle. The second example is taken from a political scandal from the 2010s—Anthony Weiner's obscene enjoyment of a picture-exchange with an underage girl. The former politician of the Democratic Party annihilated his political career by sending explicit photos of himself half-naked to a minor. With

Lacan, I will try to rationalize the behavior of these two individuals as paradigmatic examples that exemplify not only impossible jouissance (which Lacan also sees at work in what he calls "feminine jouissance" as acted out by Antigone and Teresa of Ávila), but also jouissance of enigmatic vengeance. The behaviors of the two personalities mentioned above exemplify "slight deviations" (or unpredictable swerves) of individuals, which, as traumatic and overly intense encounters of an "other" within the symbolic, give the individuals the ability to accept the full ontological weight of their world experience. A structure of agency comes to light through which, in a single moment, the subject's situation within its social framework can dramatically shift. In other words, this lecture shows how people may try, through an obscene painful-and-joyful transgression, to reenact their own genealogy of submission/subjugation in the process of civilization by suspending the normative and evaluative use-value of what is generally understood from Aristotle onwards as "the good life." Sending half-nude self-portraits to a minor (as in the case of Weiner) or starting a militarily operation with excessive casualties (as in the case of Colonel Tall) dialectically changes the lives of the subjects in a way that mirrors Lacan's fascination with jouissance as an ontological factor. It lays bare what subjectivity, at its core, is about: being a limit of the world and trying to embody an answer to a call. As such, jouissance does not so much express Lacan's Hegelian conviction that "subject and object" mediate themselves through time, but that subjects must—in order to relate to objects—try to cut the very relations that tie them to others, in order to regain or rediscover their singularity of being. Situations of acting-out can exclude individuals from the social group. What has pushed them to go that far? Which forces are accountable for apparently catastrophic results?

This lecture shows that through entering the social world (i.e., the chain of signifiers), the subject is forced to accept normative restrictions as presented in the "graph of desire." This involves the sacrifice of its pre-symbolic enjoyment which might, then, strike back. It breaks through, as jouissance, in violent moments and seeks to establish a new order of being—one in which both the rules and the specific jouissance of the subject get their share. But let's go step by step.

3

In the critically acclaimed film *The Thin Red Line*, an ambitious U.S. Army colonel named Gordon Tall (played by Nick Nolte) who wants to further his career forces his unit to conquer a steep grassy hill densely covered with vegetation during the so-called "Guadalcanal campaign" against Japanese forces. Against his captain's objections that the risk of losing is too high, the colonel bursts out angrily: "I've waited all my life for this! I've worked, I've slaved, I've eaten untold buckets of shit to get this opportunity, and I'm not passing it up now!" Soldiers, who fear for their lives, try to argue the colonel out of his decision with cost-benefit calculations, but the "call" of the hill proves to be stronger. The hill, the colonel admits, is *his* hill, as if his personal life condenses into this catastrophic situation in which the hill's capture, though absurd and dangerous from the perspective of the *Lustprinzip*, shall not be missed. Since the colonel sees the embattled hill not exclusively as a strategic point of conquest in the fight against the Japanese, but also as an individual bastion of his life, his rage exemplifies Lacan's understanding of jouissance as an excess that transgresses the limits of Freud's pleasure principle.

It appears as if Tall's life has the chance to somehow be granted consistency after a long and painful period of submission, and the colonel explicitly says as much to his confused captain's face. With a reference to a famous quote from Lacan's *Seminar XI*, one could say: the image of the hill is in the colonel's eye, but he himself "is in the tableau" (Lacan 1981, 96, trans. changed). Thus, for a moment, the colonel embodies a trait that Lacan describes as paranoia, for "contrary to the normal subject for whom reality is always in the right place, [the psychotic subject] is certain of something, which is that [what] is at issue—ranging from hallucination to interpretation—regards him. Reality isn't at issue for him, certainty is" (Lacan 1993, 75). Indeed, for the colonel, certainty is at stake. Suddenly, his miserable life of forced choices has the chance to experience a form of absolution from another dimension of reality.

The hill literally becomes what Freud calls "das Ding" in a sidenote of his *Project for a Scientific Psychology*. Lacan takes up this concept in *Seminar VII* to explain the psychological source of surplus enjoyment. He even links Freud's term to Kant's fascination with "the Law" which, through unachievable injunctions, by definition overburdens the subject. The Thing is nothing less than the "primordial pivot around which the effects of the unconscious revolve" (Boothby 2019, 166). "Das Ding," Lacan says, "is a primordial function which is located at the level of the initial establishment of the gravitation of the unconscious *Vorstellungen*" (Lacan 1992, 62).

Precisely because the Thing occupies the most obscure core of the unconscious, it deserves to be identified as the most elemental motive cause of human behavior. The Thing stands for the eroticization and the transgression of limits. It features a transgressive quality, and Lacan's main concern is how this quality overflows the mind with pleasure by overstepping existing moral and legal laws. In the words of Jacques-Alain Miller: "What is then meant by *das Ding*, the Thing? It means that satisfaction, the truth, the drive, the *Befriedigung*, is found neither in the imaginary or the symbolic, that it is outside what is symbolized, that it is of the order of the real. . . . Everything in the two-level assembly of Lacan's great graph [of desire] is set up against real jouissance, in order to contain real jouissance" (Miller 2000, 7).

Here the Thing functions as a melancholy object of loss that can never be incorporated by the subject, since its loss is an a priori condition of subjectivity. Yet it must be fantasized as lost, since a subject who is not forever plagued by the experience of having been robbed of its substance would not be a subject at all. As such, we are compelled to reach out for the Thing, and since we cannot attain it, we limit our desire with the help of substitutions of *das Ding*: various objects of desire hiding what Lacan calls *objet a*. "Normal jouissance" (to quote Miller's fifth paradigm of jouissance) can attach itself to *objet a*, but "mad" desire of jouissance cannot. It strives for more.

One could also say that something in Colonel Tall has failed to be expressed in the order of the signifier and that the situation of life-threatening stress in which he finds himself is an escape from this impasse at whatever cost. So while, in this account, desire operates according to Lacan's so-called "three registers" (the symbolic, the imaginary, the real) via the imaginary and the symbolic as some kind of barrier against the real, it is, by contrast, jouissance that becomes the driving force of the real against the registers of the imaginary and the symbolic. A new form of singularity finds shape. It is, as Eric Santner asserts, "a non-relational excess which is out-of-joint with respect to . . . any form of teleological absorption by a larger purpose" (Santner 2005, 96). Arbitrary life stages are about to fall into a totality that suddenly makes sense for Tall. All that has to be done is to put everything in jeopardy, so that everything that can be risked becomes, in the moment of a potential failure, what it may already be: actually nothing, the prevented enjoyment of a badly treated soldier, who has not had a chance to get a share of "suum cuique" from the Lacanian big Other. Here, in the form of the colonel's excessive desire, jouissance confronts us as a traumatic element, a core of intensity, which contradicts moderation. *Das Ding* names the inaccessible yet determinative engine of desire, and as such the core question constitutive of subjectivity itself. "Das Ding has to be posited as exterior, as the prehistoric Other that is impossible to forget—the Other whose primacy of position Freud affirms in the form of something *entfremdet*, something strange to me" (Lacan 1992, 71).

For Gordon Tall, the hill is this exterior. It is both a phantasmagoric placeholder for multiple deprivations that have shaped his life and a surface for the projection of a prehistoric and a priori desire that only opens up through the aforementioned experience of lack as an extra-symbolic aim that must be seized.

14

In Violation of the Pleasure Principle

(Lecture 15)

1

One feature of Lacan's concept of jouissance is to underscore that, for us humans, the world in the common, everyday sense cannot be experienced as coherent. If this is true, then this insight into a certain form of incoherence has the paradoxical quality of sanctioning our lives, especially when we find life miserable and are threatened by failure, or suffocated by too much perfection and harmony. This may explain why Lacan interprets jouissance from the 1960s onwards as a form of "moral masochism" (Freud) and asserts, with regard to Kant, that "if one eliminates from morality every element of sentiments, if one removes or invalidates all guidance to be found in sentiments, then in the final analysis the de Sadeian world is conceivable—as one of the possible forms of the world governed by a radical ethics, by the Kantian ethics as elaborated in 1788" (Lacan 1992, 79).

Lacan's reference to Kant's moral law is important here, as it actually is a law out of human reach, a law of anticipated inaccessibility that carries an infinite desire (especially in comparison to Aristotle's ethics) or, better, that carries an infinite and excessive demand within itself. As such, the law can be a paradoxical inspiration of restlessness, an existential electricity that serves the subject even in situations when, through abjection, it risks its own life or the well-being of a community (see Finkelde 2016, 2018). Jouissance, as both the enigma of vengeance and the act of abjection, does not refer us to small pleasures or forms of excitement that are collectively celebrated, for example, on New Year's Eve. Rather, in his "retour à Freud," Lacan means especially life-threatening forms of enjoyment—like Colonel Tall's obsession—that are fundamentally based on a radical questioning of the symbolic order the subject is a part of. It is worth mentioning that this kind of jouissance is uncovered by Lacan within Teresa of Ávila's spiritual "mystical ejaculations [which] are neither

idle chatter nor empty verbiage" (Lacan 1998, 76). Lacan speaks of a jouissance beyond the phallus (ibid., 77), that is, a jouissance that the signifier is unable to restrict and/or delimit. Because, as Lacan says regarding
Bernini's sculpture of Teresa, "she is having jouissance [. . . but knows]
nothing about it" (ibid., 76). As Lucie Cantin has shown, the Catholic
nun of the Carmelite order is intensely concerned with her honor and
the importance of her words, as she was ordered by her superiors to write
her experience down. But while Teresa's autobiographical notes and her
confessions obliged her to reveal everything, she was limited by jouissance
itself. "She could not free her from that capture in a jouissance that disor-
ganized her" (Cantin 1993, 135).

2

An example similar to Colonel Tall's excessive enjoyment, which carries
a pleasure-in-pain economy beyond "the good life" (more on this below),
can be elaborated upon through the tragicomic fate of the American
politician Anthony Weiner. The Democrat ruined his career and that of
his wife—one of Hillary Clinton's closest advisors from 2015 to 2017—
by repeatedly sending a photo of himself with a bath towel around his
waist to a minor girl from his mobile phone. The published pictures of
Weiner were amusing to a wide audience as, in one of the photos, Weiner
literally grabs himself by his genitals. Curiously, however, it was not so
much the fact of his questionable behavior that ended his public career,

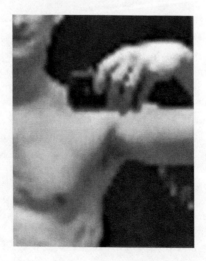

but that he was caught again in a similar pose several months after the scandal calmed down. The photos were published in the *New York Post* on June 12, 2011.

My admittedly speculative thesis (which asks for a maximally charitable reading) is that Weiner, as in the case of Colonel Tall, *had* to act as he did against all odds of cost-benefit calculations, since his world experience could receive its ontological consistency in his mind only through this form of a constitutive violation of the symbolic order and his role within it—touching the circles of a potential president (Hillary Clinton). The violation of the pleasure principle, which, as a principle of suffering, aims at a place-out-of-place, "keeps us in this world," as Lacan says (Lacan 1992, 185, trans. changed). We live to destabilize living, since life would be unbearable without its other, life-threatening counterpart.

Since, from *Seminar VII* onwards, Lacan understands jouissance even as an ethical principle (which is not the same as being a principle within ethics), his distance from Aristotle and the peculiar pleasure-and-desire administration within the Aristotelian understanding of "the good life" could not be more extreme. Near the beginning of book 6 of the *Nicomachean Ethics*, Aristotle repeatedly defines the concept of "right" desire as a necessary condition for successful practical thinking and moral excellence (ibid., p. 103, 6.1139a21–31). He writes: "moral virtue is a state of character concerned with choice, and choice is deliberate desire, therefore both the reasoning must be true and the desire right, if the choice is to be good, and the latter must pursue just what the former asserts" (Aristotle 2009, p. 103, 6.1139a21–25). The enjoyment of buying a house is not supposed to carry us away beyond the limits of reason. In this sense, right desire is restricted by practical reasoning. It needs limits to arrive at a level of true satisfaction and true enjoyment that helps the individual to flourish. Right desire, then, fits our basic enjoyments as needs that are features of our human nature. In this sense, the notion of a good choice is truly objective insofar as it is grounded in facts about the world (including facts about my place in this world) and in facts about what constitutes human flourishing. When our choices conform to these facts, then our desire is right. As such, practical thought and desire are directed toward the same goal (*eupraxia*, or "acting well"). Desire and intellect share the same content.

So it is no wonder that perfect enjoyment is personified in the "unmoved mover." One can also find it, according to Jonathan Lear, in true contemplation (Lear 2002, 99). This in part explains why Aristotle repeatedly questions the Sophists in his *Ethics*, since they present themselves as the enemies of true rest by promulgating a false and vain understanding of enjoyment for enjoyment's sake through truth-relative talk. "For if the nature of anything were simple, the same action would always be most pleasant to it. This is why God always enjoys a single and simple pleasure; for there is not only an activity of movement but an activity of immobility, and pleasure is found more in rest than in movement" (Aristotle 2009, 6.1154b25–29). The Aristotelian immobile mover embodies a particular unity of homeostatic enjoyment, being, and thinking. Aristotle distinguishes this pleasure of calmness within the balance of the good life from the understanding of the Sophists. Their philosophizing disturbs the homeostatic order of being. It does not articulate itself for the sake of truth, but produces the pleasure of speaking in favor of an enjoyment free of normativity—enjoyment for enjoyment's sake. This is one reason why, from the 1960s onwards, Lacan compares Aristotle with the Kantian moral law, as we mentioned earlier.

Weiner's lifeworld may have contracted into an experience of libidinal intensity in the moment when the mentioned photo was sent—an intensity that no longer knows any pleasure principle in its ordinary form of "right desire." From this intensity, which is experienced with sexual relish, the individual may suspect that he/she can no longer catch up with the coming catastrophe, and yet cannot refuse the command—to send the photo. We find here jouissance in its purest form: a minimal ontological inconsistency injected into a seemingly homeostatic basic structure of being by a "slight deviation" (Lat. *clinamen*; Lucretius and Epicurus) triggered by pushing the "send" button.

But, one might argue as a good Aristotelian and as a proponent of the good life, why is jouissance not simply an affect that is part of our psychic furniture, which, according to a long philosophical tradition from Plato to Kant, is attributed to the soul beside reason and emotion? Enjoyment would, in this line of argument, be a continuation of the classical triad of *epithymetikon* (appetite), *thymos* (temper), and *logos* (reason) which, when triggered, is nothing more than "weakness of the will" or a "syllogistic bastard" (Davidson 1982). For Lacan, though, this subjugation of jouissance into either appetite or temper neglects its reasonable employment: to help to settle the account of an individual's lifeworld as forced choice by an individual's questioning of the entire symbolic universe through a trifling deviation.

I mention this Aristotelian tradition of thought to underline how the abject-inspired behaviors of the two individuals presented here (Tall and Weiner) articulate a longing to break through the "forced choice" of selfhood. It is assumed in the process of civilization within the signifying chains of universally recognized equations. Since my remarks on Lacan's notion of forced choice go back several lectures, the next lecture will begin with a reminder of what the theory is about.

15

The Thing

(Lecture 16)

1

Central to Lacan's understanding of the ego's process of socialization is the description of a sacrificial situation (my example was the fate of Prince William). In this situation, a pre-symbolic life-substance of enjoyment, which paradoxically emerges with the development of the symbolic order as the other side of the ego's self-reflexivity, must be given up. (Lacan describes the concept of forced choice in multiple ways, from his "graph of desire" to his slogan "Your money or your life!" [Lacan 1981, 212].) The sacrificial situation is constitutive and, in the context of various social contract theories, concerns the incorporation of the subject into the administered form of communal enjoyment and communal reasons.

In the formation of the ego function, something is always excluded. Not all desires of the individual (be they psychological or biological) can be carried over into the ego function. Some desires, for example, those for an intimate love relationship with the mother, must be sacrificed. The sacrificial setting is constitutive and, in the context of various social contract theories, concerns the involvement of the subject in the administered form of communal enjoyment and communal reasons and justifications of what it means to exist.

Donald Davidson speaks of "triangulation" to describe the change of a sentient being into a sapient one. The latter subjugates him- or herself to multiple justified true beliefs within chains of signifiers and communitarian rule-patterns (Davidson 1982a). This process of sacrifice is what Lacan calls "forced choice" (also referred to as "your money or your life!").

Prince William, Duke of Cambridge, is forced to be himself—and that is great. The subject, who is supposed to freely choose her or his community (for only a free choice is morally binding), does not exist before this choice (Žižek 1992). It is constituted by it. The choice is therefore paradoxical in principle. Insofar as the single individual retains the freedom of choice, it does so only if it has already made the right decision of subordination to the community's preexisting social contract. If I choose the "other" of community, I risk forfeiting the freedom of the choice itself. "Clinically speaking, I choose psychosis" (ibid., 75).

Hegel is clearly one of Lacan's sources since, according, to the latter, spirit incorporates sacrifice as its formal structure. The different sensations that the individual receives through sense-perception are not only perceived and experienced directly by the individual, but are also conveyed as a moment of the ego-function's self-reflexivity in its codependence on others (*Sittlichkeit*). That is, rudimentary acts of cognition are part of a collective training in which split subjects emerge together with their corresponding split facts, split values, and split states of affairs. According to Lacan's theory of the act of choice, sacrificed is the aforementioned "thing," which he discusses with reference to Kant, as well as Heidegger and Freud. The "thing" is the incestuous object in which an impossible enjoyment in the mind-world relationship is inscribed, while at the same time the fullness of this enjoyment is fantasized as the lost object of one's self. The Thing, as the impossible, is "that which I call the beyond-of-the signifier" (Lacan 1992, 54). Striving for this impossible

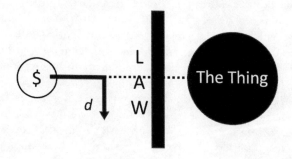

enjoyment becomes our fundamental task. It leads to the fact that we all participate in *Kulturarbeit* (Freud) in its various forms as a means of compensation for the unreachable surplus enjoyment of pleasure that, annoyingly, always remains at a radical distance, apparently out of reach. And, of course, it must be out of reach. Only an impossible object can be the proof that there is more in the subject than the subject itself.

Lacan expresses this idea, among others, in the *graph of desire* (Lacan 2006d). You may remember: the so-called split subject must—in the context of the aforementioned forced choice—plunge into the symbolic order of the big Other, so that in the end, the small vegetative organism that is a toddler emerges as, for example, Prince William, Duke of Cambridge, with all his insignia transmitted to him by the House of Windsor. An organism sacrifices a pre-symbolic life-substance of enjoyment not only to play a prince's role, but to enjoy a prince's symptoms *as his own*. An epistemic remainder, like an irresistible itch, alludes to an Other that coagulates out of subjectivation and is expressed only in symptoms—including social symptoms.

Robert Brandom describes these processes of sacrifice analogously in his theory of inferentialism. Sapient beings are trained so long as their sentient properties are subordinated to "right moves" in a game of mutual "scorekeeping" of giving and asking for reasons (Brandom 2000, 163–65). This process, though, has antinomic dimensions that were acknowledged already by Rousseau and transmitted through Kant to Hegel as the paradox of autonomy—which is the paradox of "forced choice" seen from a different angle. This antinomic character stands out when one tries to pin down the aforementioned competence with a certain date, a certain age, or a final exam. Kant circumvents the problem by emphasizing, against Brandom, that, for example, morality cannot be learned, since it depends on a "revolution of disposition" (Finkelde 2017, 46–49). Morality is presented as an excess of life within nature's causes and effects. In other words, the human being always comes (even for Brandom) too late to his "correct moves," and this unsettles him. The threshold between the place where we are trained as moral beings and the place where we are autonomous in our moral behavior (properly playing the game of giving and asking for reasons) is surrounded by a principle of uncertainty, which again plays into the condition of being forced to choose one's "character" (Kant), one's life, one's morality. Lacan: "Desire is a relationship of being to lack. This lack is the lack of being . . . This lack is beyond anything which can represent it" (Lacan 1988b, 223).

2

With Lacan, therefore, one could say that the subject will retrospectively open up the big Other (the moral law, in Kantian terms) according to the subjectivation thesis of the graph of desire, as the individual itself is unconsciously posited by the big Other (the Law).

After all, such positing is "forced choice." In this positing, self-images play a crucial role that are co-defined by the big Other and confirmed from the so-called mirror stage onwards. The self-image sets a primary bifurcation into the totality of the organism's libidinal energies. One result is that the unity of the imago must, according to Lacan, always be inadequate to the abundance of desires that waggle on in our pre-symbolized bodies, which carry, through multilayered processes of transference, the unconscious patterns of our educators and the social world surrounding us.

In this sense, following Franz Rosenzweig's talk of an "immortal self" (Rosenzweig 1985, 79) in distinction from the mortal individual, one could say that the unconscious is not mortal for the very reason that it does not exist, in the strict sense, within chains of what is universally defined as an entity bound like a variable to a system of identification. And how should something that does not exist be able to die?

There is always a desire left over, that is not taken care of within the rise of the imago. It is this desire that, in the lives of Colonel Tall and Anthony Weiner (but ultimately, of course, in every individual human mind-world relationship), is able to emerge as the part that has no part in the share of what universally has reason to exist.

Lacan: "This image is the ring, the bottleneck through which the confused bundle of desire and need must pass through to be it, that is, to reach its imaginary structure" (Lacan 1988a, 176). The imago or gestalt stands for a standstill. This structural process of subjectivity is always a path of suffering, since the psyche is, allegorically speaking, pushed through the aforementioned "ring" in order to be recognized and symbolically equipped with a joyful investment that binds the individual to fantasies that are at the borderline of individuality and sociality. The forced choice cannot be put to rest. It lingers on in self-reflexivity, causing the lustful pain of the ego's self-relation to that which—coming from the unconscious—it is not.

Tall and Weiner thus exemplify subjectivity's dependence on jouissance as an ontological factor with regard to "forced choice" in a way that transcends Lacan's more clinical comments on excessive desires personified in both Antigone and Teresa of Ávila.

Now, it is interesting that Kant also grounds his theory of the moral choice with the help of a purely a priori theory of a revolutionary choice of character. Before we became empirical subjects, we have—according to Kant—chosen our "disposition" with regard to the moral law (Kant 1996, 72–74). Kant speaks of an a priori choice between good and evil, since this choice is, for him, a necessary condition in grounding the moral subject in a noumenal realm outside of space and time. Only this choice can guarantee that we, as empirical beings within the causal structures of nature, can claim responsibility for our evil deeds. In other words, something else in us has chosen our moral disposition without an empirical proof of this primordial "forced choice."

But the Kantian choice in its noumenal dimension is always in the making (Finkelde 2017, 69–82). The "forced choice" of disposition has taken place, yet at the same time, it haunts us each and every time the moral law confronts us. As we never know what kind of disposition our noumenal self has chosen, we never know how we will choose in the present. Indeed, we are apparently predestined, but exactly *how* this Kantian predestination has turned out, for the good or for the bad, can only be realized too late. In the individual's life, this choice is, as it were, permanently in the suspension of our choosing, because "I still live" and therefore I must repeatedly face the moral law again and again. But, as I said, this applies not only to the moral law, but also to the "forced choice" in the Lacanian sense. It has always taken place (in the past) and is still in the making (in the present), simply because the ego is an intersubjective entity incorporating an epistemic remainder which, as a part that has no part, in-exists in its existence.

3

Colonel Tall and Anthony Weiner grab on, to speak speculatively, to this "forced choice" in the making. "Untold buckets of shit" are supposed to be transubstantiated into surplus enjoyment, whatever may be the costs of life for Colonel Tall. The goal is a transcendental fantasy: the reestablishment of Tall's or Weiner's sufficient reason for their surplus enjoyment-deprived existence. The mind's higher-order abilities may truly have "forgotten" what it had to choose in the process of entering into (and establishing) a frame of certainty, but this does not mean that unconscious parts of the psyche share the imposed process of forgetting/choosing. An anti-Platonic "anamnesis" sets in with consequences that crisscross everything that the Platonic understanding of anamnesis stands for. No clearly defined universals are found, except for forces of a nether-world within the ego and its communal dis-functioning. Those parts of the psyche that resisted forced choices can continue to in-exist in the aforementioned form of a lustful disturbance of pain and pleasure that is both troubling and electrifying for the mind. For these reasons, we can be terrified and bewildered by our dreams, but also by our actions, exemplified above by Colonel Tall and Anthony Weiner. What do actions like these stand for? They may stand for an unconscious objection to the forced choice by an apparently minor deviation.

In line with the arguments presented above, I understand jouissance (1) in accordance with many scholars in the field of Lacanian philosophy of psychoanalysis as a painful lust in the psyche's libidinal economy. In particular, "impossible jouissance" (Miller) captures a paradoxical and ultimately necessary obscene operation of our mind to transgress certain legal and homeostatic forms of the internalized symbolic norms to which our psyche, in its self-relation, had to submit. Subsequently, however, I understand jouissance (2) as an enigmatic desire of vengeance that tries to reenact the forced choice that the individual experienced through "abjection."

The subject which is more than the subject itself not only feels the lustful urge to transgress normative limits, to slash out against the investiture of the self, but also wants to repeat the forced choice (through abjection), though this time from an allegedly empowered position that gives the individual a proper option—whatever it may cost for her or his life, or the lives of others. Here jouissance can be defined as an urge to suspend the original and ultimately unconscious gesture of forced choice—of submission. It aims at resetting the conditions of submission that gave away to this life for the individual by resetting the big Other.

It is via obscene enjoyment that people will get to know the deeper Truth intimated for them by their regime's master-signifiers: "nation," "God," "our way of life," and so forth. Žižek argues that it is such ostensibly nonpolitical and culturally specific practices as these that irreplaceably single out any political community from its enemies. (Culture itself is, according to Freud, a pleasure-deferring and propulsion-repelling form of sublimation and, therefore, a symptom of instinctual desires.) But what Žižek says about jouissance as a political factor is even more valid for the subject's libidinal economy toward him- or herself in an ontological sense. Therefore it is, as already mentioned, indeed too easy to reduce irrational patterns of behavior to emotions and affects that conquer reason and produce a syllogistic bastard (Davidson 1982). Reason itself conquers affects in the name of the deviation for the latter's sake. If Tall's or Weiner's superego could speak in the situations mentioned above, it might say: "For a fraction of a second, disrupt everyday life and all its normative burdens that you depend on. Now everything depends on you." Or: "Show what no one is allowed to see. Expose your desire in its purest form to all symbolic claims against you." "Touch the thing. Touch what you had to sacrifice to be in this (miserable or so-called perfect) life, that is yours."

As already discussed, Lacan detects similar kinds of enjoyment beyond pleasure, aside from Teresa of Ávila, in the sublime personality of Antigone. But these examples of unrestrained enjoyment, prominently commented on by Lacan in his *Seminar VII* and subsequently by many Lacanian scholars, often compel us to overlook too quickly that jouissance need not favor sublime ideas, as Antigone does, but also obscene and even horrific ones: the death of others or child pornography.

Having said this, it must be emphasized here too that even if, in my line of argument, the "good life" serves as a foil to the work of jouissance in its all-or-nothing form, we of course encounter certain aspects of joyful rebellion against parts of the established good life all the time. Miller's fourth and fifth paradigms, called "normal jouissance" and "discursive jouissance," can be mentioned here together with Slavoj Žižek's (1991a), Mari Ruti's (2012), Jodi Dean's (2006), and my own references to enjoyment as a political factor (2016, 2018). "Normal jouissance" is explained by Miller with regard to *Seminar XI*, in which Lacan breaks jouissance up into various *object a(s)*. This kind of "jouissance is not reached by heroic transgression, but by the coming to mind of the drive, by the drive which makes a return trip" (Miller 2000, 9). Here, jouissance obviously plays a less destructive role. People have accepted the ready-made symbolic order received from birth and now cope, in the pursuit of touching the Thing, with jouissance, without risking all for nothing. My focus on jouissance as enigmatic vengeance (against "forced choice") does not want to diminish these lesser forms. Its focus on the jouissance of enigmatic vengeance is grounded exclusively in the aspiration to outline the concept's hidden ontological implications in the subject-world relation as much as possible through acts of abjection.

4

Weiner followed, speculatively thinking, an unconscious command to be a-rational (not irrational): to risk everything for nothing: because, as I said, he did it again ("encore"). Jouissance is included in the pleasure principle, but does not belong to this principle. It is an excess that cannot be seen as excess because its scale falls into its own form detached from the norm. And this *form out of form* is reflected upon by Kant in his moral law, since it is especially in its "holiness" (Hegel) that it is most akin to Kant's concept of the "devilishly evil" (*das teuflisch Böse*; see Zupančič 2000).

Colonel Tall's destiny, which bears a resemblance to Ernst Jünger's fate as described in a famous 1925 text entitled *Copse 125: A Chronicle from the Trench Warfare of 1918*, illuminates this. For Tall, everything depends on getting his share out of untamed logics of worlds that, until now, could not guarantee him an unbiased distribution of well-being or a place to enjoy himself being himself. The same may be true for the fate of Anthony Weiner in the perspective presented above. In sending the aforementioned erotic photos, he can prove his ability to accept the full ontological weight of his symbolic world by risking his reputation, the reputation of his wife, and the reputation of a potential president of the

United States by touching the "send" button. Not only for Lacan—but also for Kant—are humans haunted by what they are not responsible for and yet must take responsibility for. Lacan invokes the symbolic order to underline how the "forced choice" has turned out yesterday or will turn out tomorrow—allegedly. Jouissance is ever-present here in the human libidinal economy, since subjects strive, inspired by a call, for the truth of their being and seek to liberate themselves from the aforementioned choice that never was a fair or truthful one, a choice that granted subjectivity its "suum cuique." One could also say with another concept of Lacan that we as human beings strive for the "thing," that is, the entity from which we as subjects were deprived within the aforementioned sacrificial structure that brings subjectivity to the fore. Jouissance strives to get a grip on the noumenal realm of this thing as that (noumenal entity) which had to be rejected for subjectivity so that objectivity could emerge. The "thing" is the phantasmagoric archetype of a lost object through which absolute enjoyment would be possible. And this is what "small deviations" (Lat. *clinamen*) or "trifling irritations" of the symbolic universe, mentioned above, strive for: to touch upon a spectral entity that haunts us; to lay a sufficient ground of reason.

As such, jouissance can urge someone who leads a happy family life, who has a fulfilling job, or who is, on all levels of his fate, apparently a happy person, to risk everything for nothing—a nothing that incorporates a particular nugget of enjoyment. In situations like these, the "clinamen," or the "deviation/excess," attempts to touch upon the lost and forbidden thing from which one was separated. The goal is to give consistency to the contingent reality from a place out of place, without which even the most beautiful family idyll can be felt as an unsupportable hell. But this subjectivity must be willing to enjoy risking everything for nothing. Jouissance, here, enjoys its own form of reinstalling the symbolic. This, though, works only when the forbidden thing is felt coming closer into the subject's range. The picture-message is sent, the command to conquer *Copse 125* is given. Abjection accomplished. The psyche may be flooded by an autonomizing elixir of life in sending the image, since now it is the individual who can subjectivize everything for nothing. Then, the outcome could still be horrible, but at least it was the result of a choice, not the collateral damage of a forced choice.

In jouissance-charged actions, the psyche recovers part of the disciplinary costs passed on to him or her by the big Other. The psyche seeks to retrieve the credit imposed on itself, which is only possible if a cost-and-benefit calculation in the symbolic-libidinal household of the individual is rejected completely. In this way, jouissance tries to find a space of an existential auto-creation in which everything in relation to pure nothing must be at stake. Think again of Weiner's fate. I do not want to deny that a pathological addiction to sexual arousal may have driven the man. But I think sexuality as an affect can just be one of many variables in a complex equation that can have strong ontological components, with unacknowledged desires beneath the ego's reasons. In jouissance, and in the rejection of the symbolic order by an obscene and liberating gesture of excess, an unconscious act of freedom may be hidden. Incidentally, Lacan sees such an act of freedom in the work of the Marquis de Sade. The latter does not want to create lust or eroticism, but, as Lacan says, "approach [the reader] to a burning center or an absolute zero. . . . Sade's work belongs to the order of what I shall call experimental literature. The work of art in this case is an experiment that through its action cuts the subject loose from his psychosocial moorings—or to be more precise, from all psychosocial appreciation of the sublimation involved" (Lacan 1992, 201).

It does not matter if we approve of this or not. For Lacan, the ethics of psychoanalysis is not linked to "right desire" within a plurality of forms of the "good life." In jouissance we are essentially dealing with the subject as a limit to the world. The desire of jouissance is an uprising of the unconscious against the costs of submission into chains of signifiers.

5

Terrence Malick's movie title evokes the ambivalence of a *Thin Red Line*. The latter has an outstanding property since it can be seen only when it has been violated or crossed. The line literally separates human reason from jouissance. Its relation to the Lacanian "thing" does not exist as a boundary between rationality on the one hand and jouissance and temper on the other. Rather, the reference to the line's thinness means more: namely, that we cannot make it out. It becomes visible only in looking back. Malick underlines this insight in an important scene in the last part of the movie. We see Colonel Tall in a sitting posture of exhausted contemplation almost reminiscent of Albrecht Dürer's angel in *Melencolia I* The battle has been fought successfully, although with high losses of American lives. Corpses and battle debris lie around like senseless props with an expired meaning. Did Colonel Tall really have to go that far? Of course he did, since the red line can, as I said, be measured only through looking back. Tall had to equip an inconsistent outside world with consistency. He had to save his life by risking (at least from his perspective) everything for nothing. A seemingly small deviation of a soldier's career

became the sufficient reason to tie together subjectivity and objectivity, for a decisive moment. After such battles, no one thinks to say things like "since 5:45 a.m. we have been returning fire," or asks who is actually responsible for the Syrian civil war. All the circumstances are somehow clear, now that jouissance has come to an end. Tall is sad, but satisfied mentally and bodily. The battle gave his miserable life an ontological contact with reality. This may underline Lacan's insight that subjectivity must time and again make the experience of madness in order to step out of itself and into the corset of the symbolic order anew. Indeed, jouissance is the painful libidinal fuel that is required within the mind in order to go so far. It is the only substance that psychoanalysis claims exists. As I understand Lacan here, substances are immutable bearers of change, according to the classical definition. Jouissance belongs to the basic structure of reality, since it remains the same basic feature in the subject-object dichotomy in all possible worlds. Hegel has given us an ingenious formulation of this power of jouissance as negativity's driving force for spirit that also knows no dependence on the pleasure principle. In the preface to the *Phenomenology of Spirit*, he famously writes sentences that could well have been cited as a voice-over to Colonel Tall's contemplative silence. "Death, if that is what we want to call this non-actuality, is of all things the most dreadful, and to hold fast what is dead requires the greatest strength. . . . But the life of Spirit is not the life that shrinks from death and keeps itself untouched by devastation, but rather is the life that endures it and maintains itself in it. Spirit only wins its truth by finding its feet within its absolute disruption. . . . This tarrying with the negative is the magical power that converts it into being" (Hegel 1977, 19, §32).

We should not take Hegel's understanding of spirit as an instance of divine sublimity, but rather in Lacan's sense, as a power source of raging jouissance, which blurs the line between rationality, affect, and irrationality, thus destabilizing the subject-object dichotomy ad infinitum. The colonel did not know where the red line between jouissance and reason was hiding. He discovered it as an unconscious desire looking back after trying to touch upon the Thing as the sufficient cause of reality. The colonel had to carry out his act because the symbolic order, at its core, carries even these insane formations at its origin. And jouissance repeatedly draws us back to this source of a forced choice, which we are called upon to reset. The battle is an encounter with the real without the need for the colonel to know what the real is. Similarly, for a politician, a priest, or an actor, a nude photo of an underage girl or boy may be such an encounter with the real. The lustful real presence can forcefully extinguish the symbolic order because it is able to make the world coherent. In other words, when I am confronted with this lustful presence of utmost danger for my own symbolic role, I experience pleasure, because I can (allegedly) renegotiate the social contract that has been done unto me.

Works Cited

Adorno, Theodor W. 2004. *Negative Dialectics*, trans. E. B. Ashton. London: Routledge.

Allison, Henry. 2004. *Kant's Transcendental Idealism*. New Haven, CT: Yale University Press.

Amnesty International. 2022. *Israel's Apartheid Against Palestinians.* https://www.amnesty.org/en/latest/campaigns/2022/02/israels-system-of-apartheid/.

Aristotle. 2009. *Nicomachean Ethics*, trans. David Ross. Oxford: Oxford University Press.

Bahr, Petra. 2004. *Darstellung des Undarstellbaren*. Tübingen: Mohr Siebeck.

Benjamin, Walter. 1986. "Critique of Violence." In *Reflections. Essays, Aphorisms, Autobiographical Writings*, trans. Edmund Jephcott, 277–300. New York: Schocken.

Benjamin, Walter. 1999. "Experience and Poverty." In *Walter Benjamin: Selected Writings, vol. 2, 1927–1934*, ed. Michael Jennings, 731–36. Cambridge, MA: Belknap Press of Harvard University Press.

Benjamin, Walter, and Gershom Scholem. 1989. *The Correspondence of Walter Benjamin and Gershom Scholem, 1932–1940*, trans. Gary Smith and Andre Lefevere. New York: Schocken Books.

Benoist, Jocelyn. 2021. *Toward a Contextual Realism*. Cambridge, MA: Harvard University Press.

Bentham, Jeremy. 2001. "Appendix A: Legal Fictions." In *Bentham's Theory of Fiction*, ed. C. K. Odgen, 141–50. London: Routledge.

BonJour, Laurence. 2010. "Externalism / Internalism." In *A Companion to Epistemology, Second Edition*, ed. Jonathan Dancy, Ernest Sosa, and Matthias Steup, 364–69. Malden, MA: Wiley-Blackwell.

Boothby, Richard. 2019. "Lacan's Thing with Hegel." *Continental Thought & Theory* 2, no. 3: 164–79.

Bourdieu, Pierre. 1991. *Language and Symbolic Power*, trans. Gino Gaymond and Matthew Adamson. Cambridge: Polity.

Brandom, Robert. 1998. *Making It Explicit: Reason, Representing, and Discursive Commitment*. Cambridge, MA: Harvard University Press.

Brandom, Robert. 2000. *Articulating Reasons: An Introduction to Inferentialism.* Cambridge, MA: Harvard University Press.

Brandom, Robert. 2019. *A Spirit of Trust: A Reading of Hegel's Phenomenology.* Cambridge, MA: Harvard University Press.

Braunstein, Nestor. 2003. "Desire and Jouissance in the Teachings of Lacan." In *The Cambridge Companion to Lacan,* ed. Jean-Michel Rabaté, 102–15. Cambridge: Cambridge University Press.

Cantin, Lucie. 1993. "Femininity: From Passion to an Ethics of the Impossible." *Topoy* 12: 127–36.

Cassirer, Ernst. 1944. *An Essay on Man: An Introduction to a Philosophy of Human Culture.* New Haven, CT: Yale University Press.

Castoriadis, Cornelius. 1987. *The Imaginary Institution of Society.* Cambridge: Polity.

Castoriadis, Cornelius. 1994. "Radical Imagination and the Social Instituting Imaginary." In *Rethinking Imagination: Culture and Creativity,* 136–54. London: Routledge.

Castoriadis, Cornelius. 1997. "The State of the Subject Today." In *World in Fragments: Writings on Politics, Society, Psychoanalysis, and the Imagination.* Stanford, CA: Stanford University Press.

Chidester, David. 1988. *Salvation and Suicide: Jim Jones, The Peoples Temple, and Jonestown.* Indianapolis: Indiana University Press.

Chiesa, Lorenzo. 2015. "The First Gram of Jouissance." *The Comparatist* 39: 6–21.

Confino, Alon. 2014. *A World Without Jews. The Nazi Imagination from Persecution to Genocide.* New Haven, CT: Yale University Press.

Dalzell, Thomas. 2011. *Freud's Schreber Between Psychiatry and Psychoanalysis.* London: Karnac Books.

Davidson, Donald. 1982. "Two Paradoxes of Irrationality." In *Philosophical Essays on Freud,* ed. Richard Wollheim and James Hopkins, 289–305. Cambridge: Cambridge University Press.

Davidson, Donald. 1982a. "Rational Animals." *Dialectica* 36, no. 4: 317–27.

Davidson, Donald. 2001. "The Myth of the Subjective." In *Subjective, Intersubjective, Objective,* 39–52. Oxford: Clarendon.

Davidson, Donald. 2001a. "A Coherence Theory of Truth and Knowledge." In *Subjective, Intersubjective, Objective,* 137–53. Oxford: Clarendon.

Deacon, Terrence. 1997. *The Symbolic Species: The Co-evolution of Language and the Brain.* New York: W. W. Norton.

Dean, Jodi. 2006. *Žižek's Politics.* New York: Routledge.

de Landa, Manuel. 2017. *The Rise of Realism.* London: Polity.

Dennett, Daniel. 1991. *Consciousness Explained.* New York: Little, Brown.

Dennett, Daniel. 2014. "Reflections on Free Will: A Review by Daniel C. Dennett." https://www.samharris.org/blog/reflections-on-free-will.

Dennett, Daniel, and Gregg D. Caruso. 2021. *Just Deserts: Debating Free Will.* Cambridge: Polity.

Depoortere, Frederiek. 2007. "The End of God's Transcendence? On Incarnation in the Work of Slavoj Žižek." *Modern Theology* 23, no. 3: 497–523.

Dolar, Mladen. 2006. *A Voice and Nothing More.* Cambridge, MA: MIT Press.

Durkheim, Émile. 1995. *Elementary Forms of the Religious Life.* New York: Free Press.

Esposito, Roberto. 2010. *Communitas: The Origin and Destiny of Community.* Stanford, CA: Stanford University Press.

Evans, Dylan. 1999. "From Kantian Ethics to Mystical Experience: An Exploration of Jouissance." In *Key Concepts of Lacanian Psychoanalysis*, ed. Dany Nobus, 1–28. New York: Other.

Evans, Dylan. 2005. "From Lacan to Darwin." In *The Literary Animal: Evolution and the Nature of Narrative*, ed. Jonathan Gottschall and David Wilson, 38–55. Evanston, IL: Northwestern University Press.

Finkelde, Dominik. 2016. *Phantaschismus: Von der totalitären Versuchung unserer Demokratie.* Berlin: Verlag Vorwerk 8.

Finkelde, Dominik. 2017. *Excessive Subjectivity: Kant, Hegel, Lacan, and the Foundations of Ethics*, trans. Deva Kemmis and Astrid Weigert. New York: Columbia University Press.

Finkelde, Dominik. 2018. "The 'Secret Code' of Honour: On Political Enjoyment and the Excrescence of Fantasy." *Culture, Theory and Critique* 59, no. 3: 232–61.

Finkelde, Dominik. 2019. *Logiken der Inexistenz. Figurationen des Realen im Zeitalter der Immanenz.* Vienna: Passagen Verlag.

Finkelde, Dominik. 2020a. "Non-Wakefulness: On the Parallax between Dreaming and Awakening." *The Philosophical Journal of Conflict and Violence* 3, no. 2: 92–107.

Finkelde, Dominik. 2020b. "Zur Notwendigkeit eines Ministeriums für kollektive Phantasiepflege und Transgression." In "On Institutions," special issue, *Metodo: International Studies in Phenomenology and Philosophy* 8, no. 1: 79–104.

Finkelde, Dominik. 2021a. "The Dream That Knew Too Much. On Freud, Lacan, and Philip K. Dick." In *Parallax: The Dialectics of Mind and World*, ed. Dominik Finkelde, Christoph Menke, and Slavoj Žižek, 239–49. London: Bloomsbury.

Finkelde, Dominik. 2021b. "Introduction." In *Parallax: The Dialectics of Mind and World*, ed. Dominik Finkelde, Christoph Menke, and Slavoj Žižek, 1–12. London: Bloomsbury.

Finkelde, Dominik. 2022. "Das Imaginäre (bei Sartre, Barthes, Lacan, Iser)." In *Handbuch Literatur und Philosophie*, ed. Sarah Schmidt and Andrea Allerkamp. Berlin: De Gruyter.

Finkelde, Dominik. 2023. "Fantasy Fatigue." *Philosophy Today* 67, no. 2: 311–29.

Finkelde, Dominik. 2024. "The Pathological A Priori. On Guilt and Shame in Creaturely Life." *Angelaki. Journal of the Theoretical Humanities* 29, no. 3: 73–81.

Finkelde, Dominik. Forthcoming. "Are All Things Contradictory? Žižek and Brandom on the Materialist Legacy of Hegel's Metaphysics." In *The Bloomsbury Handbook of Slavoj Žižek*, ed. Dominik Finkelde. London: Bloomsbury.

Flisfeder, Matthew. 2021. *Algorithmic Desire: Toward a New Structuralist Theory of Social Media.* Evanston, IL: Northwestern University Press.

Foucault, Michel. 1989. *The Order of Things: An Archeology of Human Sciences.* London: Routledge.

Frege, Gottlob. 1984. *Collected Papers on Mathematics, Logic, and Philosophy*, trans. Max Black et al. New York: Basil Blackwell.

Freud, Sigmund. 1981, vol. 2. *Studies on Hysteria*. In *The Standard Edition of the Complete Psychological Works of Sigmund Freud*, trans. James Strachey et al. London: Hogarth.

Freud, Sigmund. 1981, vol. 4. *The Interpretation of Dreams II*. In *The Standard Edition of the Complete Psychological Works of Sigmund Freud*, trans. James Strachey et al. London: Hogarth.

Freud, Sigmund. 1981, vol. 5. *The Interpretation of Dreams II*. In *The Standard Edition of the Complete Psychological Works of Sigmund Freud*, trans. James Strachey et al. London: Hogarth.

Freud, Sigmund. 1981, vol. 14. "Mourning and Melancholia." In *The Standard Edition of the Complete Psychological Works of Sigmund Freud*, trans. James Strachey et al., 243–58. London: Hogarth.

Freud, Sigmund. 1981, vol. 16. *Introductory Lectures on Psycho-Analysis (Part III)*. In *The Standard Edition of the Complete Psychological Works of Sigmund Freud*, trans. James Strachey et al. London: Hogarth.

Freud, Sigmund. 1981, vol. 18. *Beyond the Pleasure Principle*. In *The Standard Edition of the Complete Psychological Works of Sigmund Freud*, trans. James Strachey et al., 1–64. London: Hogarth.

Freud, Sigmund. 1981, vol. 23. *Moses and Monotheism: An Outline of Psycho-Analysis and Other Works*. In *The Standard Edition of the Complete Psychological Works of Sigmund Freud*, trans. James Strachey et al. London: Hogarth.

Freud, Sigmund. 1981a. "Introduction" to *Psycho-Analysis and the War Neurosis*. In *The Standard Edition of the Complete Psychological Works of Sigmund Freud*, vol. 17, trans. James Strachey et al., 207–10. London: Hogarth.

Freud, Sigmund. 1981b. "The Economic Problem of Masochism." In *The Standard Edition of the Complete Psychological Works of Sigmund Freud*, vol. 19, trans. James Strachey et al., 159–70. London: Hogarth.

Freud, Sigmund. 1981c. *Project for a Scientific Psychology*. In *The Standard Edition of the Complete Psychological Works of Sigmund Freud*, vol. 1, trans. James Strachey et al., 281–391. London: Hogarth.

Freud, Sigmund. 1981d. *The Unconscious*. In *The Standard Edition of the Complete Psychological Works of Sigmund Freud*, vol. 14, trans. James Strachey et al., 159–216. London: Hogarth.

Fukuyama, Francis. 1992. *The End of History and the Last Man*. New York: Free Press.

Gabriel, Markus. 2016. *Sinn und Existenz*. Berlin: Suhrkamp.

Gamm, Gerhard. 1997. *Der Deutsche Idealismus: Eine Einführung in die Philosophie von Fichte, Hegel und Schelling*. Stuttgart: Reclam.

Gramsci, Antonio. 1977. *Quaderni del Carcere (Quaderni 1–5)*, vol. 3. Rome: Einaudi.

Greene, Graham. 2015. *The Power and the Glory*. New York: Penguin Books.

Habermas, Jürgen. 1990. "Grenzen des Neohistorismus." In *Die nachholende Revolution*, 149–56. Frankfurt am Main: Suhrkamp.

Harman, Graham. 2018. *Object-Oriented Ontology: A New Theory of Everything*. London: Pelican.

Harris, Sam. 2014. "The Marionette's Lament: A Response to Daniel Dennett."
https://www.samharris.org/blog/the-marionettes-lament.

Hegel, Georg W. F. 1977. *The Phenomenology of Spirit*, trans. A. V. Miller. Oxford:
Oxford University Press.

Hegel, Georg W. F. 1986. *Vorlesungen über die Geschichte der Philosophie III*. In *Werke
in zwanzig Bänden*, vol. 20, ed. Eva Moldenhauer and Karl Markus Michel.
Frankfurt am Main: Suhrkamp.

Hegel, Georg W. F. 2010a. *Encyclopedia of the Philosophical Sciences in Basic Outline:
Part I: Science of Logic*, trans. and ed. Klaus Brinkmann and Daniel O.
Dahlstrom. Cambridge: Cambridge University Press.

Hegel, Georg W. F. 2010b. *The Science of Logic*, trans. and ed. Klaus Brinkmann
and Daniel O. Dahlstrom. Cambridge: Cambridge University Press.

Hegel, Georg W. F. 2011. *Lectures on the Philosophy of World History, Volume 1*, ed.
and trans. Robert F. Brown and Peter C. Hodgson. Oxford: Clarendon.

Heidegger, Martin. 1990. *Briefwechsel mit Karl Jaspers 1920–1960*, ed. Walter Biemel
and Hans Saner. Frankfurt: Pieper Verlag.

Heidegger, Martin. 1993. "The Self-Assertion of the German University." In *The
Heidegger Controversy: A Critical Reader*, ed. Richard Wolin, 29–39. Cambridge, MA: MIT Press.

Hume, David. 1985. *A Treatise of Human Nature*. London: Penguin.

Hutton, Christopher M. 2005. "The Myth of an Aryan Race." In *Race and the Third
Reich: Linguistics, Racial Anthropology and Genetics in the Dialectic of Volk*, 80–
100. Cambridge, MA: Polity.

Jacobi, Friedrich Heinrich. 2019. *David Hume über den Glauben oder Idealismus und
Realismus, Jacobi an Fichte (1799)*. Hamburg: Meiner Verlag.

Jünger, Ernst. 1928. *Das Wäldchen 125: Eine Chronik aus den Grabenkämpfen 1918*.
Berlin: E.S. Mittler.

Kakel, C. P. 2013. "Nazi Discourse: Colonial Fantasies of 'Space' and 'Race.'" In
The Holocaust as Colonial Genocide: Hitler's "Indian Wars" in the "Wild East,"
58–74. London: Palgrave Macmillan.

Kant, Immanuel. 1996. *Religion within the Boundaries of Mere Reason*. In *Religion
and Rational Theology*, ed. Allen W. Wood and George di Giovanni, 39–215.
Cambridge: Cambridge University Press.

Kant, Immanuel. 1998. *Critique of Pure Reason*, ed. and trans. Paul Guyer and Allen W. Wood. Cambridge: Cambridge University Press.

Kant, Immanuel. 1999. *Practical Philosophy*, trans. and ed. Mary Gregor. Cambridge: Cambridge University Press.

Kant, Immanuel. 2006. *Groundwork of the Metaphysics of Morals*, trans. and ed.
Mary Gregor. Cambridge: Cambridge University Press.

Koch, Anton Friedrich. 2016. *Hermeneutischer Realismus*. Tübingen: Mohr Siebeck.

Kristeva, Julia. 1982. *Powers of Horror: An Essay on Abjection*, trans. Leon S. Roudiez.
New York: Columbia University Press.

Lacan, Jacques. n.d. "L'Identification." In "Le Séminaire IX: L'Identification
(1961–1962)," unpublished. http://staferla.free.fr/S9/S9.htm.

Lacan, Jacques. n.d. "Logique du fantasme, 1966–67," unpublished. Staferla.
http://staferla.free.fr/S14/S14%20LOGIQUE.pdf.

Lacan, Jacques. 1967. "Psychanalyse et médecine." *Lettres de l'École Freudienne* 1: 34–61.

Lacan, Jacques. 1970. "On Structure as an Inmixing of an Otherness Prerequisite to Any Subject Whatever." In *The Structuralist Controversy: The Languages of Criticism and the Sciences of Man*, ed. Richard Macksey and Eugenio Donato. Baltimore, MD: Johns Hopkins University Press, 186–95.

Lacan, Jacques. 1981. *The Seminar of Jacques Lacan: Book XI, The Four Fundamental Concepts of Psychoanalysis, 1964*, ed. Jacques-Alain Miller, trans. Alan Sheridan. New York: W.W. Norton.

Lacan, Jacques. 1988a. *The Seminar of Jacques Lacan: Book I, Freud's Papers on Technique, 1953–1954*, ed. Jacques-Alain Miller, trans. John Forrester. New York: Norton.

Lacan, Jacques. 1988b. *The Seminar of Jacques Lacan: Book II, The Ego in Freud's Theory and in the Technique of Psychoanalysis, 1954–1955*, ed. Jacques-Alain Miller, trans. Sylvana Tomaselli. New York: Norton.

Lacan, Jacques. 1992. *The Seminar of Jacques Lacan: Book VII, The Ethics of Psychoanalysis, 1959–1960*, ed. Jacques-Alain Miller, trans. Dennis Porter. New York: W.W. Norton.

Lacan, Jacques. 1993. *The Seminar of Jacques Lacan: Book III, The Psychoses, 1955–1956*, ed. Jacques-Alain Miller, trans Russell Grigg. New York: Norton.

Lacan, Jacques. 1998. *The Seminar of Jacques Lacan: Book XX, Encore, 1972–1973*, ed. Jacques-Alain Miller, trans. Bruce Fink. New York: W.W. Norton.

Lacan, Jacques. 2006a. "The Instance of the Letter in the Unconscious; or Reason since Freud." In *Écrits: The First Complete Edition in English*, trans. Bruce Fink, 412–44. New York: W.W. Norton.

Lacan, Jacques. 2006b. "Logical Time and the Assertion of Anticipated Certainty." In *Écrits: The First Complete Edition in English*, trans. Bruce Fink, 161–75. New York: W.W. Norton.

Lacan, Jacques. 2006c. "The Mirror Stage as Formative of the *I* Function as Revealed in Psychoanalytic Experience." In *Écrits: The First Complete Edition in English*, trans. Bruce Fink, 75–81. New York: Norton.

Lacan, Jacques. 2006d. "The Subversion of the Subject and the Dialectic of Desire in the Freudian Unconscious." In *Écrits: The First Complete Edition in English*, trans. Bruce Fink, 671–702. New York: Norton.

Lacan, Jacques. 2006e. "The Function and Field of Speech and Language in Psychoanalysis." In *Écrits: The First Complete Edition in English*, trans. Bruce Fink, 197–268. New York: Norton

Lacan, Jacques. 2006f. "Aggressiveness in Psychoanalysis." In *Écrits: The First Complete Edition in English*, trans. Bruce Fink, 82–101. New York: Norton.

Lacan, Jacques. 2007. *The Seminar of Jacques Lacan: Book XVII, The Other Side of Psychoanalysis, 1964*, ed. Jacques-Alain Miller, trans. Russell Grigg. New York: W.W. Norton.

Lacan, Jacques. 2013. *On the Names-of-the-Father*, trans. Bruce Fink. London: Polity.

Lacan, Jacques. 2019. *Desire and Its Interpretation: The Seminar of Jacques Lacan, Book VI*, trans. Bruce Fink. Cambridge: Polity.

WORKS CITED

Laplanche, Jean. 1989. *New Foundations of Psychoanalysis*, trans. David Macey. Oxford: Basil Blackwell.

Laplanche, Jean. 2002. *The Unfinished Copernican Revolution in Psychoanalysis: Selected Works, 1967–1992*, trans. Luke Thurston. New York: The Unconscious in Translation.

Laplanche, Jean. 2005. *Essays on Otherness*, ed. John Fletcher. London: Routledge.

Lear, Jonathan. 2000. *Happiness, Death, and the Remainder of Life*. Cambridge, MA: Harvard University Press.

Lefort, Claude. 1988. *Democracy and Political Theory*, trans. David Macey. Cambridge: Polity Press.

Locke, John. 1997. *An Essay Concerning Human Understanding*. London: Penguin Books.

Lovecraft, H. P. 2020. *The Call of Cthulhu and Other Stories*. Oviedo: King Solomon.

Macey, David. 1988. *Lacan in Contexts*. London: Verso.

Malabou, Catherine. 2016. *Before Tomorrow: Epigenesis and Rationality*. Malden, MA: Polity.

Marchart, Oliver. 2013. *Das unmögliche Objekt: Eine postfundamentalistische Theorie der Gesellschaft*. Berlin: Suhrkamp.

Marx, Karl. 1982. *Capital: A Critique of Political Economy*, trans. Ben Fowkes. London: Penguin.

McDowell, John. 1994. *Mind and World*. Cambridge, MA: Harvard University Press.

McDowell, John. 2013. *Having the World in View. Essays on Kant, Hegel, and Sellars*. Cambridge, MA. Harvard University Press.

McGowan, Todd. 2019. *Emancipation after Hegel: Achieving a Contradictory Revolution*. New York: Columbia University Press.

Menke, Christoph. 2020. *Critique of Rights*, trans. Christopher Turner. Cambridge: Polity.

Metzinger, Thomas. 2009. *The Ego Tunnel: The Science of the Mind and the Myth of the Self*. New York: Basic Books.

Miller, Jacques. 2000. "Six Paradigms of Jouissance." *Lacanian Ink* 17: 8–47.

Millikan, Ruth G. 2019. *Beyond Concepts: Unicepts, Language, and Natural Information*. Oxford: Oxford University Press.

Morris, Benny. 2004. "Survival of the Fittest." *Haaretz*. http://www.haaretz.com/survival-of-the-fittest-cont-1.61341.

Mosès, Stéphane. 2006. "Gershom Scholem." In *Benjamin-Handbuch*, ed. Burkhardt Lindner, 59–76. Stuttgart: Metzler Verlag.

Mouffe, Chantal. 2005. *On the Political*. London: Routledge.

Nancy, Jean-Luc, and Philippe Lacoue-Labarthe. 1981. "Ouverture." In *Rejouer le politique*, ed. Étienne Balibar, 11–28. Paris: Éditions Galilée.

Natanson, Hannah. 2023. "'Slavery Was Wrong' and 5 Other Things Some Educators Won't Teach Anymore." *Washington Post*, March 6, 2023. https://www.washingtonpost.com/education/2023/03/06/slavery-was-wrong-5-other-things-educators-wont-teach-anymore/.

Nicholis, Angus, and Martin Liebscher. 2010. *Thinking the Unconscious: Nineteenth-Century German Thought*. Cambridge: Cambridge University Press.

Nietzsche, Friedrich. 2002. *Beyond Good and Evil*, ed. Rolf-Peter Horstmann and Judith Norman, trans. Judith Norman. Cambridge: Cambridge University Press.

Peacocke, Christopher. 2019. *The Primacy of Metaphysics*. New York: Oxford University Press.

Pfaller, Robert. 2017. *Interpassivity: The Aesthetics of Delegated Enjoyment*. Edinburgh: Edinburgh University Press.

Putnam, Hilary. 1975. "The Meaning of Meaning." In *Language, Mind, and Knowledge*, ed. Keith Gunderson, 131–93. Minnesota Studies in the Philosophy of Science, vol. 7. Minneapolis: University of Minnesota Press.

Putnam, Hilary. 2012. *Philosophy in the Age of Science: Physics, Mathematics, and Skepticism*. Cambridge, MA: Harvard University Press.

Quine, Willard V. O. 1969. *Ontological Relativity and Other Essays*. New York: Columbia University Press.

Quine, Willard V. O. 2013. *Word and Object, New Edition*. Cambridge, MA: MIT Press.

Rancière, Jacques. 1990. "The End of Politics or the Realist Utopia." In *On the Shores of Politics*, 5–38. London: Verso.

Rancière, Jacques. 2015. *Dissensus: On Politics and Aesthetics*, trans. Steven Corcoran. London: Bloomsbury.

Reckwitz, Andreas. 2020. *The Society of Singularities*. Cambridge: Polity.

Reiterman, Tom, and John Jacobs. 1982. *Raven: The Untold Story of Rev. Jim Jones and His People*. London: Penguin.

Rosenberg, Alex. 2011. *The Atheist's Guide to Reality: Enjoying Life without Illusions*. New York: W.W. Norton.

Rosenzweig, Franz. 1985. *The Star of Redemption*, trans. William W. Hallo. Notre Dame, IN: University of Notre Dame Press.

Rumsfeld, Donald. 2002. Transcript of the Press Conference on June 2, 2002. https://www.nato.int/docu/speech/2002/s020606g.htm.

Ruti, Mari. 2012. *The Singularity of Being: Lacan and the Immortal Within*. New York: Fordham University Press.

Santner, Eric. 1996. *My Own Private Germany: Daniel Paul Schreber's Secret History of Modernity*. Princeton, NJ: Princeton University Press.

Santner, Eric. 2001. *On the Psychotheology of Everyday Life: Reflections on Freud and Rosenzweig*. Chicago: University of Chicago Press.

Santner, Eric. 2011. *The Royal Remains: The People's Two Bodies and the Endgames of Sovereignty*. Chicago: University of Chicago Press.

Sartre, Jean-Paul. 2004. *The Imaginary: A Phenomenological Psychology of the Imagination*, trans. Jonatan Webber. London: Routledge.

Scheier, Claus-Artur. 2008. "Entzweitung als Zeitalter der Bildung: Hegel und Rousseau im kulturphilosophischen Kontext." *Zeitschrift für Kulturphilosophie* 2: 235–51.

Schreber, Daniel Paul. 2000. *Memoires of My Nervous Illness*, trans. and ed. Ida Macalpine and Richard A. Hunter. New York: New York Review Books.

Sharpe, Matthew. 2004. *Slavoj Žižek: A Little Piece of the Real*. London: Ashgate.

WORKS CITED

Ver Eecke, Wilfried. 2019. *Breaking Through Schizophrenia: Lacan and Hegel for Talk Therapy.* Lanham, MD: Rowman and Littlefield.

Wittgenstein, Ludwig. 2002. *Tractatus Logico-Philosophicus,* trans. D. F. Pears and B. F. McGuinness. New York: Routledge.

Žižek, Slavoj. 1989. *The Sublime Object of Ideology.* London: Verso.

Žižek, Slavoj. 1991a. *For They Know Not What They Do: Enjoyment as a Political Factor.* London: Verso.

Žižek, Slavoj. 1991b. *Looking Awry: An Introduction to Jacques Lacan through Popular Culture.* Cambridge, MA: MIT Press.

Žižek, Slavoj. 1992. "Why Is Every Act a Repetition?" In *Enjoy Your Symptom: Jacques Lacan in Hollywood and Out,* 69–112. London: Routledge.

Žižek, Slavoj. 1993. *Tarrying with the Negative: Kant, Hegel, and the Critique of Ideology.* Durham, NC: Duke University Press.

Žižek, Slavoj. 1997. *The Plague of Fantasies.* London: Verso.

Žižek, Slavoj. 2000a. *The Ticklish Subject: The Absent Centre of Political Ontology.* London: Verso.

Žižek, Slavoj. 2000b. *The Fragile Absolute: Why the Christian Legacy Is Worth Fighting for.* London: Verso.

Žižek, Slavoj. 2002. *For They Know Not What They Do: Enjoyment as a Political Factor.* London: Verso.

Žižek, Slavoj. 2006. *The Parallax View.* Cambridge, MA: MIT Press.

Žižek, Slavoj. 2008. *Psychoanalyse und die Philosophie des deutschen Idealismus.* Vienna: Turia & Kant.

Žižek, Slavoj. 2015. "Slavoj Žižek über Charlie Hebdo." Interview in *Die Tageszeitung* from January 19, 2015. https://taz.de/Slavoj-iek-ueber-Charlie-Hebdo/!5023334/.

Image Credits

page 2   Still from the film *La Dolce Vita* (Federico Fellini, dir., 1960). Copyright © Paramount Pictures.

page 9   *Left*: Still from the film *The Little World of Don Camillo* (Julien Duvivier, dir., 1952). Copyright © Francinex. *Center*: Bororo-Boe man from Mato Grosso at Brazil's Indigenous Games. Photograph by Valter Campanato. Wikimedia Commons. *Right*: Niels Bohr and Albert Einstein in Leiden. Photograph by Paul Ehrenfest, 1925.

page 12   Still from the film *The Matrix* (the Wachowskis, dir., 1999). Copyright © Matrix Franchise.

page 13   Banknote representing one hundred million German marks. Wikimedia Commons.

page 15   Hungarian flag with the hammer and sickle emblem cutout. Photograph by Tibor Balog. Copyright © iStock.

page 18   Still from the film *Downfall* (Oliver Hirschbiegel, dir., 2004). Copyright © Constantin Film.

page 19   M. C. Escher, *Ascending and Descending*, lithograph, 1960. Copyright © 2023 The M. C. Escher Company, the Netherlands. All rights reserved. www.mcescher .com.

page 21   Graphic of Bertrand Russell's antinomy, by Max Fesl. Courtesy of Max Fesl.

page 29   Freud depicting neurons with different functions, from Sigmund Freud, *Aus den Anfängen der Psychoanalyse: Briefe an Wilhelm Fließ, Abhandlungen und Notizen aus den Jahren 1887–1902* (Frankfurt am Main: Fischer Verlag, 1962), 331.

page 44   Architectural drawing showing the vanishing point outside the piece of paper the drawing is depicted on, by Dominik Finkelde.

page 52   Still from *The Trial* (Orson Welles, dir., 1962). Copyright © Astor Pictures Corporation.

page 63   *Left*: M. C. Escher, *Ascending and Descending*. Copyright ©
           2023 The M. C. Escher Company, the Netherlands. All rights
           reserved. www.mcescher.com. *Center*: M. C. Escher, *Hand with
           Reflecting Sphere*. Copyright © 2023 The M. C. Escher Company,
           the Netherlands. All rights reserved. www.mcescher.com. *Right*:
           Hungarian flag with the hammer and sickle emblem cut out.
           Photograph by Tibor Balog. Copyright © iStock.

page 71   Kleinian bottle. Photograph by Dmitriy Moroz. Copyright ©
           depositphotos.

page 74   God emerging from immanence, by Max Fesl. Courtesy of Max
           Fesl.

page 86   *Top:* Diagram of Hegel's dialectical teleology in time, by
           Dominik Finkelde. *Bottom:* Still from *2001: A Space Odyssey* (Stan-
           ley Kubrick, dir., 1968). Copyright © Metro-Goldwyn-Mayer.

page 88   *Top:* Diagram illustrating the relationship between Hegel's
           concepts of substance and subject. Courtesy of Eric Steinhart.
           Bottom: Still (redacted) from *Alien Resurrection* (Jean-Pierre Jeu-
           net, dir., 1997). Copyright © 20th Century Fox.

page 92   M. C. Escher, *Sky and Water*. Copyright © 2023 The M. C. Escher
           Company, the Netherlands. All rights reserved. www.mcescher.
           com.

page 102   Photographic collage on the mirror stage, by Dominik Finkelde.

page 103   Photographic collage on the mirror stage, by Dominik Finkelde.

page 105   Still from *Fight Club* (David Fincher, dir., 1999). Copyright ©
           20th Century Fox.

page 110   Lacan's graph of desire (first stage), from "The Subversion of
           the Subject and the Dialectic of Desire in the Freudian Un-
           conscious," in *Écrits: The First Complete Edition in English*, trans.
           Bruce Fink (New York: Norton, 2006), 681.

page 117   Lacan's graph of desire (second stage), from "The Subversion
           of the Subject and the Dialectic of Desire in the Freudian Un-
           conscious," in *Écrits: The First Complete Edition in English*, trans.
           Bruce Fink (New York: Norton, 2006), 684.

page 118   Graphic collage on Lacan's understanding of "the voice," by
           Dominik Finkelde.

page 119   Collage on Lacan's understanding of "interpellation," by
           Dominik Finkelde, with Lacan's graph of desire (second stage)
           and the royal badge of the House of Windsor.

page 123   Lacan's graph of desire (third stage), from "The Subversion of
           the Subject and the Dialectic of Desire in the Freudian Un-

conscious," in *Écrits: The First Complete Edition in English*, trans. Bruce Fink (New York: Norton, 2006), 690.

page 124   Jean-Michel Moreau's etching from Jacques Cazotte's *Le Diable amoureux*, published in Paris in 1772.

page 125   Graphic collage of a "chain of equivalence," by Dominik Finkelde.

page 132   Negative space sketch, from Zachary Micah Gartenberg, "On the Causal Role of Privation in Thomas Aquinas's Metaphysics," *European Journal of Philosophy*, no. 28 (2020): 314.

page 147   Diagram showing Lacan's three registers of the symbolic, the imaginary, and the real, by Dominik Finkelde.

page 148   Graphic illustrating Bertrand Russell's set-theoretical paradox, by Dominik Finkelde.

page 160   Still from the documentary film *Jonestown: The Life and Death of Peoples Temple* (Stanley Nelson, dir., 2006) showing Leo Ryan, a US congressman from California. Copyright © Firelight Media.

page 161   Still from the documentary film *Jonestown: The Life and Death of Peoples Temple* (Stanley Nelson, dir., 2006) showing Jim Jones (*center, in sunglasses*). Copyright © Firelight Media.

page 170   Poster for the Hulu series *The Path* (created by Jessica Goldberg, 2016–18). Copyright © Hulu.

page 178   Graphic of the Latin term *clinamen*, by Max Fesl. Courtesy of Max Fesl.

page 184   Anthony Weiner, selfie (detail). *New York Post*, June 12, 2011.

page 188   Graphic by Fredriek Depoortere, from Frederiek Depoortere, "The End of God's Transcendence? On Incarnation in the Work of Slavoj Žižek," *Modern Theology* 23, no. 3 (2007): 518.

page 196   *Left*: Still (detail) from *The Thin Red Line* (Terrence Malick, dir., 1998). Copyright © 20th Century Fox. *Right*: Albrecht Dürer, *Melencolia I* (detail). Wikimedia Commons.

Index

abject, abjection, 175, 177–78, 183, 186, 192–94
Adorno, Theodor W., 22, 70, 86–87
Allison, Henry, 45
Antigone, 179, 190, 192
Arendt, Hannah, 107, 157
Aristotle, 73, 179; and ethics, 183, 185–86
authority, 19, 20, 34, 60, 121; hegemonic, 120, 144, 152, 157–58; obscure, 124–25, 127; paternal, 169–70; questions of, 30; symbolic, 53, 59, 118, 128, 141; virtual, 13–14

Badiou, Alain, 61, 69, 85
Benjamin, Walter, 51, 91, 125, 158
Benoist, Jocelyn, 5, 6
Bentham, Jeremy, 147
big Other, viii, 17–18, 52, 87, 93, 124, 136, 141, 164–65, 168, 177, 181, 194; as empty place of power, 53; and the graph of desire, 110, 117–18, 120–24, 188–89, 192; and recognition/interpellation, 99–100, 110, 120–22, 125–28
BonJour, Laurence, 167–68
Boothby, Richard, 180
Bourdieu, Pierre, 60–61
Brandom, Robert, vii–viii, 3, 5, 7, 59, 61, 75, 85; on commitments and entitlements, 59–61, 159; and the space of reasons, 5, 155, 189

Cantin, Lucie, 184
capitalism, 90, 136
Cassirer, Ernst, 113
Castoriadis, Cornelius, 148; and the radical imaginary, 150, 154–55
Cazotte, Jacques, 123
Chaplin, Charlie, 117

chiasmic change, 84
Chiesa, Lorenz, 175
commitments (and entitlements), 16, 61, 82, 130, 161, 165
corps morcelé, 102, 105, 133; and images of mutilation, 105

Davidson, Donald, vii, 3, 72, 85, 110, 114, 192; and radical interpretation, 6; on relativism, 72, 77–78, 85; on triangulation, 186–87; on truth, 134
Deacon, Terrence, 30
Dean, Jodi, 192
death drive, 37, 67
de Landa, Manuel, 5
Dennett, Daniel, vii, 30, 46, 152–53, 168–69
Derrida, Jacques, 117
Descartes, René, 65–66, 89, 104
desire, 11, 14, 16–18, 20–21, 28, 30, 39, 47, 53–56, 58, 64, 81, 100, 115, 157, 161, 182, 195, 197; adjusting to fantasy, 128; deliberate 185–86; and the graph of desire, 7, 107–9, 111–12, 116, 118, 162, 179, 181, 187–88; infinite, 130–37, 183, 189–90, 192; and the other's desire, 33–37, 40, 49, 101, 104, 124, 127, 165
dialectic, 79, 84, 89, 108; and Hegel, 85, 92, 133, 179
Dolar, Mladen, 3, 117
Durkheim, Émile, 147

Emma (Freud's case), 98–99, 120
enigmatic signifiers, 33–37, 39–41, 49–50, 53, 55–56, 63, 86, 116, 127, 158–59, 168
enjoyment, 183, 192, 194; excessive, 184–88; surplus, 191

Escher, M. C., 19, 63, 92–93
Esposito, Roberto, 156
Evans, Dylan, 170
extimacy, 151

fantasies, viii, 3, 7, 11, 16, 20, 27–28, 30,
    43, 49, 105, 112, 158; collective, 127, 190;
    excessive, 7, 19, 107–9, 146–47, 155–57,
    188; ideological, 17, 148–52; manage-
    ment of, 15; of reason, 43, 67, 116, 133;
    unconscious, 51, 56–57
Fight Club, 105
Flisfeder, Matthew, 53
forced choice, 99, 118–19, 121–22, 130–31,
    177, 180, 186–94, 197
Foucault, Michel, 158
Frege, Gottlob, 70, 111, 114, 135
Freud, Sigmund, vii–viii, 3–7, 21, 40–43,
    48–49, 54–58, 62–64, 67–69, 72, 80–81,
    97–99, 129, 131, 133, 169, 175–76, 180,
    182–83, 188, 192; on death drive, 37;
    on dreams, 25, 32; on Emma, 99; and
    enigmatic messages, 35; on fantasy,
    56–57; and Kant, 43–45, 47; and the
    unconscious, 10–11, 26–38, 55, 81; on
    trauma, 33, 175
Fukuyama, Francis, 15

Gabriel, Markus, viii, 5–6
Gamm, Gerhard, 80
gestalt, 93, 133; switch, 102–5, 162
God(s), 43, 45, 47, 62, 64–66, 72
Gramsci, Antonio, 93
graph of desire, 7, 107–9, 111–12, 116, 118,
    162, 179, 181, 187–88
Greene, Graham, 7

Habermas, Jürgen, 7, 26, 100, 125, 142,
    151–52
Harman, Graham, viii, 5–6
Harris, Sam, 168–69
Hegel, Georg W. F., 3, 7, 61, 63, 65, 72–77,
    99, 111, 113, 116, 133, 176, 179, 188–89,
    193, 196; and Kant, 73–76, 189; on
    consciousness, 78–79, 84, 87–92, 97; on
    negativity, 7, 80–81, 84, 87–92, 196
Heidegger, Martin, 149, 151, 158, 169–70,
    188
Hölderlin, Friedrich, 67
Hume, David, 67–68, 72, 89–90, 104

identity, 4, 55, 63, 87, 88, 99–102, 129–30;
    lack of, 81, 105, 145, 162; law of, 5–6,
    11, 19–20, 22, 28, 39, 125, 128, 141, 143,
    169; sociocultural, 60, 112, 116, 149, 178;
    split, 80, 88, 102–5, 118, 120–22, 162–65
ideology, 61, 128; as ontology, 142–46,
    155–56, 162
imaginary, the, 62, 104, 146, 152, 176, 181;
    identification, 119, 121; radical, 149–50;
    social, 148, 154–56
inferentialism, 59, 61–62, 189
interpellation, 3, 6–7, 9–11, 15–16, 20, 34,
    50, 56, 62, 73, 78, 99, 101, 104, 158–59,
    168; enigmatic, 35, 50–57; and group
    psychology, 169; and sublime objects,
    141–42; symbolic, 30, 33, 58, 61, 100,
    107–30; and transference, 64
investiture, symbolic, 4, 16, 49, 58–62
Israel: Palestine conflict, 91–93, 125–27,
    157, 166

Jacobi, Friedrich H., 146
jouissance, viii, 8, 28, 175–81, 183–86,
    191–97
Jünger, Ernst, 178, 193

Kafka, Franz, 51–58, 124
Kant, Immanuel, 3, 7, 15, 23, 36, 57, 79–
    80, 87, 89–90, 97, 108, 117–18, 136, 149,
    151, 176, 186; on epistemology, 43–48,
    64–68, 71–77, 83–85, 131, 145–47; on
    the *focus imaginarius*, 43–47, 64; and
    the moral law, 176, 180, 183, 188–90,
    193; on the transcendental "I," 15, 131
Keller, Helen, 113–17
Klein, Melanie, 105
Koch, Anton F., 5–6, 75, 110
Kristeva, Julia, 175, 177–78
Kubrick, Stanley, 85

Lacan, Jacques, 3–8, 10, 17, 19, 21, 38–39,
    49–50, 52, 57, 63, 67, 97, 112, 130–33,
    136, 163–66, 170, 180, 187, 192, 193;
    and the big Other, 100–101, 141; and
    epistemology, 3, 67–68, 98, 113–15,
    132–33, 135, 154, 194; on fantasy, 102,
    146–47, 151; and Freud, 28, 99; on the
    graph of desire, 107–11, 117–20, 122–
    28; and Hegel, 81, 91; and the mirror
    stage, 101–5; on the moral law, 183–86,

188–90, 195–96; on paranoia, 180; and
politics, 142, 148–49, 160; on the three
registers, 60; on time, 162; on transgression, 175–79, 181–82
lack, 11, 20; in being, 19, 81, 130, 135–36,
189; of identity, 102–5, 108, 131, 136, 141;
of legitimacy, 52; of meaning, 42, 50,
54; of the symbolic (order), 65, 136, 141
Laclau, Ernesto, 53, 126, 143, 145
language, 69, 110, 120; child's entry into,
112, 117, 130; and meta-language, 111,
126
Laplanche, Jean, 3, 64; and enigmatic
signifiers, 33–37, 39–40, 50, 127; and
source objects of the drives, 36; and
the unconscious, 131
law, the: of identity, 125, 128, 141, 143, 169;
and morality, 175–77, 180–83, 186, 189–
91, 193; and obscenity, 150, 157
Lear, Jonathan, 41–43
Lefort, Claude, 53
Locke, John, 69, 89
Lovecraft, H. P., 70
Lynch, David, 46

Malabou, Catherine, 79
Marchart, Oliver, 145–46
Marx, Karl, 12, 100, 130
master-signifier, 37, 120, 122, 125, 144–46,
152, 159, 192
matrix, 15, 20, 31, 151; the movie, 11–12,
16, 73
McDowell, John, vii–viii, 4–5, 69, 85, 110,
159
Menke, Christoph, 158
metaphysics, 46, 65; Hegelian, 87–89;
Kantian, 67, 70, 73, 85, 89
Metzinger, Thomas, 30
Miller, Jacques-Alain, 176–77, 181, 191, 193
mirror stage, 98, 101–5, 109, 133–35, 162,
164, 189
Mouffe, Chantal, 145, 148

Nancy, Jean-Luc, 148
nature: second, 6, 12, 15–16, 21, 28, 39,
116, 118, 122, 131, 133, 135
negativity, 65, 97, 196; Hegelian, 74, 80–
81; of thought, 135
Nietzsche, Friedrich, 25, 27, 169
non-wakefulness, 21

objet petit a (object small a), 128, 136–37,
181
ontology, 7, 68, 114–15
Other, the big, viii, 17–18, 52–53, 56, 87,
93, 99–100, 110, 117–18, 120–22, 124–28,
136, 164–65, 168, 177, 181, 188–89, 192,
194

Palestine, 91, 93
paternal metaphor, 112
Peacocke, Christopher, 79
perception, 83, 103–4, 133, 188; a priori
conditions of, 75, 80, 85; veil of, 84
Pfaller, Robert, 167
phantasm, 123, 127–28, 135, 151, 156
Plato, 4, 169, 186; and Platonism, 72, 111
pleasure, 9, 28–29, 109, 155; in displeasure, 28–31, 37–38; and pain, 31, 175,
184, 191; principle, the, 30–31, 37–40,
43, 101, 133, 175, 180, 183–86, 188, 193,
196; by transgression, 150, 181
Prince William, 119–22, 130, 133, 140,
187–89
prisoner sophism, 162–66
psychosis, 17, 188
psychotheology, 3–4, 6
Putnam, Hilary, vii, 3, 10, 168

Quine, Willard V. O., vii, 3, 6, 55, 72, 77,
85, 116; and indeterminacy of translation, 36, 119–20, 127

Rancière, Jacques, 53, 105, 145, 148
real, the, 116, 127–28, 176, 178, 181, 197;
horror of, 107
reason(s), 3, 6, 19, 37, 50, 69, 73, 76, 105,
114, 130, 147, 150, 192, 194; historicity of,
75; illusions of, 43, 47–48, 64, 70, 146;
practical, 72, 185; space of, viii, 5, 7, 26,
155, 157, 159, 189
Reckwitz, Andreas, 53
recognition, 99, 109, 112, 124, 143; and
misrecognition, 102, 121, 167
remainder: epistemic, 4, 28, 36, 39–40,
60, 64, 83, 119–20, 126, 189, 191
retrospectivity: processes of, 6, 34, 39,
41, 69, 75, 78–79, 87, 90–92, 111–12, 116,
122, 127, 135, 149, 156, 189
revelation: the nothingness of, 51–54
Rorty, Richard, 3, 72

Rosenberg, Alex, 49
Rosenzweig, Franz, 4–5, 190
Rumsfeld, Donald, 70
Russell's paradox, 20, 146, 150
Ruti, Mari, 193

Santner, Eric, 27, 30, 53, 42–43, 50,
    54–55, 58, 60, 145, 181; on excess in
    demand, 32; on symbolic investiture,
    3–4; on the "undead," 37
Sartre, Jean-Paul, 147–48
Saussure, Ferdinand de, 33
Scheier, Claus-Artur, 67
Schelling, Friedrich W. J., 5, 72, 90
Schreber, Daniel P., 4–5, 49, 57–62, 64,
    68, 107
signifier(s): the role of, 11, 14, 26, 28,
    34, 36, 40–41, 47–48, 62, 64, 68, 81;
    beyond-of-the signifier, 188; empty,
    145, 153; enigmatic, 33–37, 39–41,
    49–50, 53, 55–56, 63, 86, 116, 127, 158–
    59, 168; order of the, 91, 109–20, 141,
    179, 181, 187, 195
spirit, viii, 97, 133, 188, 196
Strawson, Peter, 3, 72, 77
subject, the: split subject, 38, 60–61, 73,
    81, 101, 103, 111, 116, 118, 122–23, 188;
    subject supposed to know, 52; of the
    unconscious, 6, 17, 99
sublime objects (of ideology), 7, 141–46,
    150, 155–56, 158
substance: as subject, 80, 84, 87
symbolic, the, 4, 14, 16–19, 28, 30, 42–43,
    60, 118–23, 154, 164, 176–77, 179, 181,
    183, 194–97
symptom(s), 55, 57, 98–100, 117, 129, 141,
    189

thing, the, 56, 131, 180–81
thing-in-itself, the, 21, 60, 66, 68, 70–
    72, 75, 80, 83–85, 89, 131–32, 134–35,
    146–47

transference: process of, viii, 7, 33–34,
    36–37, 40, 49, 60, 64, 100, 104, 128, 133,
    147, 158–60, 165, 167–68, 190
transgression, 154–55, 157, 175–76, 181,
    193; of the Law, 177
trauma, 29, 31–33, 38, 42–43, 120, 123,
    145, 175
truth, 97–99, 111, 114, 116–17, 152, 162, 181,
    192, 194, 196; and appearance, 85; in
    psychoanalysis, 97–98

unconscious, the, viii, 3–6, 10–13, 16, 25,
    28–29, 33, 35, 37, 39, 41, 60, 63, 99–100,
    121–22, 128–29, 131, 135, 158, 180, 190,
    195; structured like a language, 131;
    symbolic processes, 15–16, 21, 162;
    unconscious processes of transference
    49, 64, 165
universal(s), 4, 110, 115, 134, 143, 191
universality, 14, 155

validity (without meaning), 51–56;
    retroactive, 147
vanishing mediator, the, 37
violence, 105–6, 125–26
virtuality (of reality), 12, 21, 58, 73;
    unconscious, 13
Vorstellungsrepräsentanz, 67, 69, 131

Weiner, Anthony, 177–79, 184–86, 190–93,
    195
Wittgenstein, Ludwig, 3, 68

Žižek, Slavoj, vii, 3, 5, 7, 11, 20, 34, 52, 61,
    81, 98, 108, 126, 193; on death drive,
    37; on Hegel, 83–85, 87, 89–93; on
    ideology, 121, 124, 192; on interpella-
    tion, 54–55, 103, 127–28, 187; on Kafka,
    56–57; on pleasure, 101; on sublime
    objects, 142, 145, 150
Zöller, Günter, 79
Zupančič, Alenka, 3